The Eucharist

⊗ PROBLEMS IN THEOLOGY

In the study of Christian theology, there have been, over the centuries, a number of problems for which no adequate explanation has yet been given, or at least, none given which commands substantial agreement among those whose task it is to explain the faith. Some of these issues are central to the understanding of Christianity – the nature of Christ's presence in the Eucharist, for example, or the need for, and the achievement of, redemption. Books in this series will look at crucial topics of this kind. Written by experts, each volume will both trace the history of attempts to answer a particular problem in theology, and then propose a new understanding of the doctrine under debate. Though based upon the latest scholarship, the books are intended for the serious enquirer as much as for the professional theologian.

Already published:

The Atonement
MICHAEL WINTER

The Eucharist
RAYMOND MOLONEY SJ

RAYMOND MOLONEY SJ

PROBLEMS IN THEOLOGY

 The Eucharist

**GEOFFREY
CHAPMAN**

Geoffrey Chapman
A Cassell imprint
Villiers House, 41/47 Strand, London WC2N 5JE

© Raymond Moloney SJ 1995

First published 1995

British Library Cataloguing-in-Publication Data
A catalogue record for this book is available from the British Library.

ISBN 0–225–66758–4

Typeset by York House Typographic Ltd, London
Printed and bound in Great Britain by Biddles Ltd,
Guildford and King's Lynn

⊠ *Contents*

⊠ *Introduction*

At the time of the Second Vatican Council, one of the central issues
in theological discussion was the question of the Eucharist,
particularly as regards the meaning of Real Presence. This
discussion came to a head, not in any document of the Council
itself, but in the encyclical of Paul VI, *Mysterium fidei*. In the
following years the theology of the Eucharist entered a quieter
period, and it is only recently that significant writing on the subject
has got under way once again. The main area of progress in the
meantime has been in the experience of the liturgy created by
Vatican II, with a consequent benefit for liturgical studies. This
book hopes to make its contribution to this new wave of reflection,
drawing, as the other books do, on these recent advances in
theology and liturgy.

Theologians of the Eucharist have to take account of two
contrary aspects of their task. On the one hand, they have to study
the context, historical and liturgical, within which the understanding of the sacrament comes about. On the other hand, if their
concern is doctrinal, they have to direct their attention beneath the
surface of things, to isolate the crucial points in what is at issue, in a
way that the original authors under discussion did not necessarily
do themselves. In this book I have made a particular point of trying
to strike a balance between these two concerns.

The principal aim of this work is the better understanding of the
sacrament, in so far as that is possible at all when one is dealing
with a mystery in the strict sense of the term; and this is the special
task of the explanatory section of the book. But before one is ready
for such a reflection, one has to see the Eucharist in its context.
The mistake of the old manualists is not entirely dead. People
sometimes still approach the Eucharist by simply presenting the

evidence for doctrinal belief without situating such evidence in its time and place. It is to avoid this error that considerable space is devoted to the history of the theology of the sacrament. In particular, there is an insistence throughout that belief in Christ's presence in the Eucharist can be understood only by reference to the nature of the celebration itself.

At the same time one has to be careful not to overload the train of thought with an excess of historical or liturgical detail. The author is a professor of liturgy as well as of sacramental theology and is convinced that a theology of the Eucharist can be developed only in association with a constant study of the liturgy. For the purposes of this book, however, such reflection has been left somewhat in the background, so that the central issues of Eucharistic theology can be presented with greater clarity and subjected to deeper analysis.

In describing the history of the sacrament, one of the author's guiding principles is his notion of understanding as essentially developmental. Once the meaning of the Eucharist, as of anything else for that matter, is entrusted to human minds, it is inevitably subject to that dynamism by which we are constantly asking questions about it and pressing on to new insights and syntheses. It is the special purpose of the study of the Scriptures and the early writers to show this process at work, for this approach is not only the answer to fundamentalism in theology but is the key to doing justice to the variations of the centuries. As simply human, such a process could go astray, but as a function of life in a community indwelt by the Holy Spirit, the essential continuity of understanding is guaranteed and so becomes one of the key values to be illustrated by the scholar.

The demand for developing understanding is also the key principle behind the author's desire to explore the fundamental issues on the level of a philosophical theology. However this aspect of the work becomes predominant in only a few of the chapters. The fact of the matter is that such a theology has been one of the main influences in the understanding of the Eucharist in the Church. One cannot come to grips with the issues which have been at work in this theology unless one faces them at this level. This represents, of course, a particular difficulty today, when the kind of philosophy which lies in the background of so much of the writing and teaching on the Eucharist is not readily accessible to many of our contemporaries. Unfortunately this means that one or two of the chapters of this book may well prove problematic for some of its readers (for instance, Chapters 9 and 14), but the book should not be judged by these chapters alone. The author has endeavoured to ensure that the level of presentation and the intrinsic interest of the subject-matter will carry the average student of theology through the book as a whole.

A particular philosophical influence on the author has been the work of Bernard Lonergan. This does not mean that a familiarity with this scholar's work or an acceptance of his principles is a necessary condition for benefiting from this book. Explicit mention of his outlook has, by and large, been kept to the footnotes, but the author would wish to acknowledge his debt to the Canadian theologian's writings. Those who are interested in Lonergan's *Method in Theology* could view this book as an instance in which the principles of his method have been applied. In particular those principles lie behind the division of this book into historical and explanatory sections. The first section is predominantly, as Lonergan would say, theology *in oratione obliqua*, that is, from the point of view of what others have said. The second section is theology *in oratione recta*, that is, where the author endeavours to respond in a personal way and to speak simply for himself.

The historical section does more than simply give us the history of a discussion, but at the same time it is far from answering all the questions that arise. Perhaps its principal function, especially for one whose faith is dependent on the ecclesial community, is to establish the parameters within which reflection is to be pursued. Such parameters, as experience shows, are wide and generous; they leave room for many differences of opinion and competing schools of thought. In the explanatory section, on the other hand, the emphasis is on personal understanding. This is where everyone must try to work out for himself or herself how to understand the Eucharist today in the light of all that has gone before and of all that faces us now. In attempting this one tries to give an answer to problems which the community has left unsolved, to draw into a unity all that seems important about the Eucharist, and to project a synthesis of that with the rest of the faith and indeed with the rest of life.

Finally in this introduction I would like to express my appreciation of all those who have helped me in the writing of this book. My thanks, in the first place, go to my colleagues and confrères in Milltown, Dublin, to my Rector, Fergus

O'Donoghue SJ for his support, to my colleagues and friends in the Milltown Institute, Gervase Corcoran OSA and Philip Gleeson OP, for reading and commenting on sections of the manuscript. My thanks in particular to Mr Michael Walsh of Geoffrey Chapman for his encouragement and his advice. I dedicate the book to my departed parents, from whom I first received the inestimable treasure of Eucharistic faith.

⊠ Abbreviations

AAS	*Acta Apostolicae Sedis*
AH	St Irenaeus, *Adversus haereses*
CBQ	*Catholic Biblical Quarterly*
CSEL	*Corpus Scriptorum Ecclesiasticorum Latinorum*
CT	*Concilium tridentinum, diariorum, actorum, epistolarum, tractatuum nova collectio,* ed. Societas Görresiana (Freiburg-im-Breisgau: Herder, 1901–)
DS	*Enchiridion symbolorum,* ed. H. Denzinger and A. Schönmetzer
DTC	*Dictionnaire de théologie catholique*
GCS	*Die griechischen christlichen Schriftsteller*
ITQ	*Irish Theological Quarterly*
LThK	*Lexikon für Theologie und Kirchenwesen*
LV	*Lumière et vie*
NRT	*Nouvelle Revue Théologique*
PG	Migne, *Patrologia Graeca*
PL	Migne, *Patrologia Latina*
PLS	Migne, *Patrologia Latina: Supplementum*
PRIA	*Proceedings of the Royal Irish Academy*
RB	*Revue Biblique*
RJ	*Enchiridion patristicum,* ed. M. J. Rouet de Journel
RSPT	*Revue des sciences philosophiques et théologiques*
RSR	*Recherches de science religieuse*
SC	*Sources chrétiennes* (Paris: Cerf)
SCDF	Sacred Congregation for the Doctrine of the Faith
SCDW	Sacred Congregation for Divine Worship
SCR	Sacred Congregation of Rites
SCS	Sacred Congregation for the Sacraments
ST	*Summa Theologica*

PATRIS MATRISQUE
MEMORIAE

Historical Section

1

⊠ *From Jewish rites to Christian rites*

We pray in a tradition. As we gather for the liturgy, we are moved by memories that reach back, some of them, beyond recorded time. Unknown to most of us, the attitudes we assume in worship, and in some cases even the very shape of our prayers and gestures, have their origins, not simply in the early centuries of Christianity, but even in some of the oldest stories of the Bible.

In the Judeo-Christian tradition, for instance, worship is essentially personal. It is part of an interpersonal relationship between God and his people, an approach that has its origin in a particular experience of faith according to which God was wont to encounter his people and intervene in their lives.

Another characteristic is the sense that worship begins, not with the creature, but with the Creator. It is God who takes the initiative in this dialogue between heaven and earth, and worship is always our response – a God-given response – to the God who advances towards us. If we think of this divine initiative as God's word of love and power inviting us – using 'word' in that loose biblical sense by which it means both 'word' and 'thing' – then we can describe worship as the word of the human being in response to the efficacious word of God.

BLESSING

This is the context within which we can come to appreciate one of the most ancient forms of prayer of the Jewish people, which has in fact become central to the principal Christian act of worship, the Mass. I refer to the custom of blessing God.[1] For the believer to bless the Creator in prayer and praise is one of the oldest forms of worship in the tradition of the people of God. It is, says one Jewish scholar, the basic form – the *Grundform* – of all prayer, and is found already in some of the oldest pages of the Bible.

Chapter 24 of the Book of Genesis recounts an engaging tale of how Abraham set about finding a wife for his son, Isaac. Isaac was, of course, his heir, and for the bearer of such a destiny none of the local women in Canaan seemed acceptable. The wife of the future bearer of the promise could come only from among Abraham's own people back in his native country, Mesopotamia. So Abraham dispatched his steward on the long journey to Haran to choose a wife from among Abraham's own kinsfolk.

On arrival the steward prayed to God for success in his search and determined on a particular divine sign that would help him to recognize the girl God had decreed for Isaac. He had not finished his prayer when Rebecca is seen coming towards him. Rebecca acts just as it had been arranged in the steward's prayer. What is more, she turns out to be a relative of Abraham. Clearly this is the one chosen by God. The steward is overwhelmed by such evidence of God's mercy and by the prompt answer to his prayer. He falls on his knees and prays as follows:

Blessed be the Lord, the God of my master Abraham, who has not forsaken his steadfast love and his faithfulness toward my master. As for me, the Lord has led me in the way to the house of my master's kinsmen. (Gen 24:27)

For the casual reader of the Bible this is just another charming story, but for the student of Jewish and Christian worship we are here at the very origins of our tradition of prayer. This is one of the oldest sections of the Bible, and here in this section we find one of the earliest instances of a form of prayer which was destined to become basic to all prayer in the Judeo-Christian tradition.

This prayer is marked at once by its spirit and its structure, both of which are illustrated in our example. It is a prayer of praise and thanksgiving, giving glory to God for his providence. It enshrines a sense of wonder at the mystery of an infinite God who takes a personal interest in the life of his servants. The focus of the prayer is on the Creator, not on the creature. In this respect it differs from those long pagan petitions to which Our Lord refers, where people are absorbed in their own needs and try to make God attend to them by dint of their own verbosity (Matt 6:7).

Commonly, as in our example, this form of prayer is one of overflowing joyfulness, but it is not always so. At times some difficulty or tragedy can cast a shadow over the mood of the one who prays. One well-known example of that comes in the opening chapter of the book of Job, as calamity after calamity overtakes the sage. Nonetheless, in the midst of his distress, Job can still pray:

> The Lord gave, and the Lord has taken away;
> blessed be the name of the Lord. (Job 1:21)

Job here is important as prefiguring Christ in his passion. It is not impossible to think of Our Lord on the cross blessing his Father in similar vein. Essentially the spirit of this prayer is a positive attitude to God, implying an acceptance of whatever God sends. To bless God, come what may, will become the key to a Eucharistic attitude to life.

The Hebrew word for blessing is *berachah*. There is some disagreement among scholars as to the precise conceptual content of the term, but perhaps its meaning is best grasped by examples, such as Genesis 24:27; Exodus 18:10; 1 Samuel 25:32, 39; Psalm 65(66):20. Some think that the term is connected with the word for knee, *berek*, and it is noteworthy that Abraham's steward does fall on his knees to bless God. Imprecise as these memories necessarily are, it is still remarkable that when the people of the Bible fell on their knees before God, praise, adoration and thanksgiving were such an important part of their prayer.

In time these basic attitudes came to be formulated according to certain norms. Spontaneous expressions of praise were commonly articulated in a two-part formula, comprising an exclamation of blessing, followed by a commemoration of the particular experience of God's goodness which was the occasion of the prayer in the first place. A typical example would be Exodus 18:10, 'Blessed be the Lord, who has delivered you out of the hands of the Egyptians.' This structure is open to certain variations. The opening phrase can be in the third person or in the second. The clause of commemoration can be in an indicative or in a participial form. While scholars will discuss the norms governing such variations, of more interest to us is the particular kind of religious experience to which these expressions bear witness. It is one which takes for granted God's intervention in history, whether in the lives of individuals or of his people generally. Furthermore it sees such intervention as an expression of God's mercy and love. Confronted with such a providence, the people can only fall down on their knees and worship him. As we will see, the Eucharist will be the high-point in the history of this kind of experience of God.

There is a more extended form of prayer which is also designated by this term, 'blessing'. In this case the name is misleading, since we are dealing with prayers of differing content. Praise, thanksgiving, confession, supplication can often come together in Jewish prayer. Jewish liturgical usage did not have a special name for this phenomenon, but as long as one of the prayers was a blessing in the classical form, at the beginning or at the end of the series, then the whole series was referred to as a 'blessing'.[2]

The association of blessing and thanksgiving is of particular interest to us, since both of these terms occur in the Institution Narrative of the Eucharist. Sometimes they have been sharply distinguished. According to some scholars, 'blessing' means praising God for what he is in himself, while 'thanksgiving' means praising God for what he is for us.[3] But such a formal distinction owes more to logic than to usage. The terms seem to have been used loosely and in some circumstances were interchangeable.[4] However, certain differences in usage are to be noted as well.

Blessing is a wider concept than thanksgiving.[5] It can be understood both in an ascending and in a descending sense. As well as creature blessing the Creator, there is the Creator blessing his creation. Furthermore, blessing is more commonly seen as embodied in gesture, and even in things. For instance, 'blessing' is the word for 'gift' in Genesis 33:11 and 1 Samuel 25:27. Finally, blessing, in both ascending and descending senses, admits of human mediation, for example through priest or king or patriarch. It can establish a whole circle of blessing between heaven and earth, with God blessing people, people blessing God, and God blessing the people again, and their flocks and their fields; and all those who bless these friends of God will share in their blessing (e.g. Gen 27:27–30). In this way we see that blessing is more than just the words of a prayer. Where there is blessing, things happen! This is what we will see in a sublime way in the Eucharist.

THE TABLE BLESSINGS

One of the greatest of all God's blessings is life itself, and so the custom of blessing God is especially associated with life and the sources of life. The whole day of pious Jews is punctuated with such blessings as we have described. When he gets up in the morning, the Jewish man will bless God for the day and – *O tempora!* – for not being a woman! Similar blessings continue throughout the day as a way of celebrating the holiness of all of life. In the world of the Creator no reality is truly profane.

One of the more important occasions for blessing the Author of Life was, and is, when parents and children gather for the family meal together. Our dependence on food is one of the great reminders of our dependence on God for life and the maintenance of life. Indeed the table of the Jewish home is a kind of altar, and the food is seen as a kind of offering.[6] The father of the family is a kind of priest. He is the source of life in the family, the traditional provider of their daily bread, and so it falls to him to lead the family in prayer over their food. One writer put it well:

For the Jews every meal was a religious meal. No special rites were needed to turn a meal into a religious celebration; it was already such by its nature, antecedently to any ritual. The ritual came into being as a result of the religious character inherent in the taking of food; it did not create this character. For this reason, it is not accurate to speak of a ritual meal, but we have no other way of making our point, since for us Westerners a meal is always a secular event and any religious character it may have depends on added ritual.[7]

At this point we come to the Jewish custom of grace before and after meals, a custom which in itself is simple enough, but which was destined to have far-reaching consequences for the origins of the Christian Eucharist. The first thing we must notice about this Jewish custom is that it is not just a prayer but a ritual, comprising word and action together, carried out in a set pattern, with its own norms and rubrics. While the custom inevitably evolved over the centuries, the main clue we have to what it was like in Our Lord's time is found in the custom as it has come down to us in the rabbinical tradition, up to and including our own time. We have sufficient information to be able to say, with fair probability, that this is the kind of thing it was in Our Lord's day, while granting that some of the rubrics and especially the texts used are from a later date.

Grace before meals was a ritual with bread and a short prayer of blessing of the Creator. Grace after meals was a more protracted ritual over wine, with a somewhat longer benediction consisting of three (nowadays four) prayers arranged in a fixed pattern of intentions, namely blessing, thanksgiving and supplication. Perhaps the best way to give some idea of the kind of ritual we are referring to is to write out a sample text, also indicating some of the actions which accompany it.[8]

Grace Before Meals
– loaves placed under a napkin

P. Blessed are you,
   Lord our God,
   King of the universe,
– uncover and raise   you who bring forth bread
– break a loaf and distribute   from the earth.

Grace After Meals
– wine poured into the cup

P. Let us say grace.
R. Blessed be the name of the Lord
   from this time forth and forever.
P. With the approval of those
      present
   we will bless our God,
   him of whose bounty we have
      partaken.
R. Blessed be our God,
   he of whose bounty we have
      partaken,
   and through whose goodness we
      live.
P. Blessed be our God,
   he of whose bounty we have
      partaken,
   and through whose goodness we
      live.
R. Blessed be he, and blessed be his
      name.

– cup taken and raised

P. Blessed are you, Lord our God,
   King of the universe,
   you who feed the whole world
   in goodness, in grace and in
   mercy.

– water poured in

P. We thank you, Lord our God,

for giving us as our inheritance
a desirable, good and ample land.

P. Have mercy, O Lord our God,
on Israel, your people,
on Jerusalem, your city,
and on Zion,
the dwelling-place of your glory,
on your altar and on your
sanctuary.

Blessed are you, O Lord,
as you build up Jerusalem.

– cup consumed

In considering the above text it is important to bear in mind that it is given only as an indication of the *kind* of thing the Jewish ritual was in Our Lord's day. We are not suggesting that he would have followed this text. Indeed we are told that, as regards the actual words, a certain freedom was left to the individual, once one remained within the traditional structure. On feast-days one could expand the prayer to include references to the particular season, as we will see later in the Passover. But the structure of three prayers in the pattern of blessing, thanksgiving and petition seems to have been the expected thing. After Our Lord's day the final short blessing, such as that given above, was expanded into a fourth prayer.

The literary form of the grace at meals, just as the literary form of the Christian Eucharistic Prayer, is a separate question from the event of worship as such. Our main interest here is in the event rather than in the expression. People bless God and God blesses the people. Something happens.[9] His blessing descends on their table fellowship and on their life. So real was this for the Jew that, if members of the family were sick and unable to be present at table, a portion of the bread used was brought to them, so that they too could share in this blessing descending from God.

Finally, behind the event of worship and the understanding the people had of its efficaciousness, lies the spirituality which gives life to the whole practice. The very notion of blessing brings us back to a spirituality of creation. All blessing comes from the Creator, whose continual care of all that he has made and whose constant renewal of the gift of life are the primary blessings of God to his world. As people respond to these descending blessings by the ascending blessings of praise, thanksgiving, gifts and service, they give evidence of their creation faith as their way of finding their place in existence and of entering into the harmony of the universe.

THE BREAKING OF BREAD

'Our understanding of our forms of worship underwent a radical transformation some forty years ago when it finally occurred to someone that Jesus was a Jew.' These words of the great liturgist Dom Gregory Dix in 1949 are still worth recalling today as we come closer to the question of the Christian Eucharist.[10] It is not that we can set aside the past two thousand years and hope to arrive at the Last Supper 'as it actually was'; but if we are to interpret the documents of faith, through which alone we can understand the Lord's institution, then we must bear in mind how Christ himself, his apostles and evangelists, were all speaking and writing out of their own age-old traditions of spirituality and worship.

The question is sometimes posed as to how much the apostles at the Last Supper would have understood what Our Lord was saying and doing at the time. While it is most unlikely that they really appreciated the significance of what was happening, they would certainly have understood much more than we would of his words and actions. He was speaking and acting in the language of Jewish ritual, a language they had all learned from the time they were knee-high. Consequently, despite their basic incomprehension, it is reasonable to suppose that enough came across to them for them to be able to work it all out later, though not without the help of the Holy Spirit. According to the unanimous witness of our four basic accounts of the Last Supper, that night saw the institution of our Eucharist, but in order for us to be able to read the apostles' testimony to that fact, we must first laboriously reconstruct for ourselves the language of those rituals which they took for granted.

The Jewish table customs, described earlier in this chapter, clearly throw a lot of light on the origins of the Eucharist. A basic thesis of this book is that, in instituting an act of worship for his community, Our Lord did not begin from nothing. For the external form of his worship he turned to the familiar rituals of grace before and after meals. These he then celebrated in a new way, relating them to himself and to his death. In time, as will be suggested in the next chapter, these two rituals fused into one complex sign of Christ's death and resurrection, but at first it seems that they were celebrated before and after a communal meal. In taking these rituals Our Lord gave them a new meaning, one that immeasurably transcended their humble origins, and so there will always be an eloquent message for Christians in the notion that, in choosing an external form for his worship, Our Lord turned, not to the elaborate liturgy of the Temple, but to the ordinary family life of the Jewish people.

However our story of the New Testament witness to the Eucharist begins, not with the four accounts of the Last Supper in Paul and the Synoptics, but with two verses of the Acts of the Apostles, verses of a deceptive simplicity.

> And they devoted themselves
> to the apostles' teaching and fellowship,
> to the breaking of bread and the prayers . . .
>
> And day by day, attending the temple together
> and breaking bread in their homes,
> they partook of food with glad and generous hearts . . .
> (Acts 2:42, 46)

The phrase which draws the attention of theologians of the Eucharist to these verses is the twice-repeated formula, 'the breaking of bread'. What does it mean in this precise context? It is clear that at other levels of the New Testament tradition, and in some other early writings, it referred to the Eucharist.[11] Could this already be the case in this very early text in the second chapter of Acts?

The age of the phrase in Acts 2 is underlined by the fact that it occurs in a particular kind of text referred to as 'summaries' of the life of the early Church: Acts 2:42–46; 4:32–35; 5:12–14. These summaries seem to come from a very ancient tradition of the community. Consequently, the meaning of the phrase at a later time (e.g. Acts 20:7) is no argument for its meaning in Acts 2; but one can argue from one summary to the other in order to fill out our picture of the life of the community at that stage of what is called 'the apostolic life'.

Every conceivable interpretation of 'the breaking of bread' in Acts 2:42, 46 has had its adherents. First of all some have said that it is not Eucharistic at all but refers either to an ordinary grace before meals or to the meal itself. Now to speak of 'gathering for grace before meals' is an unlikely mode of speech in itself, while for the second interpretation there is simply no support in Jewish sources of the period. Furthermore the juxtaposition of the phrase with mention of preaching and prayer is a strong pointer to the liturgical nature of the entire context.

The majority of commentators favour some kind of Eucharistic interpretation of the phrase. Lietzmann saw in it evidence for his theory of a wineless Eucharist in the early community, but this notion has long lost the support of exegetes.[12] The effective choice seems to lie between taking the phrase 'breaking of bread' to be a name for the Eucharist by itself, or taking it as a comprehensive term to refer by synecdoche to the entire eating and drinking together of the early community, which would have opened with the Eucharistic bread ritual, continued with the community meal, and then closed with the Eucharistic cup ritual. The hypothesis that the Eucharist owes its origin to the Jewish grace before and after meals makes it highly probable that at first it was celebrated in the sequence just indicated, and this notion gives some likelihood to our interpreting the problematic phrase in the latter comprehensive sense, at least when it is used in Acts 2.

This interpretation gets some confirmation and content by setting the breaking of bread in the context of the early 'apostolic life' as illustrated by the three 'summaries' taken together. Three characteristics of this early celebration might be tentatively proposed. First of all, it is something specific of the Christian way of life, as are the other activities mentioned, notably in Acts 2:42. This is borne out also by the way this breaking of bread takes place among the baptized and apart from the Temple and the other Jews.[13] Already the Eucharist, if such it be, is one of the main expressions here below of what it is to be a Christian.

Secondly, this ritual seems to be in some sense eschatological in its content. This emerges from the spirit of exultation in which it is celebrated. The word for exultation is *agalliasis* in Greek, an unusual word, associated from the Old Testament with the coming of the kingdom,[14] but which in the New Testament comes to be focused on the Parousia.[15] A particular connection between the Eucharist and the coming of the kingdom is affirmed in other New Testament texts,[16] which is especially understandable if, with Late Judaism, one thinks of that future event, not just as a meal in the presence of God,[17] but as one with the Messiah.[18] A Eucharist with a markedly eschatological emphasis is exactly the kind of thing which the general movement of the New Testament tradition would lead one to expect in the early days of the community.[19]

However New Testament eschatology received a particular accent from the disciples' experience of the Lord as risen: they came to think of his resurrection as a kind of anticipation of the coming of the kingdom. Consequently we have here a reason for seeing this early breaking of bread as focused on the Risen Lord, and arguably on his presence, in continuity with the meals in the resurrection narratives.[20] The text in Acts 2 makes no mention of the Lord's death as figuring in their celebration, but if the resurrection is central to it, then the thought of his death cannot be far away and must soon make itself explicit, since for those early communities resurrection and death were so closely intertwined (Acts 3:18; Luke 24:26).

A third characteristic of this early breaking of bread, one which fits in even more appropriately with the Eucharistic interpretation, is the way it is closely associated with the unity of the community (Acts 2:42). Here a key word and a key theme for the whole history of this sacrament make their first appearance in what we are arguing is a Eucharistic context, namely the word and theme of *koinōnia*, communion. It is remarkable how strongly this theme of unity is stressed in each of the summaries (Acts 2:44; 4:32; 5:12). *Koinōnia* here can refer to the general spirit of fellowship among the believers, but it can also include a reference to certain specific acts, like holding their goods in common (Acts 4:32), or their eating meals together, or perhaps even to their making a collection for the needy, a custom later called *koinōnia* by St Paul (Rom 15:26). Whatever about that, the way this communion and this breaking of bread are listed in Acts 2:42 among the acts specific of the baptized shows how their breaking bread together at once expresses and deepens the unity which marks them out as Christians.

It must be admitted that the argument for a Eucharistic interpretation of this breaking of bread in Acts 2:42, 46 can only be tentative. Nevertheless it is worth making, if it really gives us our earliest Eucharistic text in the New Testament. It is also impressive in the picture it gives of the early community celebrating in eschatological joy with one mind and heart. We might also note the surprising detail it yields, namely that this celebration apparently took place *every day*, if, as seems most likely, the second phrase in verse 46 is governed by the sentence's opening adverb in the Greek.

NOTES

1   The foundational study for this subject was that of J. P. Audet, 'Esquisse historique du genre littéraire de la "bénédiction" juive et de l'"eucharistie" chrétienne', RB 65 (1958), pp. 371–99.
2   C. Giraudo, *La struttura letteraria della preghiera eucaristica* (Rome: Biblical Institute Press, 1981), p. 183, n. 7.
3   E.g. Audet, art. cit., p. 398.
4   J. Heinemann, *Prayer in the Talmud* (Berlin: Gruyter, 1977), p. 103.
5   L. Ligier, *Magnae orationis eucharisticae seu anaphorae origo et significatio* (*ad usum privatum auditorum*) (Rome: Gregorian University, 1964), pp. 3–18.
6   This is given as the reason why salt is commonly taken by Jews with bread, just as salt was once offered with the sacrifices in the Temple.
7   E. Mazza, *The Eucharistic Prayers of the Roman Rite* (New York: Pueblo, 1986), p. 17.
8   The letter 'P' in the text indicates the part recited by the person presiding; the letter 'R' indicates the reply of those present. The text given for the grace before meals is translated from the Latin of L. Ligier in A. Hänggi and I. Pahl (eds), *Prex eucharistica: Textus e variis liturgiis antiquioribus selecti* (Fribourg: Editions Universitaires, 1968), p. 7. That for the introductory dialogue in the grace after meals is taken from *The Authorized Daily Prayer Book of the United Hebrew Congregation of the British Commonwealth of Nations* (London: Eyre & Spottiswoode, 1962), pp. 376–8. In both cases other prayers precede those cited. The text for the three main prayers of the grace after meals is taken from the Hebrew given by L. Finkelstein, 'The Birkat-ha-mazon', *Jewish Quarterly Review* 19 (1928–9), pp. 211–62. A Latin version of the latter is given by L. Ligier in *Prex eucharistica*, p. 9.
9   Cf. Gen 27:33, where something happens which cannot be revoked.
10 Dix cited by T. J. Talley in *Studia Liturgica* 11 (1976), p. 138.
11 1 Cor 10:16; perhaps Luke 24:30, 35; Acts 20:7, 11; 27:35; *Didache* 14:1; Ignatius, *To the Ephesians* 20:2.
12 For a recent negative view of the notion see X. Léon-Dufour, *Sharing the Eucharistic Bread* (New York: Paulist, 1987), p. 94.
13 *Didachē* (Acts 2:42), as distinct from *kerygma*, is for the baptized.
14 Acts 2:46. Cf. Isa 29:9; 49:13.
15 1 Pet 1:6, 8; 4:13; John 8:56; Rev 19:7; Jude 24; Matt 5:12.
16 See Mark 14:25; Matt 26:29; perhaps also Luke 14:15. The eschatological logion is regarded by many exegetes as the most certain element in the Institution Narrative, e.g. R. H. Fuller, 'Jesus Christ as Saviour in the New Testament', *Interpretation* 35 (1981), p. 146.

17 Isa 25:6ff.; 55:1ff.; 65:13–14; Ps 22(23).

18 Ethiopian Enoch 62:14; Slavic Enoch 42:5; Luke 12:37; Rev 3:20; 19:9.

19 This eschatological note in the 'breaking of bread' in Acts 2 gives some basis already for rejecting the notion of a wineless Eucharist here, since the cup was especially associated both with festivity in general and with eschatological rejoicing in particular. This association was already evidenced in the Passover, as it would be later in the Eucharist, e.g. Mark 14:25.

20 Acts 1:4; 10:40–41. See also Luke 24:28–43; John 21:9–14, though these passages are, of course, from a much later time than Acts 2.

2

⊠ The Institution Narrative

From all the documents of the ancient world which have come down to us, few fragments have been more carefully studied and more passionately debated than the handful of sentences which are known to us as the Eucharistic Institution Narrative. The longest version we have, that of Matthew in the Greek, contains only some eighty words, yet it is scarcely too much to say that, wherever Christianity has found a home, these few verses have helped to change the world. To some readers the chapter which now follows may seem meticulous to the point of exaggeration, but if one bears in mind the unique importance of the subject as we have just described it, then surely such care cannot be considered excessive.

The Institution Narrative has reached us in four versions: Luke 22:19-20; I Corinthians 11:23-25; Mark 14:22-24; Matthew 26:26-28. These are the texts which scholars are constantly taking apart and putting together again, trying to assess their interrelationships and relative ages, and to identify the influences which lie behind them. There is a general consensus that recognizes two main traditions in these texts, that of Luke and Paul on the one hand, and that of Mark and Matthew on the other. One has only to read the texts, noting the similarities between them, to appreciate the reasons for that view. If however one asks, which tradition is the older, there are two schools of thought, some pointing to Luke-Paul, some to Mark-Matthew. If one asks the further question, which version within each tradition is the older, whilst most will put Mark before Matthew, the priority of Luke over Paul, or vice versa, is still subject to debate.

The main argument for the priority of Mark over Luke-Paul is linguistic, based on the number of semitisms in the Marcan text. Those who disagree with this argument will reply that the conclusion does not follow. Semitisms are part of the style of the entire gospel of Mark, so that they could be due to the translator of the passage rather than to the age of the tradition it contains. Furthermore, there are more semitisms in Luke than in Paul, yet this does not deter most exegetes from regarding Paul as more primitive than Luke.

Associated with the argument we are here questioning is the custom of some exegetes in describing the Mark–Matthew tradition as 'Palestinian' and that of Luke–Paul as 'Antiochene'. It must be said that there is less basis in the texts for such descriptions than is commonly supposed. In both traditions there are many semitisms. In both an Aramaic original has left its traces, so that both can equally well be described as Palestinian in some degree. Such descriptions only serve to create a bias, and they give the impression of a certainty which the facts scarcely justify.

The argument for the priority of Luke–Paul over Mark–Matthew depends on how one understands the history of the New Testament tradition, namely on the consideration of the influences which shaped the text and on how these can be seen to develop. It is one aspect of the interpretation of that process which we are now about to treat in this chapter.

But before getting into the issue we might point out that this division among scholars contains a salutary lesson for anyone who would approach this subject in the spirit of a naïve historicism. It is very understandable that fervent Christians should desire to reconstruct for themselves every word and gesture which occurred on that momentous night and then to play them back for themselves in the cinema of the mind. But here, as in so many places in the New Testament, the desires of our devotion have to yield to the discrimination of scholars. While it can be maintained – though this too is controversial – that the four accounts have enough agreements in their essential lines to ground an historical argument as to the general character of what actually happened on that night, it must be accepted that our knowledge of the details remains very inadequate.[1] As Léon-Dufour once said, 'The historically certain is imprecise, and the precise is hardly historically certain'.[2] All attempts to get behind the four accounts to some primitive original must fail. What exactly did Our Lord say over the cup: 'This is my blood', or 'This cup is the new covenant in my blood'? He almost certainly did not say both, but what he actually said we will never know.

Given then this impossibility, the question now arises as to what precisely the present enquiry may hope to achieve. In the first place, of course, we hope to attain a better understanding of the four versions which have come down to us, but there is more. Although access to the original event *in all its concrete details* is barred to us, these ancient texts do lead us back most of the way through the centuries, bringing us to the faith of the early communities, who clearly celebrated the Eucharist for their people and saw the events of that last night of Christ's life as the fountainhead of what they themselves were saying and doing in their worship. In the process they reveal how they themselves understood the Eucharist, and it is this Eucharistic theology of the early Christians which is the direct object of our quest. Those of us then who take the teaching of the apostolic Church as normative for our faith will find in this whole reflection an irreplaceable guide as to what the Eucharist actually is, both then and now.

It will be noticed that our attention has now shifted from the event of Christ's farewell meal with his disciples to the gatherings for worship of the early Christians. It is these gatherings which give us the 'life-situation' – *Sitz im Leben* – of our four accounts of the Last Supper. The significance of this shift will be pinpointed by a question crucial to the entire research: what is the literary genre of these four texts? A first acquaintance with them might presume that here we have four accounts emanating from eye-witnesses to inform us of what was said and done on that night. In this view the literary genre is that of historical reportage. This, however, is not the way the majority of exegetes view these texts. They see them rather as liturgical documents, fragments of early liturgy, where they were part of what was recited and proclaimed in the very celebration of these early Eucharists. This is why these texts bring us, first and foremost, into the heart of the post-Easter community. Only secondly and indirectly do they bring us to the Last Supper.

The basis for this view comes from trying to explain the differences between the four versions. If the intention of those who framed these texts was primarily to inform us of the events by which the Eucharist was instituted, then the discrepancies between them are troublesome indeed. But if their intention was rather to express the *meaning* of what was instituted on that night, then their apparent indifference to the historical details becomes that much more understandable. Furthermore, some of the differences can be explained if we regard the accounts as polished by usage, like coins passed from hand to hand. Constant repetition in liturgy would make such an alignment and ordering of the phrases intelligible. In brief, the primary purpose is, not to narrate, but to celebrate.[3]

If this liturgical nature of the four versions can be maintained, then this gives us immediately a feature of the Eucharist not without its practical implications. When we meet the early Christian liturgy in these texts, it is already being experienced in the different communities as a relatively fixed formula, constantly repeated from occasion to occasion. The variations between each version can be understood as being part of the distinctive traditions of the various communities, but the evidence is that within each community the celebrant followed a set pattern of actions, and, at least in this crucial section of the service, a set form of words. At no time is there evidence of a Christian celebrant being totally free to say whatever comes into his head!

With this view of the text's literary genre to guide us, we can now examine the four versions in more detail, attempting to clarify their interrelationships. First of all we must stress the basic unity amongst the four versions, greater than any diversity between them. As we suggested earlier, this unity is the basis for an historical argument as to the general lines of what happened on the night of institution, but our interest now is in the common structure of the four versions, the internal symmetry of which fits in with the hypothesis of their liturgical genre. This structure, though not complete in every case, can be set out as follows:

(a) Introduction
(b) Bread word— demonstrative phrase
               — participial phrase
               — command to repeat
(c) Cup word — demonstrative phrase
               — participial phrase
               — command to repeat.

When the new Eucharistic Prayers of the Roman Rite were being drawn up after the Second Vatican Council, it was decided that it would be confusing if the words of consecration, and even the doxology at the end of the canon, were different in each prayer. In this we see a practical need at work similar to that which seems to preside over the structure of our four versions. Liturgical recital favours parallelism of forms, and this we see already in the remarkable symmetry between bread-word and cup-word in the Institution Narrative.

But as well as comparing one part with another within each version, there is also light to be gained by comparing and contrasting the versions among themselves. As the symmetry between bread-word and cup-word is experienced in frequent recital, a dynamic is set up between the two sections which different communities work out differently. In so doing, not only do they betray the varying influences and mentalities behind their understanding of the tradition, but some inevitably carry the development of the text further than others. The question then arises as to what factors in these versions may be seen as benchmarks in the progress of this development. Three in particular may be picked out as follows:

— the progressive elimination of historical details;
— the setting of phrases in parallel;
— the explicitation of the implicit.

Historical details

Liturgy tends to eliminate what is not liturgically necessary. It eliminates narrative in order to highlight the significance of the rite. Everyone, after all, will be familiar with the story, but in celebration the crucial thing is to enter into the meaning of it all. Consequently, the lessening of such details in a version is taken to indicate a later stage in development. We notice that in the Marcan account there are fewer such details than in Luke–Paul: 'On the night he was betrayed . . . after the meal'.

Parallelism

Perhaps the main index of development is found in the degree to which the symmetry between bread-word and cup-word has been established. This occurs to some extent in each of the four versions. While one might hold that it is more striking in Mark–Matthew than in Luke–Paul, the sum of the data does not give a straightforward picture:

— the participial phrases are more clearly symmetrical in Luke –Paul than in Mark–Matthew;

— the command to repeat, totally absent from Mark–Matthew, is found only once in Luke, but twice in Paul;

— the verb 'to take' is repeated over each element in Mark and Matthew;

— where in Luke and Paul the demonstrative phrases focus on 'body' and 'cup', in Mark and Matthew they focus on 'body' and 'blood'. Since this latter pair are the elements of a sacrifice in Jewish ritual, some scholars detect a sophisticated theological intent in the formation of this particular parallel.

Explicitation

A later stage of development can also be suggested where the implicit is made explicit. One possible instance of this comes in the Greek of the Pauline cup-word, where the verb 'to be', absent from the demonstrative phrase in Luke, is made explicit. However, in the same two versions, a contrary indication comes in the participial phrase over the bread-word, where the participle, missing in Paul, is supplied by Luke. Since both the words under consideration come at the end of their phrases, one could argue in either case that the word, later missing, was originally present, only to drop off at the end of the phrase at some stage, perhaps simply through chance reasons. Such ambiguity in one or two pieces of evidence taken on their own underlines that the ultimate judgement has to be based on whatever theory provides the most reasonable synthesis of all the diverse data taken as a whole.

A less ambiguous instance of explicitation will be found in Matthew where the phrase 'for the remission of sins' is added to the cup-word. Another example in the Mark–Matthew cup-word is the phrase 'for many' instead of the Lucan 'for you'. Here 'for many' is Suffering Servant language meaning 'for all' (Isa 53:12), and so explicitates the long-term significance behind the Lucan 'for you'.

COMPARING THE TRADITIONS

So far we have been simply looking at the material disposition of the text. In order to go much deeper we must take more account of the ideas being expressed and of the theologies behind them. Here we meet a contrast between each of the two basic traditions, that of Luke–Paul being primarily eschatological, and that of Mark–Matthew being primarily sacrificial. The eschatological character of Luke–Paul comes out especially in the reference to the new covenant, with the context that phrase evokes in Jeremiah 31. This aspect is emphasized all the more by the fact that the reference to cultic sacrifice, so explicit in Mark–Matthew, is here much more subdued. Joined to the fact that the memory of the original meal-setting of the Eucharist is more clearly preserved in Luke–Paul (cf. 'after the meal'), this eschatological aspect inevitably evokes that feasting in eschatological rejoicing which we met already in Acts 2:42 and 46. This is yet another point in favour of the earlier dating of the tradition in Luke–Paul.

The reference to cultic sacrifice in Mark–Matthew is as surprising as it is explicit. Where Luke–Paul cites Jeremiah 31:31, Mark–Matthew takes up Exodus 24:8. The full significance of this will be developed in a subsequent chapter, but already we can see that it marks a more complicated theology of the Eucharist than that found in Luke–Paul and so arguably a later development within the Christian community. Other more obvious points of contrast in the two traditions may also be pointed out, which, as we will see later, will have their place in our hypothesis of development which is gradually emerging.

In Luke–Paul the two rituals of the original Eucharist are seen as separated by a meal. It is in line with this fact that each of the rituals on its own is regarded as a sign of Christ's death and declared to be such in the accompanying words. It also fits in that, as the bread-word on its own is a sign of death, so the word 'body' in Luke–Paul may be taken to refer directly to the whole human being. How then can we describe the relationship between the two rituals? We might say that their relationship is climactic rather than simply a synthesis of parallel statements. Each ritual on its own is a sign of Christ's death, but the ritual over the cup is so in a more developed way. The accompanying phrases in the latter case are more fulsome, for here the narrative has reached its eschatological climax.

In the other tradition the relationship between the two rituals is more puzzling and more subtle. By the time of the Mark–Matthew narrative there is no mention of the intervening meal. The two rites seem to have come together, either simply associated with a meal or totally independent of one. Nor is it a matter of the mere juxtaposition of the two rituals. The accompanying words show that these two are now understood as one complex sign of Christ's death. The clearer symmetry between the bread-word and the cup-word, which we explained above, fits in with the same intent.

Jeremias once referred to the 'enigmatic emptiness' of the Marcan bread-word, given the absence in it of any participial phrase of explanation.[4] What Jeremias failed to appreciate was the organic link between the two rituals in this tradition. The Marcan bread-word is part of the one complex sign of Christ's death, which the two rituals taken together are now seen to constitute. When we relate that fact to the highlighting of 'body' and 'blood' in each of these rituals and recall how these realities are the correlative elements of Jewish ritual sacrifice, then we can appreciate how the whole development of the Mark–Matthew tradition has been drawn into a theology of sacrifice.

THE OLD TESTAMENT BACKGROUND

One of the greatest difficulties nowadays, two millennia after the time of Christ, as people try to understand these ancient texts of the New Testament, lies in our loss of that hidden commentary on the words and deeds of Jesus which his contemporaries carried about with them as the legacy of their past. It is not only that they shared a common language, but that they also shared a common history and a whole inheritance of associations and concepts formed throughout the Old Testament. As we pointed out previously, we in our time have no alternative but to attempt laboriously to reconstruct what they knew instinctively and took for granted.

Two notions in particular from this context stand out as problematic in our contemporary world, sacrifice and covenant. Both of these were central to the Old Testament, as they are central to the Institution Narrative, but both of them imply a network of ideas and associations which have long vanished from ordinary language and consciousness. 'Covenant', in its biblical sense, is no longer part of the average Christian's religious experience. 'Sacrifice' for some has so many applied senses that its original meaning can no longer be assumed. For others, as for instance in the case of some African Christians, it can be part of their religious experience in its proper sense, but this can be as much a hindrance as a help. I recall one of my African students saying that in his culture, if you said you were going to sacrifice, people would wonder what you had done wrong! For them sacrifice is essentially expiatory. Yet since these two concepts remain crucial for the Institution Narrative, there is no alternative but to study them carefully and to explain them at some length in our preaching and religious education.

The notion of sacrifice

Sacrifice is an elusive notion. At first sight it seems obvious enough, and many a scholar has tried to define it both in theology and in comparative religion, but no acceptable definition has ever been able to establish itself. This fact is already telling us something. Sacrifice seems to be one of those primal notions of the human mind which apparently we can grasp and implement long before being able to put it into words. Bernard Lonergan speaks of defining a term by knowing how to use it, and this seems to be the case with sacrifice.[5]

It now seems that the reason for so many failures in defining sacrifice lies in the attempt to capture it in some universal concept. Of its nature, sacrifice is so much a part of human religious tradition that it cannot really be conceived in the abstract. It is essentially an empirical notion, varying in its nuances and rituals from people to people and from faith to faith.

The scriptural notion of sacrifice takes up the latter approach. It is only when theologians began to follow the exegetes rather than the philosophers that they made any headway in the matter. When the New Testament makes use of this notion, its starting-point has to be, not sacrifice as understood in some universal concept of comparative religion, but sacrifice as understood in the actual tradition of the Old Testament.

Sacrifice, as religion generally, has its roots in our deepest human instincts, but if we want to explore its meaning more closely, we must take it in the concrete, as an aspect of how the people of the Bible actually understood themselves before their Maker. Old Testament religion is built upon an interpersonal relationship between God and his people. Indeed it is a loving relationship, for in Israel's central creed, the *Shemah*, people are invited to *love* the Lord their God with all their minds and hearts (Deut 6:5). At the same time they do not lose their sense of the divine transcendence, nor do they indulge in any over-familiarity. The relationship with God is unique. Ultimately there is no adequate analogy for it, for God is not just one being among other beings.

How then do the people of the Bible come before this God of theirs? They want to give themselves to him, to belong to him, to be one with him. The religion of Israel is not just admiration of the marvels of Yahweh nor just dependence on the Lord of the universe, but it is a search for communion with the Saviour God, to become his possession for ever.[6]

Stirred by this deep movement within, the people of the Bible seek to express their inmost feelings in the most fitting manner open to them. They have various ways of representing their feelings, but most religions have what they consider their highest expression of this unique relationship, and the Israelites are no exception. That expression is ritual sacrifice, and our first description of it can be that it is simply their highest act of worship.

What then is the external form which this kind of worship takes in the concrete experience of the Bible? Its purpose, we recall, is to express the people's belonging to God and their desire to belong to him ever more fully. The way the Bible enacts that desire in ritual lies in making some form of presentation to God, a transfer of ownership over an offering. The worshipper makes a gift to God as a sign of self-giving. Other religions might organize it differently, or at least understand it differently, but this is the way Israel in fact understood it, as the testimony of modern exegetes bears out.[7]

The protocol of sacrifice among the Jews went as follows. The altar was understood as a special symbol of the divinity. To signify the transfer of ownership over the gift, the offering was brought into contact with the altar. This explains how one of the ordinary terms for offering is *corban*, meaning 'to bring near' (see Mark 7:11). In the more solemn sacrifices one offered a more precious gift, such as an animal of one's flock. In such sacrifices the most sacred part of the victim, the blood, was brought to the altar, the part standing for the whole. The Jews seem to have been unique in regarding blood in this way. In their view it meant life, for the blood is where the life is (Lev 17:11). That is why they looked on it as the most 'divine' part of the animal. In other cultures blood is a sign of death. In the Bible it is a sign of life.

Through this understanding of sacrifice, taken *a posteriori* from the concrete tradition of the Bible, we have an answer to a problem which long divided Catholic theologians. There used to be two schools of thought as to what constituted a sacrifice, the oblationist and the immolationist views. The terms speak for themselves. For the oblationists it was the giving of a gift; for the immolationists it was the destruction of the victim. Once theologians began to approach the question in an *a posteriori* manner, the arguments of the oblationists carried the day.[8]

It is true that in Israelite sacrifice there can be an element of destruction, but this is required rather as a pre-condition of the ritual than as constitutive of sacrifice as such. We can see an indication of the secondary nature of this immolation in the fact that often it was carried out by the worshippers themselves and not by the priest, whereas in the classical liturgy of the Temple only the latter could bring the blood to the altar.[9] In sacrifices for sin the destruction of the victim received added significance, as the offering was thereby removed from the worshipper's use and could be regarded as a kind of compensation for the offence.

Modern exegetes rightly stress that, in atonement, the role of blood in relation to sin is a purifying one for the Jews. This is what we mean by 'expiation'. The perspective is a descending one, and it fits in well with the sacred character we have ascribed to blood. But in so far as this takes place through an offering made to God, there is inevitably a certain 'ascending' or propitiatory aspect also. Then there is the fact that intercession was always an integral part of atonement sacrifices.[10] Many contemporary writers highlight the expiatory aspect to the exclusion of the propitiatory, but, as Schürmann once pointed out, one has to be particularly wary of theological prejudices where the question of human co-operation enters in, as it does with oblation and propitiation.[11] One must consider the sacrificial event as a whole and not just isolate one particular aspect of the ritual. It is in such an integral perspective that it becomes clear that propitiation is an intrinsic part of Jewish sacrifice for sin.

However, as well as people who underplay the propitiatory aspect of the Old Testament, there are also those who exaggerate it. This comes frequently with regard to the notion of substitution in the case of a sin-offering. The idea of a victim punished as a substitute for the sinner did exist in Israel in the case of the ritual of the scapegoat (Lev 16:20–28). Furthermore this notion is found in other religions in relation to the offering of sacrifice, and it must have been from the surrounding nations that this particular ritual entered Israel; but precisely because of the understanding of sacrifice outlined above, the scapegoat ritual was clearly distinguished by the Jews from sacrifice in the proper sense. Once the scapegoat was burdened with the sin of the people, it was considered something unholy, to be driven out into the desert. In Jewish sacrifice, on the other hand, the victim becomes the embodiment of holiness. All that is offered is holy, says the Book of Numbers 18:9. A victim in such a state is the opposite of sinful and could not be the bearer of sin.

One final common misapprehension of Jewish sacrifice to be excluded is the notion that sacrifice is a kind of meal with God. Once again, such a notion is certainly found in the history of religions, and it probably existed among the nations surrounding the Jews. Evidence of it can be detected in the crude language of Genesis 8:21, a form of speech which entered the sacrificial language of Israel.[12] But that such expressions are to be taken only in a metaphorical sense is clear once one keeps in mind the dominant concept of sacrifice in Israel. It is true that some of their sacrifices had a significant meal-aspect. It is also true that the notion of a meal with God was found in Israel, though only at some exceptional moments.[13] In the ordinary course of Old Testament liturgy, sacrifice was understood rather as a meal before God than as a meal with God, and this approach seems more in keeping with the Jews' unique sense of the divine transcendence.[14]

The notion of covenant

'Covenant' is one of the most sacred terms in the whole religious vocabulary of Israel. It is the basic metaphor that describes the framework of relationship between God and the people, solemnized in the great scene in Exodus 24:1–11, but present in their consciousness ever after. In its original meaning a covenant is a bond, though the precise etymology of the Hebrew term *berith* remains uncertain. In Greek it is translated by *diathēkē*. This is a common word in Greek for a person's last will and testament, and though this idea is sometimes associated with our term, as for instance in Hebrews 9:16–17, there is general agreement today that *diathēkē* in the Institution Narrative is to be understood rather from the Hebrew word *berith* than from the Greek notion of a testament.

From earliest times the relationship of the people with God has been spoken of under the image of a covenant, but it is understandable that, given the fundamental nature of the term, its meaning should develop over the centuries, inseparably intertwined with the people's growing understanding of their faith. In the earliest occurrences of the idea, the word is spoken with the greatest sense of awe. Often it comes out of a divine theophany. The emphasis is on the divine initiative, and the covenant is sealed in a solemn act of cult. Obligation is always central to a covenant, and in this early stage the obligation can be seen as a one-sided affair, for instance when God binds himself by oath to Noah (Gen 9:8–17).

With the passage of time, more stress comes to be placed on the human partner. The covenant is seen more clearly as a two-sided undertaking, an agreement between God and the people. The content of this agreement on God's side is the election of Israel. On the people's side it is the keeping of the Law. The famous formula of the covenant sums it up: 'I will be your God and you shall be my people' (Lev 26:12).

At this stage the covenant is beginning to look very much like a contract, but this notion could easily mislead us. Strictly speaking, in relation to a contract, the partners are equal, but in no sense can any human partner be the equal of the divine. For this reason the covenant has been compared by some scholars to a vassal-treaty rather than to a business-contract. Just as the sovereign makes a treaty with his vassals, while losing nothing of his sovereignty over them, so the freedom of the human partner in accepting the divine law takes nothing from the sovereignty of God.[15]

With this greater appreciation of the covenant as a reciprocal relationship, greater emphasis comes to be placed on the role of the word, of law and of mutual pledge. The covenant is even compared to a marriage (Ezek 16:8; Mal 2:14), though the analogy is necessarily imperfect, since the human partner is not just an individual, nor even a clan, but the whole nation.

Ultimately the covenant is about love, God's love for his people and their love for him. This is already implicit in the very origins of the idea, which seems to be based on the image of kinship and blood-brotherhood. In the final stage of development this aspect receives a new depth as the prophets and their followers hold up to Israel a new ideal of interiority. In the midst of the great scandals and disasters of the people, the prophetic eye discerns from afar a vision of a new covenant at the climax of history. In this prophetic future, belonging to the covenant will be a matter of 'knowing' Yahweh, that is of knowing and loving his will (Jer 9:23; 22:16; cf. 2:8); and this knowledge will be written by God in the human heart, as he removes from us our hearts of stone (Ezek 36:26).

Three aspects of this prophetic vision may be underlined as anticipations of the New Testament. In this new covenant, not only will God play his own part, but he will take over that of his partner as well, writing his law in our hearts. In this way the prophetic vision anticipates Paul's doctrine of grace. Then this new interiority is to be brought about by the Lord's own spirit (Ezek 36:26–27). Already the Christian Pentecost is on the horizon. Finally, in one of the last of the prophets, we read that this new age is to be marked by a new worship, spanning the world from east to west with the offering of a pure gift to God (Mal 1:11). This text was to be a favourite one in the Eucharistic theology of the early centuries.

The covenant sacrifice

If the early Christian Apologists found special Eucharistic significance in Malachi 1:11, they were not the first to look for a basis for Eucharistic offering in the Old Testament. It is remarkable how as early as the Institution Narrative in Mark and Matthew we find an explicit evocation of the great sacrifice described in Exodus 24:1–11. Since this episode of the Pentateuch is so important for a New Testament theology of the Eucharist, we must delay over it and set it in its context.

The great scene of Exodus 24 comes as the conclusion of the story of the Sinai covenant, which opens in chapter 19 of that book. On the mountain God appears to Moses and reveals the Decalogue to him. After three intervening chapters, which go into the Law in more detail, comes this scene in which the people accept the Law and their acceptance is ratified by the offering of a sacrifice.

Covenants could be ratified in Israel by various kinds of ritual. In the case of individuals it could be something as simple as a handshake (2 Kings 10:15; Esdr 10:19), or the exchange of gifts (1 Sam 18:3; 20:8). A common meal was another form of ratification, which could be sacrificial (Gen 31:54) or non-sacrificial (Gen 31:46; 26:30), depending on circumstances. Various kinds of blood-rite were also in use. The ritual in Genesis 15:9–21 is probably non-sacrificial,[16] but clearly sacrificial is that in Exodus 24.

The interpretation of Exodus 24:1–11 is complicated by the results of documentary analysis. Different verses seem to come from different traditions, as reflected in the following tentative scheme:

vv. 1–2; 9–11— Yahwist
vv. 3–6; 8   — Elohist
v. 7   — Deuteronomic Editors.

This scheme is some help in interpreting the problematic gesture in verse 8. Perhaps the best clue in understanding it is provided by the analogous ritual in Exodus 29:21 (cf. Lev 8:30). In the whole of the Old Testament there are only four instances of a blood-rite sealing a covenant, two of them probably sacrificial, Exodus 24 and 29; two of them probably not sacrificial, Genesis 15 and Jeremiah 34:19. In Hebrews 9:18–23 the ritual of Exodus 24:8 is understood as purificatory. This is probably a Christian misinterpretation. The analogy with Exodus 29 suggests that its meaning is consecratory. Some scholars question whether the ritual is intrinsic to the sacrifice or additional to it. One indication that it is intrinsic might be the fact that it can be placed in the same Elohistic tradition as verses 3–6.

This is the kind of question which brings home to us how modest we must be in making affirmations about the religious mentality of such a distant past. For instance when P. van Imschoot says that the blood-rite here makes the worshippers be all of one soul, one wonders on what evidence such a claim can be made.[17] Similar circumspection is required in interpreting verses 9–11. Is it a sacrifice or not? Strictly speaking, there is no indication in the text that it is sacrificial, and it would be in keeping with the general character of the Yahwist that it be non-sacrificial.

Such then is the general meaning of this foundational scene in Exodus 24. When we come to study the sacrificial character of the Institution Narrative, we will find that this scene provides one of the basic points of reference. The words of Moses at the rite of sprinkling will be of particular relevance.

The Suffering Servant

One further section of the Old Testament provided significant background for the Institution Narrative, namely the Isaian prophecies of the Suffering Servant.[18] While scholars continue to discuss the original meaning of these profound and mysterious texts, it is their use in the New Testament which is relevant for our purposes. Clearly the early Christians identified the Servant with Jesus, and these prophecies were one of the great Old Testament resources which enabled them to make some sense of the mystery of Our Lord's passion and death. Two aspects in particular of these prophecies are of interest to us here: firstly, the references they contain to the covenant; secondly, their expectation of an atoning death.

Some have thought that the prophecies draw some of their inspiration from the figure of Jeremiah. Certainly the Servant is presented with many of the characteristics of a prophet persecuted as Jeremiah was. He is to preach justice and law, but to work with a self-effacement and restraint which suggest the essentially spiritual nature of his mission. Indeed, according to Isaiah 42:6 and 49:8, the Servant *is* the covenant.[19] Given the spiritual interiority of his mission, he may be seen as the embodiment of the interior perfection of the new covenant, as outlined in Jeremiah 31:33 and Ezekiel 36:26–27. In praying for his persecutors (Isa 53:12), he even goes beyond the figure of Jeremiah, who did not hesitate to curse them (Jer 12:3).

But it is above all through the language of his atoning death that the Servant is significant for the New Testament generally and for the Eucharist in particular. His death is a sacrifice (Isa 53:10). The Servant is led 'like a lamb to the slaughter' (Isa 53:7) and so he is offered up in sacrifice, his life 'poured out' as a libation (Isa 53:12).

This is perhaps the earliest example in Judaism of a martyr's death understood as an atonement. Nor is it simply expiatory. The martyr's death, both here and in Late Judaism, is propitiatory. That is part of the force of comparing his death to a sacrificial *offering*. The theme of interceding for the transgressors (Isa 53:12) is also part of propitiatory sacrifice, as we have noted above. On this basis the vicarious nature of the Servant's death becomes a central theme: he was 'wounded for our transgressions, bruised for our iniquities' (Isa 53:5), bearing 'the sins of many' (Isa 53:12).

When we come to the Institution Narrative it is surely striking that, brief and all as the narrative is, these two significant themes of the Servant prophecies are there given a central place. Firstly the notion of the covenant is stated explicitly in Luke–Paul: 'This is my blood of the covenant'. Secondly, there is the notion of vicarious offering, clearly expressed in the phrases 'for you', 'for many'. Indeed this word 'many' in the Mark–Matthew versions of the cup-word is the very language of Isaiah 53:12. Both in Isaiah and here 'many' means 'all'. Finally, there may be a further echo in the use of 'poured out' in the cup-word, recalling the Hebrew of Isaiah 53:12 where it says that the servant pours out his soul, his life.[20]

With this consideration we conclude the task of this chapter, which was to lay the ground-work for the hypothesis to be put forward in the next one. As well as reviewing the Old Testament background, some idea has been given of the development of the tradition in the text of the Institution Narrative. If the view advanced here leans towards the priority of the Luke–Paul tradition over that found in Mark and Matthew, such a position can only be tentative in itself, but in fact it will be found to fit in well with the argument to be advanced in the chapter to which we now turn.

NOTES

1 'Even on the grounds of strictest historical scholarship it must be judged highly likely that Jesus originated the ritual acts of sharing bread and wine as representing his body and blood which Christians practise to this day': J. D. G. Dunn, *The Evidence for Jesus* (London: SCM, 1985), p. 27.

2 X. Léon-Dufour, 'Jesus' understanding of his death', *Theology Digest* 24 (1976), pp. 293–300, at p. 294.

3 Among scholars who defend the liturgical nature of the texts are L. Bouyer, J. Betz, J. Jeremias, E. Kilmartin, X. Léon-Dufour, L. Ligier. H. Schürmann holds that the texts are solemn speech but not liturgy: *Der Einsetzungsbericht Lk 22:19–20* (Münster: Aschendorff, 1955), p. 65, n. 239; p. 94, n. 290. D. Power believes that they are not directly from the liturgy: *The Eucharist Mystery* (Dublin: Gill & Macmillan, 1992), p. 26.

4 J. Jeremias, *The Eucharistic Words of Jesus* (London: SCM, 1966), p. 167.

5 B. Lonergan, *Doctrinal Pluralism* (Milwaukee: Marquette University Press, 1971), p. 16.

6 Deut 7:6; 26:18; Exod 9:5; cf. Tit 2:14; 1 Pet 2:9–10.

7 R. de Vaux, *Ancient Israel, Its Life and Institutions* (London: Darton, Longman & Todd, 1961), pp. 451–4.

8 Credit for this must go especially to M. de la Taille. See *The Mystery of Faith*, I: *The Sacrifice of Our Lord* (London: Sheed & Ward, 1941), ch. 1. A more recent development of the issue will be found in L. M. Chauvet, *Symbole et sacrement: Une relecture sacramentelle de l'existence chrétienne* (Paris: Cerf, 1988), pp. 104–15, 273–96.

9 Lev 1:4–5; 3:2–3, 7–8, 13–14.

10 In all three places the Septuagint translated the notion of sinners entreating God's favour as 'atonement', *hilaskesthai*: Mal 1:9; Zech 7:2;

8:22. We might add to this the remark of one author that expiatory sacrifices implicitly propitiate by removing the cause of God's 'anger': J. Galot, *Jesus Our Liberator: A Theology of Redemption* (Rome: Gregorian University Press, 1982), p. 105.

11 Schürmann, *Der Einsetzungsbericht*, p. 96, n. 235.

12 Exod 29:18, 25; Lev 1:9, 13; Num 28:2.

13 E.g. Gen 18:1ff.; also at the eschatological banquet.

14 R. de Vaux, *Studies in Old Testament Sacrifice* (Cardiff: University of Wales Press, 1964), p. 42.

15 D. McCarthy, *Treaty and Covenant* (Rome: Biblical Institute Press, 1963).

16 McCarthy, op. cit., p. 163, n. 26.

17 P. van Imschoot, 'L'alliance dans l'Ancien Testament', NRT 74 (1952), pp. 785–805, at p. 789.

18 Isa 42:1–6/7/9; 49:1–6/9; 50:4–11; 52:13 – 53:12. The break-off point in the first two of the songs in particular is open to discussion.

19 As was indicated in the previous note, the inclusion of these verses in the prophecies of the Servant is open to dispute.

20 Hebrew: *he'erah naphscho*. Notice that the word for 'soul' or 'life' here is *nephesh*, which is the same word which is the subject of Lev 17:11, 'The life of the flesh is in the blood'. 'To pour out the blood' and 'to pour out the soul' are basically identical.

3

⊠ *The notion of sacrifice in the Institution Narrative*

Few aspects of the Eucharist have been so divisive among Christians as the doctrine of Eucharistic sacrifice. The attitude to this teaching runs so deep in the minds of all Christian scholars that it inevitably raises the hazard of presuppositions in any approach to the question. Despite the scholarly objectivity which all aim at, it is tantalizing how even in the exegesis of this brief New Testament passage scholars end up only confirming the doctrinal positions with which they started out. A presuppositionless exegesis is impossible, said Bultmann, but part of the explanation may also be found in the texts themselves. They are not necessarily written from a uniform viewpoint, and divergence among exegetes may be partly explained by different people latching on to different aspects in the tradition. It is in the hope of coping with this situation to some extent, and to try to move towards a more comprehensive viewpoint, that this chapter will propose the hypothesis to be set out below.

The key to any treatment of the question is the aspect of development. Sacrifice is such a profound and complex notion for a first-century Jew that it is understandable if it is slow to find an entry into the early accounts of the Eucharist. Nevertheless, as we will see, the evidence for its eventual presence is unmistakable. What we must try to do, therefore, is to consider what was going on in the early community as the awareness of this notion was crystallizing in their minds.

Almost as difficult as the notion of Eucharistic sacrifice was the application of the concept of sacrifice to the events on the cross. This development is the underlying assumption of the Institution Narrative as we now have it. It is a theologoumenon, or theological conclusion, which we often take for granted, so familiar is it from the Epistle to the Hebrews. But it is a surprising notion for a Jew, and can only be seen as coming about through a process of gradual development. It cannot be taken for granted in the earlier texts of the New Testament tradition. Indeed part of the hypothesis which this chapter will advance is the view of a number of scholars that the appreciation of Calvary as sacrificial and that of the Eucharist as sacrificial were two intertwined notions which were only clarified for the early community through a mutual influence between the two.

The very notion of a Christian sense of sacrifice raises a prior issue concerning the attitude of the New Testament to organized external cult generally. It is easy to marshal a whole set of texts in the gospels which attribute to Our Lord a very critical attitude to the Temple and to ritual.[1] On this basis some scholars went so far as to say that Our Lord was against external cult as such and that Christianity is a purely internal religion. This argument, however, is generally abandoned today. It is clear that in this aspect of his mission Our Lord was acting in the line of the prophets. He was no more against cult as such than they were. What he was condemning was the formalism which is the cardinal temptation of all external worship. The purification of cult rather than its abolition seems to have been his real aim, and a contrary set of texts promoting forms of external worship can be gathered from the gospels as well as from the prophets.[2]

Our Lord's attitude to the Temple was a special issue. It was one of the key points raised in his trial, and it is hard to avoid the impression that Our Lord was pointing beyond the Temple to its fulfilment in the new worship of the End Times. A key text here is John 4:24.[3] Some have interpreted it as speaking of a purely spiritual, internal religion. More likely is the view that 'spirit' here refers to the Holy Spirit. The worship the New Testament favours is not spiritual in that purely internal sense, but eschatological.[4] It gives the Holy Spirit, God's gift for the End Times, and it can do this through some external rituals, of which Baptism is the clearest example (John 3:5). Our Lord's attitude then to the Temple, while critical, is not one of direct opposition, but it is one which does permit of the Temple's being eventually superseded.

AN HYPOTHESIS OF DEVELOPMENT

In order, then, to grapple with the manifold data which the New Testament offers us on the Eucharist, I would now like to propose an hypothesis as to how the understanding of the Eucharist developed in the early community. In this way I would hope to provide a framework of reflection within which many of the divergent data of the texts can be brought into a unity. The success of the hypothesis depends on the degree to which it can make sense of so bewildering a field. My hypothesis considers the development of Eucharistic understanding in the New Testament in three stages.

The first stage is that reflected in the early texts of the Acts of the Apostles. At that time the Christians were still living as Jews, and there is every reason to believe that they still took part even in the Temple's sacrificial worship.[5] Like the Essenes and other groups, they were conscious of being a sect within Judaism, and it is understandable that, as well as the forms of worship which they held in common with all Jews, they would have developed forms of worship specific of their new-found Christian identity.

This is the context for that breaking of bread in Acts 2:42 and 46, based on the Jewish grace before and after meals, which we saw in a previous chapter. In its external form such a ritual was not sacrificial for a Jew. For them sacrifice was what went on in the Temple. Indeed, so deep was this particular conviction, that the Jews of that time had difficulty in regarding the Passover as a sacrifice in the strict sense of the term, given that it was eaten as a family meal.[6] As a result, it would probably never occur to them to regard their breaking of bread as sacrificial. It did, however, embody the memory of their Lord. It would have reminded them, not only of eating and drinking with him after the resurrection (Acts 10:41), but of their last supper with him in the Upper Room, where many of the subsequent celebrations were held.[7] This relationship alone would be enough to give meaning to the celebration as a way of entering more deeply into the fruits of Christ's death, namely into the new covenant, the forgiveness of sins and union with God through his Son. It would also be seen as an anticipation of the Lord's return and of that meal with the Messiah which Late Judaism had taught them to expect.[8]

Such then is the first stage in our hypothesis. It is a stage dominated by the Temple and its cult, and by the gulf which set this cult apart from the rest of Jewish life. The early Christians, therefore, would have distinguished their worship from that of the Temple, precisely because they were believing Jews. In their case, the distinction was all the more pronounced, because they realized that Christianity was born out of Our Lord's confrontation with the Temple. Any New Testament theology of worship has to start from this great divide between the categories proper to the Temple and those appropriate to the new Christian reality. In this context, notions like 'priest', 'altar' and 'sacrifice' are so many old skins for old wine, while what is specifically Christian must be contained in categories as different as they are new.[9]

The second stage in our hypothesis is defined by the way cultic categories begin to trickle back into Christian usage, albeit in a new and perhaps figurative sense. The most likely starting point of such a development would be the way the early Christians would have continued an old tradition of finding a certain counterpart to sacrifice in the way they lived their ordinary lives. When Paul tells the Romans to offer themselves as a spiritual sacrifice to God (Rom 12:1), he is following a familiar line of thought, such as we find in Sirach 35:1–10 or in Psalm 50(51):17.

For the early Christians their breaking of bread belonged to the sphere of 'ordinary life', distinct from the sacred sphere of the Temple. Consequently it belonged to that sphere to which sacrificial categories could be applied in at least a figurative sense. Furthermore, in so far as the table-ritual contained within itself elements of an offering,[10] it is understandable that such an attitude of oblation should become attached to it in a special way, even if that had not already been suggested by the words attributed to Our Lord in the Eucharistic tradition.

A similar dynamic must have been at work in the understanding of the cross. For ordinary Jews, whether Christian or not, Calvary was not a sacrifice. For them sacrifice was essentially a ritual, and by the first century it was confined to the Temple. Calvary, on the other hand, was a secular event. For the first disciples its significance was even more negative, for it was for them a great scandal, the contradiction of all their hopes, at first totally devoid of meaning.

It was out of the experience of the resurrection rather than of the Passion that light first began to break through. The earliest christological formulae, such as those in Acts 2:23–24 and 3:13–16, contain no statement of the salvific significance of Jesus' death. But the resurrection was God's Yes to what Jesus stood for as he went to the cross. It implied that his whole life, culminating in the cross, was the source of salvation for us all.[11] For Jews the notion of sanctification flowing from a bloody death would easily call to mind the analogy of a sacrificial immolation, and so it is not surprising that, among the several images used in the New Testament for presenting Christ's death as meaningful, that of sacrifice soon became one of the dominant ones. Eventually Calvary came to be seen as the very paradigm of that offering of ordinary life to God which marks the life of the just. The term 'sacrifice' may still be applied only in a figurative sense to the cross, but this usage would have been a beginning all the same, and, what is more, it must inevitably have affected the understanding of the Eucharist.

Nor is it unreasonable to postulate an influence in the inverse sense, namely from the Eucharist to the understanding of the cross. Seeing Calvary through the lens of the Eucharist brings out the aspect of offering and reinforces the tendency to interpret it ritually. Consequently our hypothesis is that Calvary and Eucharist, being linked already by the Institution Narrative and by the meaning of ritual memorial to be explained in the next section, each affect the understanding of the other, so that the Eucharist provides the categories of ritual which were absent on the cross, and Calvary supplies the element of historical significance, which a table-rite on its own could not command.

By this stage, if not earlier, the Eucharistic Institution Narrative would have been assuming the shape familiar to us. Clearly it is an evocation of the cross and of the victory of the Just One. In such a context sacrificial notions easily suggest themselves (cf. Wis 3:6), so we need not be surprised when we find a certain resemblance between Eucharist and sacrifice emerging in Paul (1 Cor 10:18–22). I deliberately use the vague word 'resemblance', because at this stage the notion of sacrifice is still being applied, both to the Eucharist and to the cross, in a loose and largely figurative sense, as when we say of our national heroes that they 'sacrificed' themselves for their country.[12]

The key insight, which transforms the whole situation and ushers in the third stage of our hypothesis, arises out of the unity of salvation history.[13] It is an insight into God's plan for the world, and it is formulated most clearly in the Letter to the Hebrews. There we learn that Christ's death on the cross was what Old

Testament sacrifice was all about. The ancient sacrificial system of Israel was but a shadow anticipating that reality which is Calvary (Heb 10:1–10).

So familiar is this teaching that it is difficult for us to realize how much had to happen in the early community before they came to appreciate the cross in this way. For one thing, the Christology of the early community had to develop to the point where they saw that Christ's death was not just something he had to put up with but something he had embraced in sovereign freedom. It was an offering he had made of himself to the Father.

But even more relevant was their perception of the transcendence of Christ implicit in the resurrection appearances. It was only in virtue of the uniqueness of Christ which this implied that they could go on to see his central place in the whole plan of God and that he was really the meaning of the entire history of the Old Testament.

The implications of this Christology for one's attitude to Old Testament cult is what we see being worked out in the Letter to the Hebrews, and the key point for our purposes comes in the way Christ's death and resurrection are presented there as the fulfilment of the ancient sacrifices. Through the unity of God's plan, Calvary is now being presented as related intrinsically and properly to the whole sacrificial system of Israel. Consequently Christ's death on the cross is seen as a sacrifice in a proper but unique sense. It is really the prime analogate of all sacrifices, the substance of which they are only shadows. It is no longer simply a sacrifice in a figurative sense, such as might have been said of the death of the Servant (Isa 53:10). Strange as it might seem to a Jew, Calvary has to be a sacrifice in this proper sense, since it belongs intrinsically to the whole context of ritual sacrifice by being the meaning of it all. However, in saying that, one has to bear in mind our insistence that this event, albeit sacrificial in a proper sense, is so in a unique sense. The meaning of sacrifice is changed by being fulfilled. Calvary's sacrifice is unique because Christ is unique.

It is inevitable that so fundamental and far-reaching a perception should have its influence on the Christian Eucharist. This ritual, after all, was already understood to be the memorial of Christ's paschal mystery. As we will see in the following section, 'memorial' here has a pregnant meaning; at this point we will just say that this deeper sense of the Eucharistic memorial must have been a contributory factor in the development we are studying.

Certainly, the new sense of the sacrificial nature of the cross inevitably redounded on that ritual which celebrated the cross in the way we see in the Institution Narrative. If the Eucharist is the actuality of the cross, something we will consider in the next section, then the sacrificial categories which belong to the cross can understandably be extended in a proper sense to the ritual which is its prolongation and memorial.

The main witness to this development is the Mark–Matthew Institution Narrative. Though many scholars find evidence for the sacrificial nature of the Eucharist in the Luke–Paul version, the references there remain inchoative and ambiguous when contrasted with Mark–Matthew. It is not clear that the notion of sacrifice underlying Luke–Paul has got definitively beyond the figurative sense of the second stage of our hypothesis.

Two items in particular in the Mark–Matthew version reveal that the Eucharist is here being treated in the explicit terms of ritual sacrifice. First and most clearly, we have the words of Moses from the covenant sacrifice of Sinai reproduced almost word for word over the Eucharistic cup: 'This is the blood of the covenant.'[14]

Secondly there is the way 'body' and 'blood' are set in symmetry, in contrast to the 'body–cup' parallel in Luke–Paul. For a Jew of those times, 'body' and 'blood' are the elements of a sacrifice.[15] In that context a certain operational distinction between them is implied, such as the protocol of sacrifice required, but we must be on our guard against interpreting this distinction in the kind of ontological terms found in the Middle Ages, when they spoke of the 'substance' of the body and the 'substance' of the blood. The well-known text of Leviticus 17:11 makes it clear that the blood is not distinguished from the flesh as a different reality but as the inmost and most crucial part of the flesh. At the same time, the separation of flesh and blood in sacrifice is sufficiently marked to ground the later separation of the sacramental species as a sign of death. It also means that the highlighting and distinction of body and blood in the Mark–Matthew Institution Narrative are best understood in relation to this sacrificial procedure.

Some additional phrases in the narrative fit in with this sacrificial view and help to confirm it, though hardly sufficient to establish it on their own. There is the word 'poured out'.[16] It recalls immediately the gesture of Moses in Exodus 24, where cognate words are used in the Septuagint.[17]

Then there are the expressions in the narrative which present Christ's death as vicarious, 'for you', 'for many', 'for the remission of sins'. Such phrases draw their meaning, either from sin-sacrifices in the strict sense, or from the applied sense found in Late Judaism's notion of a martyr's death. Given that the sacrificial nature of the Eucharist is already clearly present in the text through the indications outlined above, these expressions of vicariousness can be taken as fitting in with this sacrificial sense and interpreting it in an expiatory and propitiatory way.[18] Schürmann makes the point that the covenant sacrifice was not regarded as expiatory by the Jews, but others hold that by the beginning of the Christian era practically all sacrificial acts were considered to have an atoning effect.[19] The presence then of the idea of vicariousness in this place can be seen as flowing from that sense of plenitude which Christians were beginning to find in Christ's death, regarding it as the fulfilment of the entire sacrificial system of Israel. Already the uniqueness of Christ and of Calvary is beginning to break the mould of the categories it fulfils.

Is it not extraordinary, given the initial gulf between the Temple cult and the emerging Christian rituals, that cultic categories should be accepted so early into Christian language, albeit in a transformed sense? Yet there they are, in the Mark–Matthew Institution Narrative, with a clarity which some Christian traditions have been very slow to accept. In such a context it is of interest to cite the words of a Protestant scholar:

The whole early Christian tradition, when speaking of the Supper, makes use of a sacrificial terminology . . . I find the New Testament terminology as well as the patristic unanimity too overwhelmingly in favour of the sacrificial theme in a balanced Eucharistic theology . . . Since the Eucharist is a sacrament of the sacrifice of Christ and a channel of the Church's sacrifice, it must also be interpreted in sacrificial categories.[20]

The sacrificial theme also serves to illustrate the whole process of developing understanding going on in the early community. Indeed the relevant texts could be listed in a tentative order that reflects this movement of thought, not implying a view as to the relative age of the texts, but only to highlight the age of the tradition on sacrifice contained within them:

Acts 2:42, 46; Luke 22:15–18; Luke 22:19–20; 1 Corinthians 11:23–25; 1 Corinthians 10:16–17; Hebrews 9:20; Mark 14:22–24; Matthew 26:26–28; John 6:51–58; Rev 5:6–14.[21]

Clearly there is an evolution of understanding going on in the early community, and one of the motor ideas in that movement seems to be the notion of ritual sacrifice. We might note in particular the following transition in language:

body–cup — body–blood — flesh–blood.

In the Mark–Matthew Institution Narrative in particular, the demonstrative words over loaf and cup reveal a consciousness of standing before God with the offerings of a covenant sacrifice in one's hands. It is striking how, in order to interpret to themselves the meaning of their actions in worship, the people of those communities have reached back to the words of Moses and made them their own. That the offering is actual in their ritual is precisely the force of the demonstrative pronouns in the interpretative words. This actuality is then seen by some as confirmed by the tense of the participle in the words over the cup: ' . . . the blood which is being poured out for many'.[22]

In the period after the New Testament, the use of cultic categories in Christian liturgy is going to develop further. Soon words like 'sacrifice', 'altar', and eventually 'priest' are going to shift from a figurative to a proper sense in Christian worship. Some may regard such a development as illegitimate, but when one sees it in continuity with a development already under way in the New Testament, then it is hard to stigmatize it as unscriptural or unchristian.

THE EUCHARISTIC MEMORIAL

Surely one of the most significant and evocative statements of Our Lord in the gospels was his description of the Eucharist as his memorial. The phrase is proper to the Luke–Paul version of the Institution Narrative, coming once in Luke and twice in Paul. If we take the expression in its obvious sense, it already lights up the Eucharist for us as the sign across the centuries of the mystery of Our Lord's love in his dying and his rising. The expression, however, has a further and less obvious meaning, one that points to a mysterious presence in our ritual, giving to our celebration a new context and a startling immediacy.

This deeper meaning of the word 'memory' in the liturgy was a factor in that development of the sacrificial nature of the Eucharist which we studied in the previous section. As we shall see, it is a word which opens up for the scholar an alternative avenue of approach to the whole question of Eucharistic sacrifice. Many would probably treat this present topic before raising the issues studied in the preceding section, since this subject seems more congenial and accessible than the other. While that is true, I preferred to discuss the question of development first, because it gives us a better view of the overall context within which the present point is to be treated. Furthermore, there is the fact that this question of memory is closely related to that of the Passover nature of the Eucharist, an aspect which is often given an exaggerated emphasis, not least by Catholic teachers and preachers, who find there what seems to me a short-cut to the doctrine of Eucharistic sacrifice.[23] The result has been that several fundamental questions, discussed in the previous section, have sometimes been lost to view.

The story of the present section brings before us one of the most unexpected and far-reaching developments in contemporary theology. It concerns the meaning of the little word 'memory' when Our Lord is represented as saying at the Last Supper 'Do this in memory of me'. When Western Christianity broke in two in the sixteenth century, the word that seemed to divide it for ever in the understanding of the Eucharist was this word 'memory'. Now it is this same word which is drawing us into a new and growing unity.

The discovery which led to this change of direction goes back over fifty years to that wave of scholarship which first took up the study of the Jewish background of our gospel texts.[24] One of the basic characteristics of all Jewish liturgy, both in the Bible and in the rabbinical writings, is the sense of salvation history as the framework of all prayer. We see this in the Psalms as well as in rabbinical texts such as those used in the table blessings. For the Jew, God is the Lord of history. This means that God intervenes in history, for instance in his great salvific acts on behalf of his people. It also means that all of history is present to him.[25] Before God, all the Jews are one people, with one destiny, every generation equally present to his all-seeing eye. When God intervened in the past, for instance on behalf of Moses and his contemporaries, he was really doing it for all the succeeding generations as well. In a sense, through the power of God, each generation was involved in the Exodus. We find this belief expressed with particular clarity in the book of Deuteronomy, e.g. Deuteronomy 6:21; 16:12.

In a similar way, just as the present generation was involved in the past, so there is a sense in which the past can become actual today. This notion runs through all Jewish prayer, but it comes to a head, with a special immediacy, in the liturgy. Something of the divine transcendence over history passes into the people's worship, and the great salvific acts of the past become actual in the midst of the celebrating community.

This is the required background for the consideration of the terms 'memory', 'commemoration' and 'memorial' in the context of Jewish liturgy. When we Westerners read 'Do this in memory of me', we think we know what 'memory' means. In fact, in the context of Jewish liturgy, it is really a technical term. As worshippers recall the events of sacred history, they enter, not only into the thought of the past, but also, in some sense, into the actuality of what happened.

A Jewish ritual commemoration, therefore, is not just a matter of thoughts and feelings and nostalgia for the past. That is what I will call an empty memorial. A Jewish ritual memorial is one filled with the reality of that which it commemorates. To express it we might call it 'a living memorial'.[26] Often when people commemorate important events in secular history, they can speak with a sense of actuality which can be very like that used in Jewish sources, but there is a key difference. In secular things it is a question of human beings in one generation recalling those of another. In liturgy God is part of it all, and that makes all the difference.

To substantiate the notion we have just outlined, one might appeal first to the rich associations of the word 'memory' throughout the Old Testament. Indeed for the Jews 'memory' is one of the basic ideas in their religious vocabulary, running right through worship from simple blessings to the psalms of sacrifice. The term does not refer merely to one cognitive faculty. It is a word that sounds like a bell through many of their most sacred texts, ultimately embracing the whole relationship between God and his people in the covenant.[27]

The key point comes with the fact that, not only is it a case of people remembering God; it is also a question of God remembering the people. Again and again God is asked to remember Israel, his covenant and his promises.[28] By the same token he is asked not to remember their sins.[29] Indeed, as the occasion demands, God remembering can be God rewarding and punishing.[30]

Stirred by God's being mindful of them, the people are charged to remember the Lord, and always to bear in mind his law and his promises. Their sins are the occasions when they fail to remember.[31] The two aspects come together in the striking verse of Isaiah: 'Even these may forget, but I will not forget you, says the Lord' (Isa 49:15). 'Memory' is really a way of designating the whole relationship between God and his people as personal and existential.

Nor does memory remain as something purely internal. As the texts just cited suggest, memory and action go together. The people's remembering means the people's doing God's will. God's remembering includes God's acting and hopefully God's forgiving. 'Memory' here is really a word for the whole covenant come alive.

MEMORY AND SACRIFICE

A high-point in the relationship of remembering comes with sacrifice. For Israel, 'memory' is a sacrificial word. Already in the book of Leviticus the portion of the victim burnt on the altar is called a 'reminder' or a 'memorial', and it is clear that it is a question of God's remembering the sacrifice.[32] De Vaux considers that it was designated in this way possibly because it was thought to 'remind' God of the whole offering.[33] The usage persists, and it can be found at the other end of the Old Testament in Ecclesiasticus 35:6. Not least of its occurrences was its use in the context of the Passover. We read in the Book of Jubilees, 'It [the Passover] shall come for a memorial before the Lord'.[34]

The expression is particularly significant for our purposes because it puts into simple language an aspect of worship often lost to view. All worship has both a descending and ascending aspect, such as we already saw in the case of Jewish blessings. The grace and efficacy of God descend on the worshippers, but as well as that the adoration and love of the worshippers ascend to God and are pleasing to him. Such attitudes are expressed ultimately in the four great ends of sacrifice (praise, thanksgiving, propitiation and petition), but we should notice that this 'ascending' aspect of worship cannot be reduced to intercession, central as that is. In sacrifice the attitudes of the worshippers are not just expressed in words. They are embodied in the act of offering and in the symbols offered. The attitudes, actions and gifts of the worshippers are all values in the sight of God. They are things he 'remembers', and to them he wills to give a place in his plan as the prior condition of the divine action which will flow from his remembering.

God's remembering, therefore, is an intrinsic part of all worship in the Bible.[35] On this basis alone Jeremias was quite right to appeal to it as part of the meaning of memorial in the Eucharist.[36] Jeremias, however, went on to claim that this divine remembering was part of the meaning intended by the phrase in the Institution Narrative, 'Do this in memory of me'. The more obvious reference in this phrase is to our remembering Christ rather than to God's remembering him. That the phrase contains the perspective of divine remembering remains controversial, and so it would be a weak basis for establishing the objective nature of the Eucharistic memorial. This is why it is necessary to fill out all we have said about the divine remembering with a consideration of the role of memory in Jewish liturgy based on salvation history. As the Passover is the clearest instance of such a memorial, we will now take up the question of the relationship of the Eucharist to that feast.

EUCHARIST AND PASSOVER

It is a commonplace of Eucharistic catechesis today to present the Eucharist as a Christian Passover. This approach has a lot to do with the memorial aspect of the sacrament, since, as we have said, the Passover is one of our clearest examples of what a Jewish ritual memorial is like. Now this fact alone is sufficient justification for introducing the Passover at this point of our study, but it also gives us an opportunity to take up a further historical question as to whether the Last Supper itself was actually a celebration of this Jewish feast. There are therefore these two reasons for looking more closely at the Jewish Passover. We will take up the second consideration first.

Given the widespread use of the notion that the Eucharist is a Christian Passover, it is surprising to find how uncertain is its basis in the New Testament. Scholars still remain divided on whether or not the Last Supper was a Passover. The doubt goes back to the New Testament itself, where the Synoptics seem to assume that it was, and the Fourth Gospel implies that it was not.[37] A

compromise solution is that of Raymond Brown in his comment-
ary on the Fourth Gospel, where he concludes that the Last
Supper was not a Passover in the strict sense but a meal that had
'Passover characteristics'.[38]

Strange as it may seem, this is a question which the systematic
theologian does not have to decide, once one accepts the
hypothesis of this book that the Eucharist was established, not on
the elements proper to a Passover, but on the grace before and after
meals common to any Jewish festive celebration.[39] If the Eucharist
was seen from the beginning as a Christian version of the Passover,
then one would expect it to be a yearly celebration rather than the
more frequent event it seems to be already in the New Testament.[40] It is also striking how little use is made of the Passover in
interpreting the Eucharist in the gospels and epistles. Indeed this
can be seen as further evidence of the initial gulf between the
categories of Old Testament cult and those proper to the new way
of faith. Perhaps only in John can some lines be established
between Passover and Eucharist, as for instance in the paschal
context of John 6.

Nevertheless the Passover remains an important subject for a
theology of the Eucharist. For one thing, it is part of that entire
tradition of sacrificial worship which the cross is to fulfil and the
Eucharist to continue in a new way. Furthermore, it is, as we have
remarked already, one of the clearest examples of what a Jewish
ritual memorial is like. It helps to illustrate the mentality with
which the apostles would have heard the words 'Do this in memory
of me'. Finally, even if in the Last Supper Our Lord did not follow
the Passover ritual, a Passover atmosphere would have been
unavoidable by any group of people in Jerusalem in that particular
week, surrounded as they were by the bustle of festive
preparations.

The Passover was one of the greatest feasts of the Jews. It evoked
some of their most sacred memories, as they looked back to those
events in the thirteenth century before our era when God first
made them a people. The Exodus could claim to be the
foundational event of the Jewish nation, containing within itself
the sign and promise of redemption. Liberation is central to its
spirit, and liberation remains one of the central themes of the
Passover. A Jewish writer describes the festival as 'the festival of all
times, in which the past deliverance blends with the future
redemption in an eternal today, in order to make present in this

way the life-giving love of God as a timeless, eternal event of salvation'.[41]

One of the key words in the Passover liturgy is 'memory'. This appears, not only in the original texts of the Bible concerning the feast, but also in the rabbinical texts with which the feast is celebrated today.[42] It is a memory embodied not only in thoughts but in rituals, as when the person presiding offers unleavened bread to the gathering, saying 'This is the bread of affliction, which your fathers ate in the land of Egypt'.[43] It is a memory not only of the past but of the future, as when the grace after the meal speaks of 'the memory of the Messiah, the Son of David' rising up and coming into the presence of the Lord.[44]

The key point concerning 'memory' in the Passover is the fact that it is understood in the pregnant sense which we have outlined above. Indeed the Passover texts are the best place for substantiating this view of memory which we are putting forward. Very clear is the belief that each generation of Jews was involved in the original events. The father of the family in the Jewish home in our day speaks in the first person plural with the contemporaries of Moses: 'Once we were Pharaoh's slaves in Egypt and the Lord brought us out of Egypt by his mighty hand' (Deut 6:21). The point is unequivocal in the rabbinical Passover text:

> In every generation each one is bound to consider himself
> as though he himself had come out of Egypt . . .
> God the Holy One, blessed be He, redeemed not only our
> fathers,
> but He also redeemed us with them.[45]

Just as the present was involved in the past, so does the past become involved in the present. Wherever a Jew experiences something of God's liberating grace, it is the working out of that blessing first given to the people through Moses. But this actuality of the past becomes true in a special way in liturgy, as the people of the present generation relive those ancient events through their worship. When the father of the family holds up before them the unleavened bread, they are living again that hasty meal of long ago, for he says to them,

This is the bread of affliction, which your fathers ate in the land of Egypt.

Or again,

On that day you will explain to your son: 'This [i.e. the unleavened bread of today] is because of what the Lord did for me when I came out of Egypt.' (Exod 13:8)

In a number of places in the Passover liturgy we notice the use of the demonstrative 'this', as in the sentences just quoted. The word indicates the intersection of the times. This day, the day of our time, is the time of liberation, says the text. In other words, the Exodus is *now*!

When we come to the Eucharist, we have at hand the category of a Jewish ritual memorial to interpret what Our Lord was saying and doing at the Last Supper. The point does not depend on whether he actually used the phrase about memory attributed to him in the Luke–Paul version. The notion would have been sufficiently present in the general Passover atmosphere of the scene and in the traditional understanding of the place of history in prayer. When we spell the thought out in the way suggested by Luke's account of the Last Supper, with its strong Paschal colouring, then we can say that, just as the events of the Exodus were made present in the Jewish celebration of Passover, so the salvific events of the New Testament, Our Lord's death and resurrection, referred to in Luke's gospel as his 'exodus' (Luke 9:31 in Greek), are to be made present wherever Christians gather for the celebration of the Eucharist. The Eucharist is not to be simply a nostalgic evocation of 'a green hill far away', but the actuality of his death and resurrection which constituted *the* great Passover sacrifice for the salvation of the world.[46]

Looking back over the path we have come in the understanding of Eucharistic sacrifice in the New Testament, we have discovered two main avenues of approach to the issue. The first one was found in the covenant sacrifice of Moses. While references to this can be detected in the Luke–Paul version of the Institution Narrative, it is clearest in the Mark–Matthew tradition. There we discovered categories of cultic sacrifice being accepted explicitly of the Eucharist.

The second line of approach lay through the notion of Jewish ritual memorial, which seems to be evoked explicitly by the command to repeat in the Luke–Paul tradition. This sense of the actuality of the past in the present was more than likely a factor in the development of the parallel with covenant sacrifice to which we have just referred. In itself, particularly when one sees a parallel with the Jewish Passover, it brings out that the Eucharist is more than an empty calling to mind of the past. If in some sense Christ's death and resurrection are actual in our celebration, and if these events constitute the Lord's sacrifice, then it follows that the Eucharist itself has to be seen as in some way sacrificial through being the actuality of the one sacrifice of the New Law.

NOTES

1 E.g. Matt 9:13, citing Hos 6:6; Matt 15:7–9; 21:12–17.
2 Mark 11:47; Luke 22:19; Matt 5:24; 28:19; John 3:5. For the Old Testament see 1 Sam 16:2; Isa 43:22–28; Mal 1:11; Sirach 7:31; 35:6–9; 38:11.
3 Also relevant is John 1:51. On this see O. Cullmann, *Early Christian Worship* (London: SCM, 1953), pp. 73–4.
4 Thus H. Schürmann, 'Neutestamentliche Marginalien zur Frage der "Entsakralisierung"', *Der Seelsorger* (Vienna) 38 (1968), pp. 38–48, 89–104, notably at p. 46.
5 Acts 21:24–26; Matt 5:24 probably refers to Temple sacrifice.
6 See the remark of R. Brown, *The Gospel According to John, I–XII* (New York: Doubleday/London: Geoffrey Chapman, 1966), p. 62.
7 O. Cullmann, *Early Christian Worship*, p. 30.
8 These ideas could have built on the prophecies of the Servant also, but it is problematic how soon these prophecies began to be invoked by Christians. R. H. Fuller, for one, thinks it was not from the beginning: 'Jesus Christ as Saviour in the New Testament', *Interpretation* 35 (1981), pp. 145–56, at p. 148.
9 In the situation postulated here there would be no room at this early stage for the kind of borrowing from the Temple sacrifices of thanksgiving suggested by H. Cazelles, 'L'Anaphore et l'Ancien Testament', *Eucharisties d'Orient et d'Occident* (Lex Orandi no. 46; Semaine Liturgique de l'Institut Saint-Serge 1; Paris: Cerf, 1970), pp. 11–21.
10 Jungmann saw this especially in the ritual of raising the cup and pronouncing the blessing over it: *Missarum sollemnia* (Vienna–Freiburg–Basel: Herder, 1962), vol. I, p. 27, n. 63.
11 Fuller, art. cit., p. 147.
12 In this context 1 Cor 5:7 is sometimes cited, but the term of comparison between Calvary and Passover in this text is not sacrifice but the introduction of a new era of salvation, as P. Neuenzeit points out: *Das Herrenmahl* (Munich: Kösel, 1960), p. 166. Hence the text cannot do more than illustrate a loose use of sacrificial language. From their dogmatic interests Catholic theologians have often given too much weight to texts like 1 Cor 5:7 and 10:18–22.

13 Some envisage this coming about by deducing the sacrificial nature of Calvary from the sacrificial nature of the Eucharist, e.g. M. Schmaus, *Dogma 5: The Church as Sacrament* (London: Sheed & Ward, 1975), p. 69. I prefer to think rather in terms of each truth helping to clarify the other in a mutual relationship. It is not then a question of a deduction but more of an insight, as Lonergan understands that word, namely a 'leap' to a higher synthesis: B. Lonergan, *Insight: A Study of Human Understanding* (London: Longmans, 1967).

14 Cf. Exod 24:8. There is a curious confirmation of this link in Heb 9:20 where the story of Moses' sacrifice is recounted, using the words of consecration almost literally in their Marcan form, beginning with the neuter demonstrative 'this', as in Mark, rather than with the Septuagint's 'behold' (*idou*).

15 A good example of this in the New Testament is Heb 13:11–12. For 'body' and 'blood', or more usually in Greek 'flesh' and 'blood', as the traditional sacrificial correlatives in the Old Testament, see for example Lev 17:11, 14; Deut 12:27; Ezek 44:7; Ps 49(50):13.

16 Greek *ekchunnomenon*, agreeing with 'cup' in Luke, and with 'blood' in Mark–Matthew: Luke 22:20; Mark 14:24; Matt 26:28.

17 See *enecheen* and *prosechee* in Exod 24:6, but *kateskedase* in verse 8. Léon-Dufour has argued that *ekchunnomenon* is more appropriate for designating a violent death than a ritualistic action: *Sharing the Eucharistic Bread* (New York: Paulist, 1987), p. 143. It does not seem, however, that the arguments in this sense can be pressed too far, since in the less ritualistic Lucan version, unlike in Mark, this participle agrees with 'cup' and so is clearly taken in a ritualistic sense.

18 I say not just expiatory but propitiatory in so far as the sacrificial remission of sins comes about through an *offering* pleasing to God. These notions, referred to already in the preceding chapter, will be discussed in greater detail in the explanatory treatment of sacrifice in Chapter 13 below.

19 H. Schürmann, *Der Einsetzungsbericht Lk 22:19–20* (Münster: Aschendorff, 1955), p. 6. For the other view referred to see R. Daly, *Christian Sacrifice* (Washington: Catholic University of America Press, 1978), p. 201.

20 J. von Allmen, *The Lord's Supper* (London: Lutterworth Press, 1966), pp. 86 and 96.

21 As regards the Luke–Paul tradition, in this list I follow the controversial opinion of Schürmann, regarding Luke as generally prior to Paul, and distinguishing the full text, Luke 22:15–20, into two juxtaposed accounts of the one event: Schürmann, op. cit., note 19 above, pp. 133–50. As regards the long text in Luke, I translate the view of Ligier: 'After the studies of J. Jeremias and H. Schürmann, the long text of Luke (Lk 22:19b–20) has regained, despite certain nuances, the confidence of the exegetes': *La Maison-Dieu* no. 87 (1966), p. 9.

22 Similarly the participles in Luke–Paul: Léon-Dufour, *Sharing the Eucharistic Bread*, pp. 188, 234.

23 Already at the Council of Trent, 7 December 1551, the Pope's theologian, James Lainez, was arguing as follows: *Eucharistiae convenit Pascha . . . Pascha autem est sacrificium . . . Ergo Eucharistia est sacrificium*: CT VII/2, p. 532.

24 An early influential study of our subject-matter was N. A. Dahl, 'Anamnesis: memory and commemoration in early Christianity', an inaugural lecture in the University of Oslo in 1946, later published in English in *Jesus in the Memory of the Early Church: Essays by Nils Alstrup Dahl* (Minneapolis: Augsburg Publishing House, 1976), pp. 11–29.

25 Pss 139(140); 32(33); Jer 32:19; Heb 4:13; Jas 1:17.

26 The phrase 'living memorial' has been applied by others to the Eucharist, but in a static sense, referring to the Real Presence, e.g. Bonaventure, *Sent.* IV, d. 12, P. 2, a. 1, q. 1 (Quaracchi edn, IV, 280). In this book the phrase is applied to the Eucharist *as action* and is best understood in opposition to 'empty memorial'.

27 The text of grace after meals in the Passover is a striking example of this, as we will see below.

28 E.g. Jer 14:21; Exod 32:13; Deut 9:27; 4:31; Lev 26:42; Ezek 16:60 etc.

29 Isa 43:25; 64:9; Pss 78(79):8; 24(25):7 etc.

30 1 Sam 25:31; Job 14:13; Jer 15:15; Neh 6:14.

31 Deut 4:23; 6:12; 8:11, 14, 19; Prov 3:1; Ps 9:6 etc.

32 Greek: *mnēmosunon*, Lev 2:2.

33 R. de Vaux, *Ancient Israel, Its Life and Institutions* (London: Darton, Longman & Todd, 1961), p. 422.

34 Jubilees 49:15.

35 For an example of this meaning of 'remembering' in the New Testament see Acts 10:4.

36 J. Jeremias, *The Eucharistic Words of Jesus* (London: SCM, 1966), pp. 244–55.

37 For the Fourth Gospel the Passover occurred on the evening of Our Lord's death: John 18:29; 19:31.

38 Brown, *The Gospel According to John, I–XII*, p. 556. For a recent defence of the Passover nature of the Last Supper, see C. Giraudo, *Eucaristia per la chiesa* (Brescia: Morcelliana/Rome: Gregorian University Press, 1989), pp. 162–86. A. Jaubert's ingenious theory that it was a question of different calendars has not met with the support of such exegetes as P. Benoit, J. Binzler, R. Brown, J. Gaechter, J. Jeremias.

39 The repetition of the command to repeat, in association with each of the table blessings in Paul's version, has been understood by exegetes to point to the independence of the Eucharist from the meal, e.g. Neuenzeit, *Das Herrenmahl*, p. 135.

40 If the breaking of bread in Acts 2 be Eucharistic, then the Eucharist is already a daily occurrence: Acts 2:46.

41 P. Lapide, *The Resurrection of Jesus: A Jewish Perspective* (Minneapolis: Augsburg Publishing House, 1983), p. 79.

42 Original biblical texts would be Exod 12:14; 13:9, 16. In citing the present day liturgy of the feast I follow the text given in A. Hänggi and I. Pahl (eds), *Prex eucharistica* (Fribourg: Editions Universitaires, 1968), pp. 13–34. My quotations will be my own translations from the Latin.

43 Ibid., p. 15.

44 Ibid., p. 27.

45 Ibid., p. 24.

46 This last point will be treated when we come to the Eucharist in the Fourth Gospel.

4

⊠ *The Eucharistic Change*

The belief that in the Eucharist bread and wine become the body and blood of Christ is one of the strangest teachings in the Christian tradition. People who have been used to it since childhood have often lost the sense of wonder at its mystery, while for those coming to the faith, it is certainly not the first truth that should be proposed to them. It is a doctrine which presupposes a whole context of other truths, which have to be appropriated first, before this one can begin to make some sense.

This state of affairs is reflected in the order of treatment in our chapters. Some readers may have wondered why it is only now that this point is being taken up, when this is the point which seems to many to be the main one about the Eucharist. The reason is that it is necessary to establish a context first before broaching this central truth. As we will see, it is the context of worship and sacrifice which helps to throw a little light on the meaning of this truth and on its purpose. To 'throw a little light' might seem an excessively modest way of putting it, but, at the end of the day, when the exegetes have done their work and the theologians have had their say, this truth remains a mystery of faith.

We have used the phrase 'the Eucharistic Change'. This phrase refers to an event which occurs every time the Christian Church renews in its liturgy the sacrifice of Christ. In the course of the centuries Christians have felt the need to devise special names for such a special event, such as transubstantiation, transignification and so on. While such terms have their usefulness, it is necessary, at the same time, to be able to describe what happens in words of one or two syllables, for this truth is a commonplace of Christian catechesis. This is why we will make use of our unpretentious phrase and we explain it in a similarly straightforward manner. By it we mean that in the Eucharist bread and wine become the body and blood of Christ and are bread and wine no longer.

It is not the purpose of our theology here to prove this truth. Those of us who believe this truth do so because this is the faith we have received. It is the way the great body of Christians, East and West, have understood the Eucharist from time immemorial. The primary purpose of theology is to make the truth a little more understandable, and in this chapter we pursue that aim in the context of the Scriptures in particular. We will examine the data to see whether or not this age-old belief of Christians has a basis in the New Testament. Many Christians would add that their faith does not stand or fall by what they find, but as regards such a rider opinions may well diverge.

Three main forms of language have been used over the centuries to express this truth. The first is the language of identity, as when the Lord is represented as saying 'This is my body . . . this is my blood'. This kind of language is traditional in the prophecy and ritual of Israel. Prophets do not indulge in nice distinctions. They speak bluntly – sometimes even without the copulative connecting subject and predicate, as when Ezekiel said over his hair 'This [is] Jerusalem' (Ezek 5:5). Somewhat similarly in the ritual of the Passover we find 'This is the bread of affliction which your fathers ate in the land of Egypt'. The precise force of the language is not immediately apparent from the terms themselves.

The second form of language is that of change. It is that which we have used in the heading of this chapter and in the explanation which we have just given above. This form of language is not found in the New Testament with regard to the Eucharistic gifts, but it begins to appear shortly afterwards, perhaps in Justin (*c.* AD 150), certainly in Irenaeus (*c.* AD 200), and is destined to have a significant place in the epiclesis of the great Eucharistic Prayers. The fact that it emerges so soon after the New Testament is an important indication that this is the way in which the language of identity was understood in the early community.

The third form of language is that of presence. This mode of speech, typified by the expression 'the Real Presence', is so familiar to us today that it is difficult to realize that, strictly speaking, it comes into use, in this precise way, only from the Middle Ages on. However, as we will now go on to see, divine presence is certainly a significant theme ever since the Old

Testament and helps to establish the context within which the issue we are discussing is to be approached.

God's presence with the people was one of the main prerogatives which Israel claimed for itself ever since their time in the desert. The very term 'the Tent of Meeting' expressed the notion as something localized and reciprocal, God present to the people and they to him. This assurance of the divine presence was one of the central attributes of the covenant, of which eventually the Temple became the symbol and the home. While the people commonly understood this presence in an absolute and empirical way, already there were those who were more conscious of how this presence makes claims upon believers and that God will be found only to the extent that one calls upon his name and searches for him with faith.[1] With the destruction of Jerusalem and the Exile of 587 BC, Israel began to develop a more spiritual view of divine presence. Some saw it as following the people to Babylon, and eventually it became associated with Israel's prayer and worship and the celebration of God's word.[2]

The divine presence was one of the prerogatives foretold for the new covenant also (Ezek 37:26–28), and some already saw that it would be identified in a special way with one individual (Isa 7:14). This is what we in fact find being claimed for Christ in the gospels (Matt 1:23). In his humanity the ancient prerogative of the presence of God finds a new centre and a new location.[3] Indeed we could describe the flesh of Christ as the first Tabernacle of the New Testament.[4]

In time the intimacy of God with his people through Jesus of Nazareth is to be extended to the Church through Christ's presence within it (Matt 28:20). In this context the ancient spiritual notion of presence is given new life by being found in a special way in Christian worship, where it is actualized in the community (Matt 18:20), in the word (John 6:26ff.) and so eventually in the Eucharistic gifts.[5]

From presence we move to change, and from the static to the dynamic. This too is part of the context from Old and New Testaments within which the Eucharist is found. We have seen it already in the notion of blessing. When people bless God, God blesses the people, and things happen! His blessing, like his word, has its effects here below (Isa 55:10–11).

Then there are God's prophets. Through them God worked his wonders. The word of Elijah brought down fire from heaven

(1 Kings 18:38) and the word of Moses changed water into blood (Exodus 7:14–25). It was generally expected that the Messiah would work similar deeds of power, and this is what we in fact find attributed to Christ in the New Testament. In particular there is the power of his blessing over the food in the desert (Mark 6:41), and there is the change of water into wine in Cana (John 2:1ff.). Once Christ is understood to be present at the Eucharistic table, it is not so surprising if similar wonders are understood to occur there. These aspects of presence and of change, when we recognize them in the New Testament context, help to level down our approach to the sublime teaching on the Eucharistic Change.

When we speak of the Eucharistic Change we are interested in things the Lord took, bread and wine, and what he did with them. But Our Lord did not simply take up these two objects to make something else of them. He took up a ritual, an action, in which things were involved. What he changed was primarily the ritual and its meaning, and in changing the ritual he changed the things as well.[6] In the Luke–Paul version of the Institution Narrative the action is clearly to the fore, and the text does not highlight the ritual objects. Some like to speak here of the 'action-symbolism' in the text. In Mark–Matthew, on the other hand, the objects are given a central place by the new formulation of the cup-word in particular: bread–wine–body–blood. It is a 'thing-symbolism'. What these elements at the centre of attention really are in themselves is felt to be significant. The implication of this emphasis can be worked out in the following way.

Our central evidence for belief in the Eucharistic Change is found in the words of the Institution Narrative, especially in the Mark–Matthew version. There are other texts in the New Testament that point to this truth, but these are really derived from the early community's use of the Institution Narrative in its liturgy and depend on the latter for their interpretation.[7] Also there is the fact that the Institution Narrative has been a pivotal text in the actual celebration of the Eucharist down through the centuries. This is the text on which the Church has rested the interpretation of its action in the very performance of the rite.

This central piece of evidence consists of two components,

(1) a key statement in two sentences:
   'This is my body . . . this is my blood';
(2) the context of that statement.

Interpretation is always a matter of setting words in their context, but this basic hermeneutical principle is nowhere more crucial than here. In themselves the words are capable of more than one meaning, as the history of their interpretation amply demonstrates. Two main lines of approach have been distinguished. In one, the words are taken in a purely symbolic way: bread and wine are simply signs of Christ's body and blood. In the second line of approach, the words are taken literally: bread and wine are not only symbolic of Christ's body and blood, but are somehow identified with them. It is the context which enables us to decide between these alternatives.

In fact the context of the words, just as the words themselves, has been interpreted in various ways by the exegetes. I now propose to consider four such approaches, according as one sees the context as didactic, prophetic, cultic, or sacrificial.

In the gospels Our Lord is presented as a master of the image. Symbols and parables flow from his tongue as he directs his teaching not just to minds but to hearts. Commonly such images are intended simply to convey an idea. Whether or not there was an actual inn on the road to Jericho is immaterial (Luke 10:34). The key thing is the idea. That is what predominates where the context is didactic.

A good example may be found in Matthew 16:5–12, where Our Lord warns the disciples about 'the leaven' of the Pharisees. Immediately the disciples take him literally and begin looking around the boat for leaven. Our Lord corrects them and equivalently says to them that he was speaking figuratively, not literally. This passage is of interest because it shows how the problem of the conflict of literal as against symbolic interpretations could be handled even within the limited vocabulary of the disciples. It also represents Our Lord as correcting people when they mistakenly take him literally. Would he do the same to those of us who take the words over bread and wine literally? The pointer in the Institution Narrative that he would *not* is the fact that, unlike Matthew 16, the context is not simply didactic but something more.

A purely didactic approach to the context in the Last Supper falls out of consideration once one appreciates that here Our Lord is acting in the line of the prophets. These redoubtable preachers often expressed their message not only by words but by what is sometimes called a 'prophetic gesture'. This device was not simply a dramatization of the prophet's meaning but a gesture which was believed to make the event dramatized something inevitable. The mime of the exile (Ezek 12:1–20), the gesture of the two sticks (Ezek 37:15–28) are two clear examples. In the New Testament we have Our Lord's dealing with the fig-tree in Matthew 21:18–19. Prophetic gestures mean more than the simply didactic in that the gesture has a real effect. Something happens! Some exegetes interpret Our Lord's actions at the Last Supper as a solemn prophetic gesture, bringing about salvation through his death.

While it can be conceded that this is a factor in the Institution Narrative, and it helps to get us beyond a purely didactic approach, it scarcely seems sufficient to do justice to the cultic nature of the context as we have already interpreted it in a previous chapter. It certainly would not be sufficient to carry us as far as the doctrine on Eucharistic Change. In Ezekiel 5:5 the prophet Ezekiel, in the course of a prophetic gesture bringing down God's judgement on Israel, says over his hair 'This is Jerusalem'. No one would claim that the efficaciousness of his action requires that the hair be transubstantiated into Jerusalem! To arrive at a basis for the notion of Eucharistic Change one needs to go beyond the category of the symbolic gesture and a context that is simply seen as prophetic.

The key factor in the text that carries us further is the cultic nature of the event within which the Dominical words are spoken. If Jewish ritual memorial implies the presence in our ritual of Christ's death and resurrection, then Our Lord himself has to be in some sense present. Thus the context is already pointing to some kind of presence of Christ before we take up our central statement at all. When then we go on to speak of his body and blood with the bluntness which we find in the Institution Narrative, it fits in that by the words of our key statement we are speaking of his body and blood as in some way present among us.

But Eucharistic Change says more than Real Presence. What finally clinches the full literal meaning of the words in the sense of Eucharistic Change is the sacrificial nature of the cult which is being carried out.

In sacrifice, what it is that is offered is important. It is by offering what it is that you offer that of which it is a symbol. The prophet Malachi certainly finds the religion of his contemporaries reprehensible because what they are offering is defective (Mal 1:8). Indeed sacrifices are commonly specified by that which is offered. A gross example would be the difference between the worship of Yahweh and the worship of Moloch (Lev 20:2–5). More significantly, the difference between the Old Law and the New is typified by the difference in what is offered. In the Old Law one offered vegetable offerings, animals and incense. In the New Law there is only the body and blood of Christ as offered on the cross (Heb 1:1–10).

The fundamental step towards the implication of Eucharistic Change was already made once we saw the Institution Narrative being understood in sacrificial terms. If the Eucharist is in some sense sacrificial, then we are engaged in an offering that is actual, and the object of such an actual offering can only be what is on that paten and in that cup. But there is no sense now in offering bread and wine, since the Lord has changed the whole sacrificial order which once made such offerings acceptable. The only offering which has any meaning now is that of Christ's body and blood. Consequently, if we are truly offering what is on that paten and in that cup, and we are doing it in the context of the New Law, then what is on that paten and in that cup can only be Christ's body and blood. This emerges from the context even before we look at the actual declarations of identity made in the Mark–Matthew Institution Narrative. It is the logic of sacrifice, built into the context, which points to our taking our central statement literally.[8]

It seems, indeed, that more can be said. If our offerings are Christ's body and blood and *not* bread and wine, as the context requires, then the notion of Eucharistic Change can be said to be implicit in the text. It is implicit in Our Lord's changing the Old Covenant into the New, and in his changing our act of worship into his own. If we think of Our Lord as saying 'This is my body . . . this is my blood', by the whole situation he is equivalently saying to us 'This is my worship', and it is out of this change of context that he can come to say 'This is my body . . . this is my blood'.

NOTES

1   1 Kings 8:29–30, 41–51; Ps 145:18; Jer 7:4.
2   H. L. Strack and P. Billerbeck, *Kommentar zum neuen Testament aus Talmud und Midrasch* (Munich: Beck, 1922–28), I, pp. 794–5.
3   John 1:51, fulfilling Gen 28:12.
4   It can be argued that this is a part of the meaning of John 1:14, especially if the Greek verb *eskēnōsen* is accepted as a deliberate echo of the Hebrew *shekinah*.

5 Kilmartin denies that Matt 18:20 refers to communal worship, preferring
   in this connection rather Matt 9:29 and John 15:7, but if one relates the
   text less to its actual context in Matt 18 than to the rabbinical view of the
   presence of God in prayer, the traditional interpretation surely retains its
   force: E. J. Kilmartin, *Christian Liturgy*, vol I (Kansas City: Sheed &
   Ward, 1988), p. 352, n. 10.

6 Here one could think of developing an old terminology of the schools in a
   new way. If the 'matter' of the Eucharist can be considered to be not just
   two objects but the two rituals which Our Lord took, then the 'form' will
   be the new meaning which he gave to these rituals.

7 E.g. 1 Cor 10:16–17; John 6:51c–58; 1 Cor 11:27–32.

8 Though the argument of this paragraph has the appearance of a
   deduction, it is really understood by the author as simply indicating the
   appropriateness of the conclusion rather than its absolute necessity.

5

⊠ *The Fourth Gospel*

The Fourth Gospel is *par excellence* the gospel of divine glory. The mystery of the divine disclosure, which the Synoptics have concentrated into one startling episode on the hill of the transfiguration, is orchestrated by the fourth evangelist from event to event in Our Lord's public life, until it reaches its climax in the paradox of the cross. Inevitably the Eucharist has its place within that story, and it will be the aim of this chapter to bring before the reader this special Johannine perspective on the sacrament.

The author of this gospel has been called 'John the Liturgist'. His precise identity may remain in dispute among the experts, but the liturgical quality of his gospel is now widely recognized. We might notice, for instance, the frequent mention of Jewish feasts, and some scholars even hold that the scriptural topics in the gospel correspond to selections in a Jewish lectionary.[1] If the author is indeed the disciple referred to in John 18:15–16, then he seems to have ready access to priestly circles, which again fits in with attributing to him a special interest in matters liturgical.

Such a way of approaching this evangelist is in marked contrast with that once put forward by Bultmann, who wished to exclude all sacramentalism from the central tradition of this gospel.[2] His point of view is less in evidence today ever since the detailed rebuttal of it by Oscar Cullmann, especially in his work *Early Christian Worship*.[3] For Cullmann the Fourth Gospel is written in two times, or, as Léon-Dufour puts it, on two keyboards, the time of Jesus and the time of the Church.[4] It is written to show that, in leaving the world, Christ did not abandon it. In describing the events of Jesus' life, the evangelist can at the same time be making a statement about the Church of the period in which the gospel is being written. The healing of the paralytic (John 5:1–9) is a statement about Baptism. The multiplication of the loaves (John 6:1–15) is a statement about the Eucharist. Indeed, says Cullmann very strikingly, these sacraments are for the time of the Church what the miracles were for the time of Jesus.[5] They are signs of the presence of the kingdom of God and manifestations of the divine glory.[6]

Raymond Brown has divided this gospel into two sections, the Book of Signs (John 1 – 12) and the Book of Glory (John 13 – 21). These 'signs' are special occasions when the glory of God, which lives in Jesus, is made manifest with particular clarity. They are also anticipations of that climax of disclosure which comes when Christ's 'hour' finally arrives in the Passion.[7] A number of these signs refer to the Eucharist, especially the two miracle-stories: the marriage-feast at Cana (John 2:1–11) and the multiplication of the loaves (John 6:1–15). In one way these signs are manifestations of power, but when we see them as leading up to the powerlessness of the cross, it comes home to us that the real point lies deeper. What we are contemplating here is the mystery of divine love, in all its majesty and beauty, unveiled for us in every gesture of Jesus. That is what is really revealed in Cana and at the feeding of the multitude. That is what is now embodied for us in the sacrament. The 'uttermost proof of his love'[8] has passed over from the cross into the Eucharist.

THE LAST SUPPER

It is surely not by chance that the verse of the gospel we have just referred to is the one which opens the 'Book of Glory'. This 'book' is the account of the paschal mystery, beginning with the Last Supper and ending with the resurrection. All of it represents the climax in the manifestation of divine love, but that it opens with the Last Supper helps to relate this whole series of events to the Eucharist.

Here we come up against one of the great puzzling questions in Johannine scholarship, namely that the Fourth Gospel, which is so permeated with a Eucharistic spirit, is the only one to draw a veil of silence over the institution of the sacrament. Various conjectures as to why this is so have been put forward by scholars. Some say simply that, by the time this gospel was written, the story was so well known that it did not need to be repeated yet again. This however seems a rather weak argument, since it could equally well have been used to exclude other episodes which in fact are retained, such as the events in John 6:1–21. More persuasive is the view which sees it as John's way of shifting attention from the sacrament to the entire paschal mystery, which is, of course, what the sacrament is all about.

This device could even have a liturgical aspect to it. It is not impossible that, then as now, the liturgy of the Eucharist was developing a life of its own and losing its sense of dependence on the events which are its meaning. By this device, then, the evangelist was bringing attention back to what Christian liturgy is all about, emphasizing his point by presenting the events of our redemption as themselves a kind of liturgy. The death and resurrection of Christ, not his actions at the Last Supper, are the paradigm of true liturgy as they are the paradigm of redemption.

Whatever the truth about such conjectures, it is certain that the author of the Fourth Gospel was familiar with some Institution Narrative and that his account of the Last Supper is deeply coloured by the missing story.[9] The discourse at the table deals with two major Eucharistic themes, love and union. The parable of the vine in John 15 inevitably evokes the fruit of the vine in the Eucharistic cup.

The final chapter of the discourse has been referred to by some as Our Lord's 'High Priestly Prayer'. It is the longest text of prayer placed in Our Lord's mouth in the New Testament, and it certainly bears some of the characteristics of a Eucharistic Prayer. It opens with a concern for God's glory, which reminds us of the spirit of blessing and thanksgiving with which Jewish table prayers normally begin. The aspect of petition comes in more quickly than is usually the case in the examples of the Eucharistic Prayer known to us, but the dominant petition is for the fruitfulness of Christ's work among his followers and for the unity of the Church. These are major themes in the great Eucharistic Prayers also, and, as in both the *berachah* and the anaphora traditions, the main body of petition in the chapter is based on an evocation of historical experience (John 17:5–14). Lastly we might note the theme of consecration, which comes to the fore in John 17:17–19. This parallels the aspect of oblation which, of course, is central to all our Eucharistic Prayers.

Before leaving this topic one should warn against trying to prove too much. Absolutely speaking, we have no idea what the Eucharistic Prayer was like at the time this gospel was written. The similarities we have discovered are loose in kind, and there is no evidence for attributing to them anything more than their sharing common roots in Jewish prayer generally and in Jewish table prayer in particular. However there is sufficient to support our main contention, which is the general Eucharistic mood of the Last Supper in John.

THE PASSION

Finally John the Liturgist brings us to the cross. To the eyes of the casual observer the events culminating in Calvary are simply the story of a brutal execution. Christ on his cross is but a wretched convict, yet another victim of the proverbial inhumanity of human beings to one another. But to the contemplative gaze of the fourth evangelist these events mark the unfolding of a great liturgy.

There is a hieratic dignity and solemnity in the way the Christ of this gospel moves towards his death. It is all according to the divine rubrics (John 19:11, 24, 36), and his passing is the completion of a ritual.[10] It takes place at the same hour as the immolation of the lambs in the Temple (John 19:14). Possibly on Calvary one could even hear their bleating. Not a bone of the victim is broken (John 19:36), but the Mishnah describes how the heart is pierced to let the blood flow.[11] Something similar happens on the cross (John 19:34), and the hyssop for the sprinkling of the paschal blood is at hand (John 19:29). Truly Christ is led like a lamb to the slaughter.[12] In death, even more than in life, he is the Lamb of God (John 1:29, 36), and Calvary is the great Passover of the salvation of the world.

But in the Fourth Gospel the cross is not only an altar but a throne. On the cross Christ reigns. There he is 'lifted up', exalted, as the commentators generally point out.[13] What this means is that, for John, the light of the resurrection is already shining through the crucified figure on the cross. Our soteriology fits in with this perception of the evangelist: if the resurrection does not in some sense begin on the cross, it will not begin at all. Christ is no merely passive victim of all that is done to him. In his heart he remains the Son of God who rises above all the sufferings laid upon him and offers them to the Father for the salvation of the world (John 10:17–18). This is the key to that dignity and self-mastery with which Our Lord goes to his death. The Fourth Gospel is like the Eucharist in presenting the death and resurrection in their unity. For Christ the cross is victory and glory.

Another expression of the fourth evangelist builds on the same point. The event of Calvary is referred to as Christ's 'hour' (John 2:4; 12:1; 17:1). His years on earth have gathered to their climax. It is the high-point of salvation history and the centre of time. Indeed, when this hour comes, it is as though time stands still. In the words of Ignace de la Potterie, this hour is presented in such a way in the Fourth Gospel that it rises above the flow of events in a 'definitive permanence outside time'.[14] As we shall see later on, the Church eventually comes to realize that something of this trans-historical quality of Christ's hour has now passed into the Eucharist.

In these various ways the fourth evangelist is indicating how the events on Calvary reach out to the four corners of the earth and to the end of time. Ultimately his perspective is eschatological. For him Calvary is the centre of the great Messianic congregation foretold for the end of the world.[15] The unity of this new people is to flow from the cross (John 12:32), a unity for which Christ prayed at the Last Supper, and for which the Church continues to pray with special urgency in all its great Eucharistic Prayers.

One final scene in John's Passion Narrative clinches the link between the Eucharist and the cross. It is the last Johannine sign before the resurrection, when the soldier opens the side of the dead Saviour (John 19:34).[16] An ancient tradition in the Church, taken up by many exegetes today,[17] interprets the blood and water from Christ's side as symbols of the sacramental life of the Church, of Baptism and Eucharist in particular. The implication seems to be that it is through these sacraments that the cross will continue to live and take effect in the minds and hearts of believers.

This notion is given a wider context by seeing Christ here on the cross as the Second Adam. Just as Eve was born from the side of Adam, so is the Church of the sacraments born from the side of Christ. The significance of the opening of the side is well captured in the teaching of the Rabbis: 'God did not create woman from man's head, that he should command her; nor from his feet, that she should be his slave; rather from his side, that she should be close to his heart' (Talmud). Putting all this together, it is hardly going too far to say that the sacraments are the gift of Christ's love to the Church, so that the power of his Passion may live on in the world.

THE SIXTH CHAPTER

On the northern shore of the sea of Galilee, amongst the ruins commonly accepted as those of Capharnaum, stand the remains of an ancient synagogue. While the present building is from two to four centuries after Our Lord's time,[18] there is some evidence that it stands on the site of an earlier building, which enables us with some probability to mark the spot of what has been called 'the most famous synagogue in Galilee'.[19] Ever since the opening miracle in the Synoptics (Mark 1:26), Capharnaum and its synagogue have been the centre and symbol of Our Lord's Galilean ministry, an activity of which the discourse in John 6 represents the climax.

Whatever claim we can make to have identified the alleged site of the discourse, tenuous as it is, to reconstruct the historical content of such a discourse, and of the events leading up to it, must be acknowledged as an impossibility. Not history but theology must be our primary concern, as we analyse the amalgam of thoughts and events which the final editor of the gospel has attributed to this occasion. The evangelist here writes more as a musician than as an archaeologist, presenting us with a symphony of concepts, images and themes.

The chapter opens with a reference to the Passover season (John 6:4), itself already a theologically significant detail, and we are then given the story of two miracles or signs, the multiplication of the loaves and fishes (vv. 5–15), and the walking on the waters (vv. 16–21). Most of the chapter is then devoted to the discourse and to the discussion to which it gives rise (vv. 22–71).

Exegetes refer to the two signs as 'the bread miracle' and 'the water miracle'. It is a way of drawing attention to echoes of the Exodus narrative, the bread miracle recalling the gift of manna (Exod 16), and the water miracle the crossing of the sea (Exod 14:22). Here in John 6 Our Lord is the New Moses, leading his people towards the final Passover. That the Eucharist should arise in this context is the clearest suggestion so far in the New Testament that the Eucharist is a Christian Passover.

The discourse in John 6 is commonly seen as the centrepiece in the Eucharistic teaching of the Fourth Gospel. This place, however, was not secured for it without some controversy. Luther wished to deny any mention of the Eucharist in this chapter, and even the Council of Trent did not settle the matter for Catholics.

Cardinal Cajetan wanted to support Luther at least in this, and so the council did not insist on the point.[20]

Luther's lead has been followed by many Protestants, but original indeed was the approach of Bultmann. He was torn between two aspects of the question. On the one hand, his interpretation of Johannine faith precluded any sacramentalism in the original tradition of this gospel. On the other hand, he realized that the Eucharistic language of verses 51–58 was undeniable. His solution therefore was to attribute these verses to 'an ecclesiastical redactor', who, he felt, had distorted the original inspiration of the gospel.[21] As we mentioned in an earlier section, the best refutation of this position came from another Lutheran scholar, Oscar Cullmann, who not only argued to the satisfaction of many that sacramentalism was intrinsic to this gospel, but even held that the Bread of Life discourse is to be treated as a unit.[22]

The unity of the discourse is the subject of much discussion. The problem can be broached by dividing the sermon into three main sections:

vv. 26–51b the Bread of Life,
vv. 51c–58 the flesh and blood,
vv. 59–66   the appeal to 'spirit'.

If the discourse is not about the Eucharist, what can its subject-matter be? The common answer is faith. Our Lord is here seen as presenting himself as the 'nourishment' of our faith. In this approach the sermon is seen as primarily Christological, inculcating a particular view of Christ as the centre and source of faith. It is Christ himself, in his very person, not necessarily in the sacrament, who is the Bread of Life. It must be admitted that this view makes a lot of sense, at least of the first section of the discourse, verses 26–51b. Furthermore, it has a significant tradition behind it in the patristic period.[23] Eating bread in this context means living the life of faith and making Christ the centre of our lives.

In the background here is the Feast of Wisdom as found in the sapiential literature of the Old Testament.[24] True life lies in eating and drinking the bread, water and wine of wisdom. The words of personified wisdom in these passages are echoed in Our Lord's Johannine discourse, so that the implication is clear: that wisdom, which was once spoken of figuratively in the Old Testament, is now literally incarnate in the Galilean ministry of Jesus of Nazareth.

A further nuance is added to the picture by recalling that for the Jews this Feast of Wisdom came to be identified with the eschatological banquet spoken of ever since the time of Isaiah.[25] Already in the major prophets the banquet had been presented under the image of Yahweh, the Shepherd of Israel, pasturing his sheep in abundance.[26] In Late Judaism the theme was developed further with the notion of the Messiah as the host entertaining his guests at table.[27] These two thoughts then come together in the multiplication narrative, where the activity of the Messiah is joined to themes of Psalm 22(23): the people resting (John 6:10), on green grass (John 6:10), near the waters (John 6:1–4), feasting in plenitude (John 6:11–13). Finally with the mention of the Passover at the beginning of the chapter (John 6:4), a further note from the same context is struck, for the Passover was commonly seen by the Jews as an anticipation of the Messianic Banquet.[28]

What then is the author conveying to us through such a chorus of associations? On one level he is showing Our Lord presenting himself to the people as the fulfilment of their Messianic hopes. This had been central to the entire Galilean ministry. Now it comes to a climax in a dramatic combination of word and sign worthy of a great prophet. The people had long looked forward to a Messiah who would renew for them in their day something of the wonders wrought under Moses in the desert. Here Our Lord is revealed as fulfilling these expectations in an absolute way. He is the divine wisdom itself, to eat of which by faith is life for the believer (Prov 8:35; Sir 24:29). Firstly, by the prophetic banquet in the desert, then by the challenging teaching in the synagogue, all the benefits which they were expecting for the Messianic times are shown to the people to be within their grasp, if only they would believe in Jesus.

On another level, however, the discourse is about the Eucharist. This meaning emerges in an unambiguous way in the section verses 51c–58. Ironically the person who did most for establishing this view in contemporary exegesis was Bultmann.[29] He realized that the language of this section was clear evidence of the existence of an Institution Narrative in the community reflected in this gospel. The echoes are unmistakable.[30] From this Bultmann went on to conclude that these verses are not part of the original and authentic tradition of the gospel but are an insertion by one of the later editors. We have already spoken of how this anti-sacramental view of the Fourth Gospel has been commonly set aside by scholars, but his perception of the essentially Eucharistic nature of verses 51c–58 remains influential. Raymond Brown accepts that this section may be a parenthesis inserted from elsewhere, but he would insist that these verses represent authentic Johannine material.[31]

However one sorts out the various documentary hypotheses, once one is satisfied that verses 51c–58 are authentic, the theologian will press on to decipher the meaning bequeathed to the Church in the providential juxtaposition of material left to us by the final editor. Immediately there is the Eucharistic teaching conveyed to us by verses 51c–58, but as well as that there is the Eucharistic colouring which the presence of these verses lends to the rest of the discourse. A theologian might leave open the question whether verses 26–51b, 61–65 had an explicit, if secondary, Eucharistic intent in their original form, but, in the final state of the text which has come down to us, Eucharistic overtones can reasonably be found to pervade the words attributed here to Our Lord. If Our Lord's incarnation has established him as the nourishment of our faith, then clearly the Eucharist is one of the highest expressions of that relationship. The text could also be seen to imply that a living faith is a necessary prerequisite for a fruitful celebration of the sacrament.

For the Eucharistic theologian, however, verses 51c–58 remain the centre of interest in this chapter. This is where the realist conception of the identity of the Eucharist with the flesh and blood of Christ is expressed with an insistence almost to the point of crudeness. When Our Lord speaks of the eating of his flesh (v. 51c), the Jews are presented as taking him in a literal way. Often before, Our Lord's fondness for symbolic language had been misinterpreted in a literal sense, but when that happened Jesus had no hesitation in correcting the misunderstanding.[32] In this instance, far from softening his language, he is represented as insisting on it all the more, and, if anything, heightening the realism and scandal: 'My flesh is real food; my blood is real drink.' More than once he uses for this eating a word originally used of animals.[33] It could be translated as 'munching' or 'chewing'.

But perhaps the most extraordinary expression in this extraordinary passage is that in verse 57: 'He who eats *me* . . .'. Though the background may be sapiential rather than Eucharistic (Sir

24:21), the occurrence of the phrase here, where the last editor has left it, inevitably both shocks and yet yields the valuable insight that eating the sacrament is ultimately for personal encounter rather than for the consumption of an object.

While the realism of these expressions seems unavoidable, the scandal they create, not least for Jewish ears, is almost unbearable. It is striking that where wisdom literature speaks of wisdom in language with favourable associations, the gospel here seems to set out to be provocative.[34] All the associations of eating flesh and drinking blood are revolting, not only in the Old Testament, but in our own time also. The suggestion of cannibalism is never far distant. How can this be the language of revelation?

The contrast between the phrasing of Paul and that of John is noteworthy. In 1 Corinthians 10:16–17 Paul seems to preserve a certain delicacy of expression, speaking of 'communion with' the body and blood rather than of eating and drinking them. That by the time of the Fourth Gospel such sensitivity can be set aside is indicative of how much has happened in the intervening years. Not only has the early Christians' grasp of the implications of Christ's resurrection strengthened, but also their sense of the break with the old cultic order and with the synagogue has deepened. It would seem that the spiritual nature of this eating and drinking is now so clearly established that it can be taken for granted. Indeed there is some force in the argument that this Johannine passage was framed deliberately against the language of Deuteronomy 12:23, for the terms being used are similar: flesh, blood, life.

The Eucharist is not cannibalism, because Christ's flesh and blood are made present in a sacramental way, not in a crudely physical sense. The eating and drinking are a means of union with the person, not for acquiring a particular quantity of sacred nourishment. Some of the patristic writers[35] have seen in the text itself a refutation of the crude interpretation, when Our Lord appeals to the spiritualized nature of his ascended flesh in John 6:62–63. Though this approach has received some support in modern theology,[36] many scholars today relate John 6:63 exclusively to John 6:35–51b. The point then is similar to that in Matthew 16:17. Humanity on its own cannot lay hold of the Bread of Life, but only in so far as it is aided by the Spirit.[37] In this view there is no reference to the Eucharist in John 6:60–65.

THE FRUITS OF THE EUCHARIST

In the history of spirituality the Fourth Gospel has always had an outstanding place by reason of its teaching on the fruits of the Eucharist. The relevant texts for this subject are the Capharnaum Discourse in John 6 and the Last Supper Discourse in chapters 14 to 17. The former is, of course, the more explicit in its references to the sacrament itself. In the Last Supper Discourse the thought of the Eucharist arises in a more indirect way. It is there, not only because of the setting in which the discourse is delivered, but also because the subject-matter of these chapters is so often the same as that to which the sacrament is related in John 6.

In a word, the fruit of the Eucharist, according to the Capharnaum Discourse, is 'life'. This fact is already implied in the kind of signs which Our Lord chose for this sacrament, the bread and wine which sustain life. Then this life is described as an 'indwelling' (John 6:56), a point which will be particularly important at the Last Supper. But the key text is surely John 6:54, which deserves to be quoted:

The one who eats my flesh and drinks my blood has eternal life.

The force of this statement lies in the contrast between the adjective before the noun and the tense of the verb. Eternal life is the life of heaven, the life of the future, which each of us is called to share with God for all eternity; but the one who partakes of Christ's Eucharist here below *has* that future here and now! It is not an exaggeration, therefore, if one describes the Eucharist as heaven on earth, an anticipation here below of our eternal communion with God.

This epithet attached to the word 'life' in John 6:54 indicates that the life which the Eucharist is to nourish is not simply human life as we know it from the created order. Does not St Paul speak of 'a new creation' (Gal 6:15)? St John, then, speaks of this life from above, a 'born-again' life (John 3:3), which we can only call the divine life, a life of indwelling, the dimensions of which he expands for us in the great Trinitarian revelations of the Last Supper.

In these final hours of Our Lord on earth, his actions are lit up from within by the radiance of his relationship to his Father. Entering, as he does, into the Great Passover of the salvation of the world (John 13:1–3), the way before him is to be understood as his 'return' to the Father (John 16:28). To give glory to the Father is revealed as something uppermost in the mind of Christ at the Supper (John 17:1; 15:8; 12:27–28), just as it will later be uppermost in the intention of every Eucharist. As will be maintained in Chapter 15 below, the glory of the Father can be seen as the first fruit of the Eucharist, since it is the first fruit of that Supper on which the Eucharist is based. It is a fruit we give to God in the Eucharist as a basis of the fruits which are to come to us, for in this, as in everything else, it is in *giving* that we receive.

As we have said, the fruits of the Eucharist in the Fourth Gospel are summed up in the word 'life', but our notion of this life is significantly expanded in the Last Supper Discourse by the concept of 'indwelling', and precisely by the indwelling of the three Divine Persons. Father, Word and Holy Spirit live in the Son, but through the believer's response in faith this divine indwelling is shared with the ordinary Christian. Father and Son make their home in every lover (John 14:20–23);[38] and where Father and Son are present, so too is the Holy Spirit (John 14:17, 26; 16:13–15).

A further fruit of this divine indwelling is a new power of love and union among people. The paradigm of this union is as exalted as it could be, nothing less than that obtaining between Son and Father (John 17:21). Indeed, in one reading of that verse, the union between Father and Son is not only the exemplar but the cause of the union of the people with one another.[39] This prospect of love and union, to be set out so magnificently in the First Letter of John, is developed at the Last Supper by the parable of the Vine, John 15:1–17. In this parable the Eucharistic overtones are unmistakable,[40] and so it helps to confirm our interpretation of the Last Supper Discourse as indirectly throwing light on the fruits of the Eucharist.

In this Johannine approach to the sacrament there is a certain contrast with that of Paul as found in 1 Corinthians 10:16–17 in particular. Where in Paul the horizontal aspect of the Eucharist is more to the fore, the approach in John may be described as more vertical. Paul emphasizes what the Eucharist symbolizes, John emphasizes what it is. The sacramental body in Paul points to the ecclesial body.[41] In John the focus is more on the individual participant. However there is no contradiction between the two perspectives. Each is complementary to the other, and both are required for an integrated view.

CONCLUSION ON THE NEW TESTAMENT

With the treatment of the Eucharist in the Fourth Gospel, our survey of the Eucharistic theology of the New Testament comes to an end. Looking back over the path we have pursued, I would wish to underline the notion of development as a key to unravelling and knitting together again a unified view of the sacrament at this early stage. By this means, aspects, which in themselves can only be suggestions or pointers, gain in force from being fitted into a moving viewpoint. Indeed what is true of individual moments is true of the whole period: when set beside the later developments of tradition, the general shape of the Eucharist in its classical form emerges as significantly grounded in the data of the New Testament.

This notion of development is of particular usefulness in handling the controversial issue of the sacrificial nature of the Eucharist. Allowing that at an early time this notion was scarcely present at all, one can still make room for its emergence at a later period, albeit in varying degrees of clarity and force. This same perspective absolves one from having to maintain that the development was fully formed by the end of the New Testament period. It was a question of a process of developing understanding, begun in the New Testament itself on the basis of determinations of the tradition from the outset, but left to later reflection to be refined and worked out in all their implications. Certainly, as we will see, the notion was much more clearly and emphatically developed in the patristic Church, but the key point we have established is that these later developments already existed in germ in the New Testament community, and even in the determinations of the Institution Narrative.

The doctrine of what we have called 'the Eucharistic Change' is even more problematic, and for that reason the perspective of development is here all the more crucial. Textually we have principally the affirmation of identity in the Institution Narrative. Undoubtedly these early Christians had their own way of interpreting these words, and that through a symbolic mentality much richer than ours; but for us now to find incontrovertible evidence, to answer not their questions but ours, is surely to ask too much. The best we can do is to gather together the various pointers and to see them in continuity with the viewpoint which later becomes clearer. If one believes in the presence of the Holy Spirit in the community to guide it in questions such as these, then the hypothesis of continuity will stand. If one does not so believe, then one is left in the shifting sands of individual scholarship and conjecture.

NOTES

1 A. Guilding, *The Fourth Gospel and Jewish Worship* (Oxford: Clarendon, 1960); R. Brown, *The Gospel According to John, I–XII* (New York: Doubleday/London: Geoffrey Chapman, 1966), pp. 278–80.
2 R. Bultmann, *The Theology of the New Testament*, vol. II (London: SCM, 1955), p. 59; *The Gospel of John: A Commentary* (Oxford: Blackwell, 1971), p. 472.
3 O. Cullmann, *Early Christian Worship* (London: SCM, 1953).
4 Ibid., pp. 56–9.
5 Ibid., p. 118.
6 The theme of glory here is taken rather from von Balthasar than from Cullmann.
7 On this 'hour' see John 2:4; 12:1; 17:1, and commentaries, e.g. *The Jerusalem Bible* ad locum.
8 John 13:1 in the Knox translation.
9 Echoes of an Institution Narrative in John 6:51–58 will be described below when that passage is being discussed.
10 John 19:30: 'consummating' is a word associated with ritual.
11 'He [that slaughtered the lamb] slit the heart and let out its blood' (Tamid 4:2, on the Daily Whole Offering), in H. Danby (ed.), *The Mishnah* (Oxford: Oxford University Press, 1964), p. 585.
12 Isa 53:7 and Jer 11:19.
13 See, for instance, *The Jerusalem Bible* on John 12:32; 3:13–14; 8:28. The glorification of Jesus begins already in his Passion: John 13:31–32.
14 I quote from notes on the Johannine Passion Narrative given by de la Potterie to students in the Biblical Institute, Rome in the 1960s. They are no longer available to me.
15 Jer 23:2–8; 31:8; Isa 10:10–12; 43:5–8.
16 John 19:34–36 should be read in conjunction with 1 John 5:6 and John 7:37, taking the latter in the Ephesine reading, preferred, for instance, in *The Jerusalem Bible*.
17 Cullmann, Barrett, R. Brown, Macgregor, Stanley, Schnackenburg etc. Among the Fathers see St Augustine, *Treatises on John* 9, 10 (PL 35, 1463D); ibid., 120, 2 (PL 35, 1953B); Chrysostom, *Homilies on John* 85, 3 (PG 59, 463B–C).

18 J. Murphy-O'Connor, *The Holy Land: An Archaeological Guide from Earliest Times to 1700* (Oxford: Oxford University Press, 1980), p. 169.

19 Ibid., p. 165.

20 E. Kilmartin, *The Eucharist in the Primitive Church* (Englewood Cliffs, NJ: Prentice-Hall, 1965), pp. 105–6. For Luther on the subject, see *Luther's Works*, vol. 36 (Philadelphia: Fortress, 1959), p. 19.

21 Bultmann, *The Gospel of John*, pp. 10–11.

22 Cullmann, *Early Christian Worship*, pp. 95–102.

23 H. de Lubac, *Corpus mysticum: l'eucharistie et l'église au moyen-âge* (Paris: Aubier, 1944), p. 13. See for instance Augustine: 'For to believe in him is to eat the living bread': *Treatises on John* 26, 1 (PL 35, 1607).

24 Prov 9:1–5; Sir 15:3; 24:19–21.

25 Isa 26:6–8; 54:11 – 55:3; 65:11–13.

26 Isa 49:10; Ezek 34:13; Ps 22(23).

27 Ethiopian Enoch 64:10; Slavic Enoch 42:5. Cf. Mark 14:25; Luke 12:37; Rev 3:20; 19:9.

28 If an association between the Passover and the Eucharist can be conceded for the Fourth Gospel, then we have here a further link between this chapter and the Eucharist, additional to the points which are about to be considered.

29 Bultmann, *The Gospel of John*, pp. 218–19; 234–7.

30 'Flesh' and 'blood' – 'body' and 'blood'; 'the bread which I will give'– 'bread . . . he gave'; 'for the life of the world' – 'for many'; 'eat' (*phagein*) John 6:52, 53, 58 – 'eat' (*phagete*) Matt 26:26–27.

31 Brown, *The Gospel According to John, I–XII*, pp. 285–7.

32 A good example is Matt 16:5–12. From Johannine material we have John 11:14. For an example of the opposite, that is of Christ, as in John 6, reinforcing a literal meaning when it has been called into doubt, see John 5:18ff.

33 Greek: *trōgein* – vv. 54, 56.

34 'There we find love in its most provocative form', says Hans Urs von Balthasar of this passage, in *Prayer* (New York: Paulist, 1961), p. 130.

35 For instance, Augustine, *Enarrationes in Psalmos* 98, 9 (PL 37, 1264); Cyril of Alexandria, *Commentary on John*, bk IV, chap. 3, on John 6:62–64 (PG 73, 600B–605A).

36 E.g. M. Schmaus, *Dogma 5: The Church as Sacrament* (London: Sheed & Ward, 1975), pp. 75–6.

37 Brown, *The Gospel According to John, I–XII*, p. 300.

38 Cf. John 15:4–5; 17:21–26. See also 1 John 2:24–25; 4:5–6.

39 This follows from taking *kathōs* in the Greek as not only comparative but causal, e.g. Brown, *The Gospel According to John, I–XII*, p. 769.

40 On the parable of the Vine as Eucharistic, see Brown, *The Gospel According to John, XIII–XXI* (New York: Doubleday/London: Geoffrey Chapman, 1966), p. 673.

41 One should notice that both in 1 Cor 10:16–17 and in 11:24 the language
    is held to be that of pre-Pauline cultic formulae. The corporate notion
    of Christ's body is seen as a Pauline theologoumenon, which thus can
    be argued to have grown out of the Eucharistic sense rather than vice
    versa: P. Neuenzeit, *Das Herrenmahl* (Munich: Kösel, 1960), pp. 162,
    169.

6

⊠ *Eucharistic sacrifice in the early centuries*

In these days of ecumenism it has been remarked that, as well as an ecumenism in space, there is also an ecumenism in time. This is a way of bringing out the importance of tradition in theology, and in particular the importance, both for theology and for faith, of the witness of the patristic Church. The Eucharist is a good example of what this assertion might mean. Since this sacrament was so central in the ordinary life of the Church in those early centuries, it certainly loomed large in the reflection and catechesis of bishops and theologians and so benefits from their gift for bringing out the central lines of our belief. This means that a consideration of the patristic Eucharist has an irreplaceable value for the theologian of this sacrament.

But as well as drawing our attention to the enduring substance of Eucharistic faith, the study of the ancient writers also helps to illustrate that principle of development to which reference was made at the end of the preceding chapter. Not only were there the changes that came about when the faith passed among these writers themselves, from country to country and from culture to culture, but earlier there was the crucial period when Christianity emerged out of the chrysalis of its New Testament origins into the following century. Perhaps more than at other times, what was happening at this crucial moment helps to underline the continuity between the later and the earlier periods and to demonstrate how development is an intrinsic part of the living of the Christian faith.

One of the main innovations in the story of this sacrament concerned the growing stress on the cultic aspect of the Eucharist. Here the words of such a careful scholar as Jungmann are striking for their emphasis and their clarity:

The great change which occurred in liturgical practice, *the greatest perhaps in the whole course of the history of the Mass*, was the abandonment of the meal as a setting for the Mass. With the gradual enrichment of the prayer of thanksgiving and, at the same time, the continual growth of the convert communities, which became too large for a domestic table-gathering, the supper character of the Christian assembly could and did disappear, and the celebration became in truth a Eucharistic celebration. This change had occurred already at the end of the first century.[1]

It does not seem unreasonable to postulate that the innovation to which Jungmann refers was but the outward expression of a process of developing understanding. We have already detected this process within the Institution Narrative, but we can now affirm it with more confidence as we see it subsequently affecting a number of liturgical and theological points. The first witness to be brought forward is the *Didache*, where, for the first time, we find the term 'sacrifice' applied to the Eucharist.[2] A development of understanding is under way which will eventually accept into Eucharistic practice a number of cultic terms and concepts which the initial differentiation from the Temple had excluded from Eucharistic usage. Shortly, too, the word 'sanctuary' is found in the context of the sacrament.[3] Eventually 'altar' and 'priest' will be accepted also, even though the accent and the context will be new.[4]

Underlying all these developments is the sacrificial nature of the sacrament. This, as we have seen, is one of the central dogmatic issues concerning the Christian Eucharist. We have already studied the germ of the idea in the New Testament. It is now time to see its full emergence in the writings of the early centuries.

One of the basic points made by the early writers in this context lies in their description of the Eucharist as a sacrifice which is 'spiritual'. In itself this notion has a long ancestry, going back to the polemic of the prophets against the decadence of the Temple. The key point in the notion lay in finding the moral values of sacrifice embodied in non-sacrificial acts such as repentance, almsgiving and prayer.[5] This idea was taken up especially by Jewish groups disaffected from the Temple, such as those in Qumran. Later, in the Hellenistic sphere, it found echoes in the writings of philosophers critical of sacrifice.[6]

The most immediate influences on the early theologians were obviously Christian. The basic thrust of the New Testament on the matter saw the fulfilment of the ancient cult in the totality of Christian life.[7] If, as we have just seen, this kind of approach was not entirely new, it was now put forward on a radically new basis as grounded in Christ's death 'outside the gate' (Heb 13:12), in his resurrection and in his gift of the Holy Spirit. Behind this lay the early history of Christian worship, already described in Chapter 3 of this book, and in particular the way it arose in differentiation from, and later in opposition to, the Jewish Temple. The new notion of spiritual sacrifice is thus clearly distinguished from traditional cultic sacrifice, and it acquires a specifically Christian nuance by being grounded in the eschatological gift of the Spirit. This then is the broad meaning of 'spiritual sacrifice', and it is the predominance of this sense of the term which is the characteristic feature of this earliest post-New Testament stage in the development of Christian cultic language.[8]

Only within this wider, existential sense of the expression does the phrase come to be applied to the Eucharist is a specific way. For one thing, the Eucharistic action is one of the many kinds of act in which the broad sense of 'spiritual sacrifice' is verified. In addition, ordinary Christian living was expressed and celebrated in the Eucharist, so that the Eucharist came to participate in that fulfilment of sacrifice which Christian living represented. But perhaps the key point was the fact that, from its origins, the Christian ritual had been sacramental in the sense that, beneath the outward non-sacrificial appearances, there was a hidden reality grounded in Christ's death and resurrection, its presence betrayed by elements of the old cultic language of sacrifice preserved in the Institution Narrative.

Only gradually do these various factors come together to form a coherent view of the Eucharist as sacrifice in some proper sense of the term. Eventually even the external ritual would be reinterpreted according to some of the language and protocol of traditional oblation. But early on, in a man like Clement of Alexandria, these factors are hardly considered at all. In Hippolytus on the other hand, as we shall see, they count for much more. It is really only if one stands back and tries to view the tradition as a whole that one can appreciate that the general sense of its movement was towards a notion of the Eucharist as sacrifice, neither univocally of the same genre as that of the Jews or pagans, nor in a totally different or metaphorical sense, but in an analogous sense which has to accommodate itself to the unique meaning of sacrifice inaugurated on the cross. This is the development which will be traced in this chapter.

St Justin

A good place in which to see this whole process under way is found in the work of St Justin. He is the first Christian writer to take up the idea of sacrifice as a theological question and to attempt to define the nature of Christian sacrifice over against that of Jews and pagans. Central is the prophecy of the perfect worship of the End Times in Malachi 1:10–12, a text which was destined to become a standard one among the writers on this subject. These verses had already been referred to in passing in *Didache* 14, but Justin makes them central, and indeed, according to one writer, most of what Justin has to say about sacrifice and the Eucharist can be seen as a Christian interpretation of this text.[9] The application of these verses to the Eucharist gave the Fathers a scriptural basis for their spiritual–eschatological notion of Eucharistic sacrifice.

For Justin, as for the Apologists generally, Jewish and pagan sacrifices are equally objectionable. They are the works of the devil, their primitive state being typified by the crude and bloody ritual they involved. Christian sacrifice requires no such gory protocol. It is brought about simply by the word, by prayer and thanksgiving, not by fire and blood.

This emphasis on the constitutive role of prayer and thanksgiving in the Christian sacrifice has led some theologians to interpret a writer such as Justin as holding that the Eucharist is a sacrifice only in the sense of the offering of these prayers, but not in any strictly ritual sense by which gifts are presented to God.[10] It is true that some of Justin's statements could have been read in this way, but if these theologians were correct, then the Eucharist would be sacrifice for Justin in a purely metaphorical and improper sense of the term. Wieland tried to maintain that Justin really rejects all sacrifice and regards prayer by itself as the only form of sacrifice for Christians. Such a point of view seems an over-simplification. It does not take account of the fact that Justin was writing in the middle of an incomplete process in which the categories and terms of worship were being radically remoulded in the light of a fundamentally new reality.

Theologians who take a different view to that of Wieland, just as those of an approach similar to his, can invoke a number of factors in Justin in their support. One has always to bear in mind that the immediate context of the prayer and thanksgiving to which Justin is referring is the celebration of the sacrament in bread and cup; it is not just prayer and thanksgiving on their own. Particularly striking is *The Dialogue with Trypho* 116–117, where Malachi 1:11 is explained in a text which can be translated literally as follows:

Therefore all sacrifices through this name, which Jesus required to be carried out, namely in the thanksgiving (*eucharistia*) of bread and cup, which are carried out everywhere by Christians, God testifies beforehand that they are pleasing to him.[11]

Here we see that in Justin's mind the sacrificial thanksgiving he is referring to is not just a matter of words or attitudes but is embodied in the Eucharistic ritual.

The same point is even clearer in chapter 41 of the same work, again with reference to Malachi 1:11, when Justin identifies the notion of sacrifice with the Eucharistic bread and cup:

Concerning the sacrifices offered by us, the Gentiles, to God, namely [the sacrifices] of the bread of thanksgiving and of the cup similarly of the thanksgiving, he spoke then beforehand, saying that we praise his name but that you [the Jews] profane it.[12]

In writing on this point against Wieland many years ago, Jungmann appealed to the pregnant sense of memorial which, as we have seen, entered the Christian liturgy from that of the Jews. Jungmann is confident that this notion remained alive in the consciousness of the second century and can be seen in the continuation of the first text cited above, again translated very literally:

That both the prayers and the thanksgivings, carried out by worthy people, are the only perfect sacrifices acceptable to God, I myself declare. For these things alone have Christians also learned to carry out, even through the commemoration of their food, solid and liquid, in which they commemorate also the passion which the Son of God endured on their account.[13]

If the prayers and thanksgivings of Justin's Eucharist are carried out only within the 'living memorial' of Christ's sacrifice, then it is difficult to see why the author should confine the fulfilment of Malachi 1:11 simply to an offering of prayers and not in so far as these prayers are part and parcel of their setting in that ritual memorial of sacrifice.

In this matter the key thing is to see Justin in the movement of his time and so in continuity with what went before in the Christian community and with what was to come afterwards. In this perspective it is clear that, side by side with a constant emphasis on the Christian sacrifice as 'spiritual', the whole thrust of development in the early Church was towards explicitating and expanding the values contained in the central reality of Christian sacrifice hidden beneath the surface of the rite.

St Irenaeus

In the writings of St Irenaeus the clarification of the notion of Eucharistic sacrifice is carried a stage further.[14] Irenaeus gives us the lengthiest discussion of the subject to be found in the first two centuries. If he is well described as 'the father of Catholic dogmatics',[15] it is fitting that we find in him the first attempt at a coherent theology of sacrifice.

Where Justin was reacting against exaggerations of a materialistic kind, Irenaeus is concerned at the spiritualizing tendencies of Gnosticism. As is well known, the Gnostics taught a dualism of creation and redemption, Old Testament and New Testament, matter and spirit. Strange as their theories seem to us, they were providential in providing the occasion for the first Christian theology of the created order. This is the context in which the sacrificial nature of the Eucharist was destined to grow in emphasis and significance. Stressing the unity of creation and redemption, it is grist to Irenaeus' mill that the created order should be drawn into the ritual instituted by Christ. Phrases of his like 'this bread which is of creation', 'this cup which is of creation', make the point clearly.[16]

Consequently, for Irenaeus, material creation is good; grace builds on or perfects the world of nature. In this line of thought it fits in that Irenaeus should be the first Christian theologian after the New Testament to speak positively of the rituals and sacrifices of the Old Testament, seeing them as foreshadowings of the New Law.

This assertion of the goodness of material creation must have been an important element in opening up Christian language to the categories of oblation, a notion deeply rooted in natural religion. In Irenaeus himself it is evidenced in his presentation of the Eucharist as the offering of first-fruits.[17] Certainly it is noteworthy that shortly after Irenaeus we can detect a heightening of the notion of oblation in our sources as we move from the global offering for the people, such as we have found in the New Testament, to an offering for the needs of individuals.[18] The custom of the faithful bringing bread and wine for the Eucharist comes to be referred to as their 'offering' these gifts.[19] Eventually *oblatio* and *sacrificium* come to be ordinary names for the Eucharist in the Western tradition, until they are superseded by terms derived from *missa*.[20]

David Power has remarked that Irenaeus' text 'does not seem to intend an offering of the body and blood of Christ, but one of bread and wine'.[21] Prior to him Robert Daly had implied that for Irenaeus the Eucharist is a sacrifice in the offering of prayers and thanksgiving.[22] It is certainly true that by the time of Irenaeus there is no evidence that authors had clearly formulated the notion of offering Christ's body and blood in the sacrament, but this limitation should not be seen in isolation from the other aspects of the Eucharist which reveal the way these authors viewed the whole celebration as something very special.

Both in Justin and in Irenaeus, for instance, one has to bear in mind the strange usage that identifies thanksgiving with the sacramental gifts themselves when the term *eucharist* is applied to them. With Irenaeus there is the additional fact that what is offered in the Eucharist is said to be 'the new oblation of the new testament', and this is asserted, in a context not simply of prayer and thanksgiving or of bread and wine, but of the Eucharistic Change in the words of the Institution Narrative.[23] In the same writer one should also notice that in offering *eucharistia* one will be offering that in which there is both 'something earthly' and 'something heavenly'.[24] This is surely saying more than simply offering bread and wine.

In a surprising phrase, Irenaeus characterizes the offering of Christians as 'the offering of the free'. Jewish sacrifices were carried out under the slavery of the Old Law, but Christian sacrifice he sees as the total gift of self in a spirit of joy and freedom.[25] Now freedom is one of the central issues in the theology of Eucharistic sacrifice, but it is surprising to find it highlighted in this way at such an early stage. More than likely, Irenaeus was stimulated in this direction by the discussions among the Jews and pagans on related questions.

The opposition between material sacrifice and the offering of prayers, which we have seen already in Justin, had its parallels in a number of ancient philosophers. The crux of the problem was the unchangeability of God, such as was taught in Platonism. The consequence of this truth was that sacrifices were considered useless.[26] The Stoics were as much against prayer as against sacrifice, also Platonists like Maximus of Tyre.[27] In Judaism the principle of material sacrifice was never rejected, but the comparable, if not superior, value of prayer and good works came to be stressed, first by the Jews of the Diaspora, then by the Essenes, and finally by all after AD 70. After the time of Irenaeus the discussion continued in the work of the Neo-Platonists. Porphyry ruled out sacrifice in the case of the Supreme God. God, he said, can be worshipped only by silence.[28] According to the *Corpus Hermeticum*, since God is in need of nothing, material sacrifices are to be abolished. Instead there are to be 'spiritual sacrifices' (*logikai thusiai*) only. God is to be adored simply by the giving of thanks.[29]

Again and again in his discussion of sacrifice Irenaeus makes the point that God, in his transcendence, has no need of our offerings.[30] He derives this teaching from a florilegium of texts culled from the prophets and Psalms, culminating in Our Lord's use of Hosea 6:6 in Matthew 12:7. It is in this context that he treats of the Eucharistic oblation according to the principle that God requires offerings from us, not for his own sake, but for ours, *a nobis propter nos*, so that we might not be unfruitful.[31] Irenaeus is surely close to the crux of the whole matter when he says that it is a question not just of our knowing God but of God's honouring us.[32] Far from manifesting an imperfect and needy divinity, the order of New Testament sacrifice points rather to God's concern for our progress. Far from robbing the divinity of its sovereignty, this exercise of our freedom demonstrates all the more the considerateness of divine love.

In the light of later difficulties about the whole principle of Eucharistic offering and the use of freedom it implies, it is indeed remarkable to find such a serene appreciation of freedom in so early a writer. His contribution must have been a key factor in that strengthening of the notion of the Eucharist as oblation which was to mark the third century. Even though the notion of spiritual sacrifice must still be said to predominate in Irenaeus, it is but a small step from him to his intellectual heir, Hippolytus, where the cultic understanding of the Eucharist reaches a certain climax.[33]

Hippolytus

The story which we have been tracing in this chapter has all along been one of a tension between the cultic and the spiritual aspects of the sacrament. The advent of the third century marks the end of that situation and the beginning of a new one, for from now on, in writers such as Hippolytus, Tertullian and Cyprian, cultic terminology begins to be normal in the case of the Eucharist.[34]

The point is well illustrated in the first of these authors, where cultic language is applied both to the sacrament itself and to its principal minister, the bishop. In Hippolytus' Eucharistic Prayer, the Eucharistic bread and wine are clearly offered to God, and in his ordination prayer the bishop is referred to as high priest and as offering the gifts of the Church.[35] But perhaps what above all marks out Hippolytus in relation to the previous authors we have been studying is the way cultic language is applied by him exclusively to the liturgy. Now there is no significant mention of the ordinary life of Christians as a sacrifice. The Christian sacrifice simply is the Eucharist. The wheel has come full circle.

THE CLASSICAL PATRISTIC APPROACH
TO EUCHARISTIC SACRIFICE

As we study the growth of Eucharistic theology, we cannot leave out of account the context of Christian theology generally, which at this time was undergoing some of the most decisive developments in its history. The principal issue of the age was of course the formulation of the mystery of God as triune, leading on later to the mystery of person and nature in Christ. Inevitably these discussions had their influence on Eucharistic theology, and to an extent an influence in reverse was at work also.

Both Trinitarian and Eucharistic theology had a special interest in seeing Christ as High Priest of the new dispensation. It has been suggested that this kind of language goes back to the speculations of the Hellenistic Jews, by whom Divine Wisdom was already compared to the High Priest (Sir 24:10). This points to Alexandria as a centre of interest for this kind of approach. Certainly a similar parallel was found meaningful by the author of the Letter to the Hebrews, and the idea is taken up by some of the earliest witnesses.[36] Another version of this analogy is found in Philo's theology of the Word. Though this Word is for Philo an impersonal reality, yet he calls it the High Priest of creation.[37] Clement of Alexandria also writes of the Word, but insists that the Word is personal.[38]

When we come to Origen, we find the notion drawn into the tensions of his Christology. That this writer was not entirely free from subordinationism is well known. For a time he held that we could not pray to Christ but only *through* him.[39] In Origen's view of things, the real activity for our salvation goes on in eternity, and so the High Priest is clearly identified with the Word of God in his *eternal* being. If the mediator is the Word as eternal, this easily suggests that, even within the godhead, he is less than the Father. It is out of elements like this in the tradition that Arianism would shape its own position.

At the same time, this background enables Origen to develop the language of Eucharistic sacrifice. He is the first to bring out in a clear way that Christ is the mediator of Eucharistic thanksgiving.[40] He is also the first to reflect explicitly on the propitiatory aspect of the Eucharist, not as though he were the inventor of this notion, as some have said, but as explicitating what is already implicit in the New Testament.[41] As was already suggested in Chapter 3 above, once the sacrifice of the cross is seen as the fulfilment of the sacrificial system of the Old Law, and in particular of the sacrifice of atonement, as emphasized in the Letter to the Hebrews, propitiation has to be part of the meaning of the cross, and so, by extension, of the Eucharist.[42]

In St Athanasius we enter the world of the anti-Arian reaction, which was so influential on the theology and forms of worship. In response to subordinationism and Arianism the orthodox had come to see that mediatorship had to be based on Christ's humanity. For Athanasius the Word became High Priest only when he was robed in the 'vestment' of his flesh.[43] This lent a new emphasis to a notion of worship, present since the New Testament, according to which our liturgy rests on Christ's exalted humanity in heaven interceding on our behalf.[44]

St John Chrysostom is a crucial figure for the further development of these notions. In him we can, with Betz, distinguish two periods. As a teacher and bishop in Antioch, he follows the ordinary theology of his day, in which the Mass is centred on the heavenly liturgy. In the Eucharist the exalted Christ is the host at the table entertaining his guests, and they are worshipping with him and through him.[45] That this approach is traditional is shown by its occurrence earlier even in Origen.[46] Indeed Betz has written of Chrysostom at this stage that 'he emphasizes the direct activity of Christ as host to a degree unequalled in all Greek patristics'.[47]

By the turn of the century (AD 400), John was installed as bishop of Constantinople and he was at the height of his powers. The imperial city had a very different history to Antioch. The predominance of Arianism in the capital was a matter of recent memory, since it had ended only with the accession of Theodosius I to the imperial throne. Chrysostom is one of the witnesses to what Jungmann has called the 'anti-Arian reaction' in the liturgy. One result of this was an increasing emphasis on the divinity of Christ and a heightening of the language of reverence and awe. In the Eucharist 'the death of Christ is carried out, the awesome sacrifice, the ineffable mysteries'.[48]

Associated with this, however, was another development, with far-reaching consequences for the theology of the Eucharist in the West, and one which alone would merit for Chrysostom the title sometimes given him of 'Doctor of the Eucharist'. From the final year before his exile in 403 come his 34 homilies on the Letter to the Hebrews, our only full-length commentary on that epistle which has come down to us from the ancient Church. It was the subject-matter of this epistle which finally made Chrysostom face the question of the real meaning of Christ's heavenly mediation. It seems that it was the possible Arian implications of taking that mediation literally which moved Chrysostom in a new direction.

For him now Christ's sitting at the right hand of the Father is a sign of passive, not active cult.[49] The notion of his mediating in heaven is but an adaptation of language to our limited mode of understanding, according to an act of divine 'condescension'.[50] As we would say today, it must be 'demythologized'. Not only must mediation be situated in the humanity of Christ, but specifically in his activity here on earth. The centre of gravity for the Eucharist now shifts from the liturgy of heaven to the sacrifice of the cross.[51] Directly active in the Eucharist is the ordained priest. Christ remains the High Priest of our offering, but primarily in virtue of his activity on the cross. The Eucharist is that once-for-all sacrifice made actual through the power of *anamnesis*. Thus Chrysostom becomes what Betz has called 'the theologian of the anamnesis'.[52]

The model for this notion of the Eucharist is clearly the Jewish Passover. The significance of this lies in the fact that Chrysostom is drawing his inspiration from the biblical tradition and not from any pagan cultic form, such as Casel had suggested.[53] We should bear in mind that Chrysostom was by birth a Syrian of Antioch. Antiochene theology generally always had closer links than Alexandria with the semitic background of the New Testament.[54]

The classical passage in Chrysostom on the Eucharistic memorial occurs in his seventeenth homily on Hebrews.[55] We might translate it as follows:

What then? Do we not carry out an oblation every day? We do indeed, but by carrying out the commemoration (*anamnēsis*) of his death, and this commemoration is one, not several. How one and not several? Because he was offered up once only, like the offering in the Holy of Holies. The one is the type of the other, and so is the Eucharist also. We are always offering the same victim, not one sheep today and another tomorrow, but always the same one, so that the sacrifice (*thusia*) is one. Now in virtue of this argument, since the sacrifice is offered up in many places, are there many christs? By no means, but everywhere there is one Christ, as complete in one place as in another, one body. Therefore as he who is offered up in many places is one body and not many bodies, so is it one sacrifice. He is our High Priest who offered up the sacrifice which purifies us. This is that which we also now offer up, the one formerly offered up, the inconsumable offering. This comes about for the commemoration of what once took place, for he says, 'Do this in commemoration of me'. We are not carrying out yet another sacrifice, as the High Priest did on the former occasion; rather are we always carrying out the same sacrifice, or, to be more precise, we bring about the commemoration of sacrifice.[56]

While scholars might be slow to regard Chrysostom as a great speculative thinker, the fact of the matter is that the shift of perspective in Eucharistic theology reflected in this passage contains in embryo the whole medieval view of the Eucharist in the West. The passage came to figure in the catenae of patristic texts available to the scholastics and is cited, for instance, by Aquinas, though attributed to Ambrose.[57] Of course, this Western development is not due simply to this passage, but it is remarkable to find our medieval emphasis on the cross anticipated in one of the greatest figures in Eastern Christianity, a Christianity which itself kept the Eucharist focused on the heavenly liturgy in a way no longer true in the West.[58]

NOTES

1 J. Jungmann, *The Early Liturgy: To the Time of Gregory the Great* (London: Darton, Longman & Todd, 1960), pp. 37–8 (emphasis added).

2 *Didache* 14:1 in A. Hänggi and I. Pahl (eds), *Prex eucharistica* (Fribourg: Editions Universitaires, 1968), p. 68.

3 Greek: *thusiasterion* – St Ignatius of Antioch, *To the Ephesians* 5, 2 (PG 5, 649A); *To the Philadelphians* 4 (PG 5, 700; RJ 56). This term could also be

translated 'altar'. In Ignatius it is used figuratively either of Christ or of the Church at worship, not of the Eucharistic table.

4 Such usages develop only in the third century, e.g. in Cyprian, *Letters*, *passim*. The mention of an altar in Irenaeus, *Against the Heresies* IV, 18, 6 (Har 2, 210 [see note 14 below]; SC 100, 614) refers to the altar in heaven.

5 Ps 49(50):13–14, 23; 50(51):17; 68(69):30–31; Sir 35:1ff.

6 See Frances M. Young, *The Use of Sacrificial Ideas in Greek Christian Writers from the New Testament to John Chrysostom* (Patristic Monograph Series No. 5; Cambridge, MA: The Philadelphia Patristic Foundation Ltd, 1979). A shortened presentation of the same ideas will be found in Part I of the same author's book *Sacrifice and the Death of Christ* (London: SCM, 1983), but references below will be to the first of these two works.

7 Rom 12:1; 15:16; 1 Pet 2:4–10; Heb 13:10–16. The phrase 'spiritual sacrifices' occurs in 1 Pet 2:5. In Rom 12:1 Paul speaks of 'spiritual worship' using for 'spiritual' the Hellenistic term *logikos*. See Chapter 3 above, especially on John 4:24.

8 An equivalent expression is 'unbloody sacrifice', found already in the second century and destined to figure prominently in a Eucharistic sense from Eusebius of Caesarea on. See K. Stevenson, ' "The unbloody sacrifice": the origins and development of a description of the Eucharist' in G. Austin (ed.), *Fountain of Life* (Washington: The Pastoral Press, 1991), pp. 103–30.

9 R. Daly, *Christian Sacrifice: The Judaeo-Christian Background Before Origen* (Washington: Catholic University of America Press, 1978), p. 333. A shorter version of this work was also published: R. Daly, *The Origins of the Christian Doctrine of Sacrifice* (London: Darton, Longman & Todd, 1978).

10 Jungmann cites for this view the work of one Franz Wieland, a Catholic theologian early in the century, and refers to the account of the controversy surrounding his views in G. Rauschen, *Eucharistie und Bußsakrament in den ersten sechs Jahrhunderten* (Freiburg: Herder, 1910): thus J. Jungmann, *The Early Liturgy*, pp. 45–6. See also R. P. C. Hanson, 'Eucharistic offering in the pre-Nicene Fathers', PRIA, vol. 76/C (Dublin, 1976), pp. 75–95. R. Daly is close to this view also, on the basis of the Eucharistic Prayer's being a prayer of thanksgiving: op. cit., pp. 505 and 335. However he acknowledges that this prayer must always be dependent on its ritual context and so he can differentiate his position from that of 'later radically spiritualizing interpreters of early Christian literature' (p. 333, n. 22), but, unlike Jungmann, he does not spell out the way this ritual context makes a difference.

11 Justin, *Dialogue with Trypho* 117 (PG 6, 745B).

12 *Dialogue with Trypho* 41 (PG 6, 564). Thus L. Lies, *Wort und Eucharistie bei Origenes* (Innsbruck: Tyrolia, 1978), p. 25.

13 Ibid., 117, 2–3 (PG 6, 745C). Betz agrees with Jungmann, op. cit., I/1, p. 213, n. 245.

14 In the citing of St Irenaeus two editions of the *Adversus haereses* (*Against the Heresies*) will be consulted: that edited by W. W. Harvey in the last century (see Bibliography) and the recent edition prepared for *Sources chrétiennes*. The two volumes of the former will be referred to by the abbreviation 'Har 1' or 'Har 2', followed by the page reference, while the latter will be referred to by the letters 'SC'. The chapter divisions used are those of the edition of R. Massuet (Venice, 1710) made familiar by Migne in PG 7.

15 W. Kasper, *Jesus the Christ* (London: Burns & Oates, 1976), p. 189.

16 Irenaeus, *Against the Heresies* V, 2, 2 (Har 2, 319; RJ 249; SC 153, 32).

17 *Against the Heresies* IV, 17, 5 (Har 2, 197–200; SC 100, 590ff.). According to Young, op. cit., p. 261, Irenaeus is the clearest instance of this notion in the early tradition. This author finds evidence of the same interpretation already in *Didache* XIV when seen as following on *Didache* XIII: Young, op. cit., pp. 260 and 98.

18 The clearest early instances of offering the Eucharist for individuals are in Tertullian, *De corona* 3, 3 (PL 2, 79B); *De exhortatione castitatis* 11, 1–2 (PL 2: 926C); perhaps *Ad scapulam* 2, 8 (PL 1, 700). Some authors refer to the Eucharist at the graveside on the third day after death, as found in *The Acts of John* 72, dated AD 150–180, but the notion of an offering for the dead is here, at best, implicit: *New Testament Apocrypha*, ed. E. Hennecke and W. Schmeelcher, trans. R. McL. Wilson (London: Lutterworth, 1965), vol. II, p. 248.

19 The earliest instance cited by Jungmann is Hippolytus, *La tradition apostolique de saint Hippolyte*, ed. B. Botte (Münster: Aschendorff, 1963), p. 44. The usage is clear in Cyprian, *De opere et eleemosynis* 15 (PL 4, 612–613). Discussion in J. Jungmann, *Missarum sollemnia* (Vienna–Freiburg–Basel: Herder, 1962), vol. II, p. 4. Also in Jungmann, *The Early Liturgy*, p. 67.

20 For *sacrificium* Jungmann cites Cyprian and Augustine; for *oblatio* Aetheria: *Missarum sollemnia*, I, 226. *Missa* comes from the dismissal, and probably derives from the dismissal of the catechumens at the conclusion of the Liturgy of the Word: N. M. Denis-Boulet in A. Martimort (ed.), *L'Eglise en prière* (Paris: Desclée, 1965), p. 261. Earliest instance extant is in Ambrose, Letter 20 (PL 16, 995). The Celtic languages in their word for Mass still preserve the link with the usage of Aetheria: Modern Irish, *Aifreann*.

21 D. Power, *The Eucharistic Mystery* (Dublin: Gill & Macmillan, 1992), p. 116.

22 R. Daly, *Christian Sacrifice*, p. 506.

23 Irenaeus, *Against the Heresies* IV, 17, 5 (Har 2, 199; SC 100, 592).

24 *Against the Heresies* IV, 18, 5 (Har 2, 205–8; SC 100, 610–12). Recalling that for Irenaeus the Eucharist is the offering of 'the first-fruits', we can see in the light of these texts that we are not far removed from Hippolytus where 'the first-fruits' are identified with the humanity of Christ: see Daly, *Christian Sacrifice*, pp. 362 and 372.

25 *Against the Heresies* IV, 18, 2 (Har 2, 201; SC 100, 598).

26 See Clement of Alexandria, *Stromata* VII, 6 (PG 8, 440–449).

27 Maximus, *Dissertations* XI. This writer was a second-century rhetorician, representative of the Middle Platonism of the period. On this see Young, op. cit., pp. 19–20.

28 Young, op. cit., note 6 above, p. 26.

29 Young, op. cit., pp. 21–22.

30 Irenaeus, *Against the Heresies* IV, 17–18 (Har 2, 193–210; SC 100, 594ff.).

31 *Against the Heresies* IV, 18, 6 (Har 2, 209; SC 100, 612–14).

32 *Against the Heresies* IV, 18, 1 (Har 2, 201; SC 100, 596).

33 On Hippolytus see Daly, *Christian Sacrifice*, pp. 360–72.

34 For Tertullian, see *The Prescription of Heretics* 41 (PL 2, 57A); *The Exhortation to Chastity* 11 (PL 2, 926C); *On Baptism* 17 (PL 1, 1218A); *On Modesty* 21 (PL 2, 1026B). For Cyprian, see note 4 above.

35 *The Apostolic Tradition*, ed. B. Botte (Münster:Aschendorff, 1963), pp. 16 and 8–10; R. Jasper and G. Cuming (eds.), *Prayers of the Eucharist, Early and Reformed* (London: Collins, 1975), p. 23.

36 See Polycarp's prayer in the *Letter to the Smyrnaeans* 14, 3 (PG 5, 1040); also *I Clement* 36, 1 (PG 1, 280).

37 Philo, *De fuga et inventione* 108; *De Spec. Leg.* I, 230; *De gigantibus* 52; *De migr. Abr.* 102. On this see R. Fuller, *The Foundations of New Testament Christology* (New York: Scribners, 1965), pp. 78–81.

38 Clement of Alexandria, *Stromata* VII, 2 (PG 9, 413A).

39 Origen, *De oratione* 15 (PG 11, 465–467).

40 Lies, op. cit., p. 89. See also R. Daly, 'Sacrifice in Origen', *Studia Patristica* XI (1972), pp. 125–9; 'Sacrifice in Origen and Augustine: comparisons and contrasts', *Studia Patristica* XIX (1989), pp. 148–53.

41 Origen, *Homilies on Leviticus* 9, 10 and 13, 3 (PG 12, 523 and 547; SC 287, 120–122 and 208). The second reference is noteworthy for the idea of the Eucharist being propitiatory *as memorial*. For the Jewish and possible scriptural background of memorial as propitiatory see R. Daly, 'The soteriological significance of the sacrifice of Isaac', CBQ 39 (1977), pp. 45–75.

42 The next significant application of the notion of propitiation to the Eucharist comes in Cyril of Jerusalem where he speaks of our 'offering Christ sacrificed for our sins' – 'that victim of propitiation for the common peace of the Church': *Mystagogical Catechesis* V, 10 and 8 (PG 33, 1116–1117; RJ 853, 851).

43 Athanasius, *Against the Arians* II, 8 (PG 26, 164A).

44 Heb 7:25; Rom 8:34; 1 John 2:1; Rev 1:18.

45 John Chrysostom, *Homily on Judas's Betrayal* I, 6 (PG 49, 380); *Homilies on John* 46, 3 (PG 59, 260–261); *Homilies on Matthew* 82, 4–5 (PG 48, 743–744); *Homily on the Baptism of Christ* (PG 49, 371); *On the Priesthood* (PG 48, 642).

46 John Chrysostom, *Commentary on Matthew*, series 86 (GCS XI, 198, 13–17, 22–28; 199: 4–12, 17–25).

47 J. Betz, *Die Eucharistie in der Zeit der griechischen Väter*, I/1 (Freiburg–Basel–Vienna: Herder, 1955), p. 102.

48 John Chrysostom, *On the Acts of the Apostles*, Homily 21, 4 (PG 60, 170). This view of Chrysostom was called in question by Fittkau, but Betz is confident that on this matter Fittkau can be set aside: op. cit., I/1, p. 126. See G. Fittkau, *Der Begriff des Mysteriums bei Johannes Chrysostomus* (Bonn: Hanstein, 1953).

49 John Chrysostom, *Homilies on Hebrews* 18, 1 (PG 63, 135).

50 The Greek word is *sugkatabasis*: *Homilies on Hebrews* 13, 3 (PG 63, 106); Betz, op. cit., I/1, p. 128.

51 John Chrysostom, *Homilies on Hebrews* 13, 3 (PG 63, 107).

52 Betz, op. cit., I/1, p. 192. *Anamnēsis* is the ordinary Greek word for 'memory'.

53 The criticism of Casel's interpretation of Chrysostom, along the lines suggested here, is the main point in Fittkau's work.

54 Betz, op. cit., I/1, p. 194.

55 John Chrysostom, *Homilies on Hebrews* 17, 3 (PG 63, 131). Other passages on the same theme are: *Homilies on 1 Corinthians* 27, 4 (PG 61, 230); *Homilies on Matthew* 82, 1 (PG 58, 739).

56 The word 'commemoration' in this passage translates the Greek *anamnēsis*. The word 'sacrifice' translates the Greek *thusia*. Fittkau held against Casel that *thusia* in this passage is equivalent to *thuma* and refers to the victim. Betz, rightly in my view, supports Casel in taking *thusia* in the sense of the *act* of offering the victim; otherwise there is no progress in the argument, ' . . . so is it one sacrifice', and it would give a questionable sense to the final phrase in the paragraph. For the discussion see Fittkau, op. cit., pp. 173–5, and p. 185; Betz, op. cit., I/1, pp. 190–4.

57 ST III, q. 83, a. 1.

58 The treatment of Eucharistic sacrifice in Ambrose and Augustine will be incorporated into the discussion of those Fathers at the end of the next chapter.

7

⊠ The Eucharistic Change in the patristic Church

The story of the Eucharistic Change in the patristic period begins, like our account of Eucharistic sacrifice, in the categories of the New Testament. We have already given some notion of the course of the development when we spoke of the different kinds of language in which the mystery was expressed. Foundational to the whole development – and always liable to recur at any time subsequently – was the language of identity as found in the Institution Narrative and in John 6:52–58. This was taken up, with uncompromising bluntness, in one of the earliest witnesses after the New Testament, Ignatius of Antioch: 'The Eucharist is the flesh of our Saviour, Jesus Christ, who suffered for our sins, which the Father raised up in his goodness.'[1] Similarly in the Apologist, St Justin: 'This food is the flesh and blood of that Jesus who was made flesh.'[2]

With the second kind of language, that of change, the perspective moves from the static to the dynamic. We see this beginning in the writer we have just mentioned, St Justin. The main passage may be translated as follows:

We call this food the Eucharist, of which only those can partake who have acknowledged the truth of our teachings, who have been cleansed by baptism for the remission of their sins and for their regeneration, and who regulate their lives upon the principles laid down by Christ. Not as ordinary bread or as ordinary drink do we partake of them, but just as, through the word of God, our Saviour Jesus Christ became incarnate and took upon himself flesh and blood for our salvation, so, we have been taught, the food which has been made the Eucharist by the prayer of his word, and which nourishes our flesh and blood through a change, is both the flesh and blood of that Jesus who was made flesh.[3]

Not everything in this passage is unambiguous, but the following points seem reasonably clear. As a result of the thanksgiving said over them, the bread and wine have been changed and are no longer ordinary food and drink. For this change we are given an analogy in the action of the Word of God in the Incarnation. Just as the Word descended into the womb of Mary and there brought about the flesh and blood of the Saviour, so through the word of prayer are his flesh and blood brought about in the sacrament.[4] The objective action in the one event suggests the objectivity of the action in the other.

Some commentators find a second analogy for the Eucharistic Change suggested in the text. It comes in the obscure phrase about the food which nourishes our flesh and blood. The suggestion is that the way the bread and wine are changed into Christ's body and blood is like the way the food we consume is changed into our flesh and blood. This analogy is certainly found in later writers. If it is true that it is here also, then it is a strong confirmation of the perspective of change in the text.

Two other features in Justin's writings underline the objectivity of the change which takes place in the sacrament. The first is the way the term *eucharistia* has undergone a development. From designating an action, that of giving thanks, it now designates things, the Eucharistic food.[5] Secondly there is the custom of bringing the 'eucharistized' food to the absent, presumably the sick.[6] This is an important indication of the objectivity and permanence of the new status of the elements as the flesh and blood of Christ.

Though it is remarkable how much we can find in this early text of Justin, yet one must admit once again that, taken in itself, it still leaves unanswered many of the questions which a later theology would like to raise. This is why its basic significance comes only by setting it in its context within the whole movement of early theological reflection. Later theologians will speak of the Eucharistic Change with much greater precision than did Justin, but at least his writings show us that Eucharistic understanding in the Church was already moving in their direction as early as the middle of the second century.

The next witness we meet in the history of the sacrament is St Irenaeus. We have already seen the depths he brought to the understanding of sacrifice. In the question which now concerns us his contribution is similarly remarkable. Just as Justin deepened the theology of the status of the elements by setting it in the context of the Incarnation, so Irenaeus carries it further by relating it to the resurrection and divinization of Christians. Against the dualism of the Gnostics, he is the theologian of unity, the unity of creation and redemption, of divine and human, of flesh and spirit. But Irenaeus' viewpoint is essentially developmental. For him redemption is a process of the transformation of the world. Our destiny means the transformation of the human condition into divine life, life in the Spirit, and at the centre of that process he sets the Eucharistic Change. The following key text will illustrate the point for us, though it is a passage not without its problems.

For we offer to him that which is his, proclaiming in an harmonious way the communion and union of flesh and spirit: namely that, just as the bread of the earth, on receiving the invocation of God, is no longer ordinary bread but Eucharist, consisting of two realities, the one earthly, the other heavenly, so our bodies, on receiving the Eucharist, are no longer destined for corruption, having the hope of an eternal resurrection.[7]

For us the main point in this text lies in the analogy between the change brought about in the elements and that brought about in us by the general resurrection. The connection between the two truths is, however, even more intimate, since the new status of the elements is a cause of the new destiny of Christians. Indeed, as other texts in Irenaeus make clear, he understands the whole process in a very physical way. Just as the general resurrection will be a new physical state, so are we prepared for that in a physical way by our flesh and blood being nourished and increased through the flesh and blood of the sacrament.[8] Just as heaven and earth will come together in the general resurrection, so have they already come into one in the Eucharist. Christ himself was defined for Irenaeus by the mingling and communion of divinity, *pneuma*, with humanity, *sarx*. But this took place only within the perspective of the ultimate union 'of the end with the beginning', that is, of the human race with God, so that we should 'embrace the Spirit of God' and so pass into the glory of the Father.[9]

Often in reading these early writers we are frustrated by their ambiguities and their lack of system. They do not quite answer the questions we have in mind, for instance our questions about the status of the elements. In this context, what they understand the elements to be is often revealed more clearly by what they say the elements bring about. Clearly in Irenaeus the Eucharistic gifts are central to and symptomatic of the whole divine economy. They unite us with the world of the divine Spirit, because they themselves already embody the union of flesh and spirit. They bring about in us a real change, because they themselves have been really changed. Changed into what? What else, if not into that which all our texts proclaim them to be – the body and blood of Christ? What really establishes the notion of the Eucharistic Change as the acceptable interpretation of Irenaeus' view of the sacrament is the whole movement of his thought on the divine economy. This becomes clear independently of how one understands 'the earthly reality' and 'the heavenly reality' in the text cited above.[10]

Some will try to press these texts further to answer later questions, such as whether or not they can imply a Lutheran consubstantiation.[11] A similar falsification of horizons is illustrated by Schmaus, who holds that Irenaeus excludes the notion of concomitance in the sacrament.[12] Surely the fundamental mistake here lies in attributing to early writers a degree of precision which could only be attained as the fruit of later controversies. It is as wrong to say that they exclude the one view as to expect of them a clear statement of the opposite.[13]

The second main contribution of Irenaeus focuses on the language of change. From an economy of change to a language of change there is a natural progression. As we will see, the importance of this mode of expression lay in the role it was destined to play in the great liturgies of the Church, and specifically in the epiclesis of the Eucharistic Prayer.[14] Irenaeus stands at the watershed of this liturgical tradition in that all the elements of the terminology of epiclesis can be found in him, waiting to be drawn together. In the passage we have given above, the Greek word *epiklēsis*, meaning there simply 'invocation', is found for the first time in a Eucharistic context. The usage is open to an invocation either of the Word or of the Spirit. In fact Irenaeus speaks of the advent of both the Word and the Spirit in the Eucharist. In particular, his view of the dynamic role of the order of *Pneuma*, which we have described above, provides a pertinent background for the eventual emergence of the theology of the Spirit in the Eucharistic Change, which will mark the epiclesis of the Eastern liturgies.

Then there is the word 'become' which he uses of the bread and wine.[15] This is destined to be one of the standard terms for the

Eucharistic Change in liturgical speech. In addition, if one can accept Fragment 36, which is included at the end of his book by Harvey, the great nineteenth-century editor of Irenaeus, that gives us yet another classical expression: May the Holy Spirit 'show' the bread and wine to be the body and blood of Christ.[16]

Having raised the question of the epiclesis in the context of St Irenaeus, I would like to append to our discussion at this point a brief survey of the way the Eucharistic Change is spoken of in general in this section of the liturgy. The petition that our bread and wine become the body and blood of Christ is normative in the generality of the great Eucharistic Prayers both East and West. Since so many of these prayers were formed in the patristic period, they are a convenient indication of how the Church of those times understood the Eucharist in the very celebration of it. The fact that the continuing custom of the epiclesis has preserved this notion of the Eucharistic Change at the heart of all the great liturgies down to our own day serves to underline how this perception of the sacrament is fundamental to the Eucharistic faith of historical Christianity.

As an instance of this usage, already in the fourth century, we can point to the Euchologion of Serapion in the Egyptian Church.[17] The Alexandrian Anaphora of St Basil can also lay fair claim to a fourth-century origin.[18] For the Western tradition, down through the centuries, there is, of course, our Roman Canon, and as a counterpart in the Eastern tradition we have the fine epiclesis of the anaphora attributed to St John Chrysostom:

> Send your Holy Spirit on us and on these gifts laid out;
> make this bread [be] the precious body of your Christ,
> changing it by your Holy Spirit – Amen;
> and that which is in this cup [be] the precious blood of your
>   Christ,
> changing it by the Holy Spirit – Amen.[19]

The language of the epiclesis has attained a new importance in our own day in the context of the ecumenical movement. One of the striking developments of recent years has been the attempt of different Churches to reach agreed statements on Eucharistic faith. It is our sad experience, particularly in the West, that the language of theology often serves to divide rather than to unite. In this perspective the language of the epiclesis acquires a new significance. Surely the kind of language which sufficed to express the mystery in the context of the liturgy should be sufficient for this new context also. A case in point is the Agreed Statement on the Eucharist between Anglicans and Roman Catholics of 1972, where the authors confined themselves to the terminology of Scripture and liturgy. This is one good reason why the origin and history of the language of the epiclesis are deserving of study in the way we have indicated above.[20]

THE LANGUAGE OF THEOLOGY

Early on in the patristic period, another way of speaking of the Eucharistic mystery emerged, which was destined to pass into general currency in the following centuries. The first recorded instances are found in the writings of Clement of Alexandria. Scripture, he says, has designated wine as the mystic 'symbol' of the holy blood, and the blood is itself 'symbolic' of the Passion.[21] Given the symbolic mentality of people in the ancient world generally, and given further the widespread influence of Platonism with its characteristic philosophy of the sign, it was inevitable that the language of symbolism should come to loom large in the work of the theologians of antiquity.

Various terms were used. We might set them out, first in Greek, and then in Latin, as follows:

homoiōma – *eikōn* – *typos* – *antitypos* – *symbolon*
similitudo – *imago* – *figura* – *exemplum* – *symbolum*.

With terms such as these the ancient writers were able to handle some of the antinomies of the faith. Such expressions underlined that things are not what they seem. The truth of reality is often hidden beneath the surface, and this was particularly true of the sacraments, where there was such a gulf between external appearances and what the faith claimed to be the reality. In the case of the Eucharist, the Christians seem to have realized that the historical body and the Eucharistic body of Christ were in one sense the same and in another sense different. The language of symbolism enabled them to give expression to such a paradox.

However, when these terms are used by the ancient writers, they are not to be understood in the way most people spontaneously understand symbolism today. We so easily oppose the symbolic to the real. We tend to assume that sign and reality are adequately distinct. Not so the ancients! For them a symbol participates in the reality of that which it symbolizes. While this viewpoint of theirs was supported by the Platonic theory of participation, its origins were probably wider than that, part of the common view of things in a pre-rationalistic mentality. The ancient world, said William Barclay, was simply 'saturated in sacrament'.[22] This was as true of the world of the Old and New Testaments as it was of the patristic period. We saw something of it already in the biblical notion of memory, and it can be added as a factor to our account of the New Testament understanding of the Eucharistic gifts. With the language of symbolism the patristic writers were simply systematizing and deepening something which was there from the beginning.

Nonetheless it would be wrong, of course, to give the impression that the patristic witness to the faith is a straightforward matter. Many of these writers were brilliant thinkers in their own right, and so it is not surprising if some of their statements can cause us problems. In reading them it is useful to keep in mind a distinction between their witness to the faith and their personal speculation.

Origen is a case in point. For him the Eucharist is 'the typical and symbolic body'.[23] On the level of his own theory, however, contrary to the general tendency of the ancient world, he at times seems to distinguish too sharply the inner meaning from that of the material symbol and so threatens the whole concept of sacramentality.[24] On the other hand, he provides us with a good example of witnessing to the ordinary faith of the Church when, for instance, he speaks of his reverence for any particle of the sacrament lest it fall to the ground.[25] He himself makes the same distinction we have made between writing as a speculative theologian and bearing witness to the faith.[26]

A classical passage on the contrast in the Eucharist between outward appearance and inner reality is found in the fourth of the *Mystagogical Catecheses* attributed to Cyril of Jerusalem.[27] Since this passage is at once an instance of the use of symbolic language and at the same time demonstrates with unusual clarity how such symbolism was understood, it is worth quoting:

So let us partake with the fullest confidence that it is the body and blood of Christ. For his body has been bestowed on you under the figure of bread, and his blood under the figure of wine, so that by partaking of Christ's body and blood you become one body and blood with him . . . You have been taught and fully instructed that what seems to be bread is not bread, though it appears to be such to the sense of taste, but the body of Christ; that what seems to be wine is not wine, though the taste would have it so, but the blood of Christ . . . So strengthen your heart by partaking of that spiritual bread, and gladden the face of your soul.[28]

In this passage we see how new forms of language exist side by side with earlier forms, in this case the symbolic side by side with the language of identity. The language of change also continued in use among the writers of the fourth and fifth centuries, in some cases achieving a new clarity.[29] Worthy of note also is the way some of these writers are so struck by the extraordinary nature of the Eucharistic Change that they seek out new and strange terms with which to describe it. St Gregory of Nyssa speaks of the 'trans-elementation' of the bread and wine, and St John Chrysostom speaks of their 'transrhythmization'.[30]

Where the Platonic tradition was strong, the language of symbolism remained in possession. Where, however, that tradition was not so dominant, the symbolic approach began to seem somewhat less adequate. We see this happening in the Antiochene school, and in influences stemming from there, in a passage from Theodore of Mopsuestia:

He did not say 'This is a symbol of my body and this is a symbol of my blood', but rather 'This is my body and my blood', thereby teaching us not to look at the nature of what lies before us but that through the event of the Eucharist it is changed into his flesh and blood.[31]

A similar caution is expressed by Cyril of Alexandria, who is concerned at the Eucharistic implications of Nestorianism generally.[32] Indeed it seems that, in the wake of Nestorianism, there arose a curious anticipation of later theories of consubstantiation. An analogy was established between the duality of natures in Christ and a duality of substances in either of the Eucharistic elements, bread and body, or wine and blood.[33] Where Christology veered to the other extreme in Monophysitism, even the later notion of 'impanation' is anticipated, some holding for a certain mixture of substances in the Eucharist on the analogy of a Eutychian mixture of divine and human in Christ.[34]

In this way the vicissitudes of controversy can disturb the consensus of tradition as to how the mystery of the Eucharist is to be expressed. It would be wrong however to give the impression that there were two equal and opposed streams of tradition on the matter, one asserting change and the other denying it.[35] Clear expressions of the latter approach are the exception and are located largely in the fifth century, whereas expressions of change and of symbolism are found throughout the patristic period and in all the main regions of Christendom. It is striking also that in those very passages where the continuing reality of the *ousia* or *substantia* of the bread and wine is asserted, the language of change can still break through, underlining the exceptional nature of the former assertions and the predominance of the latter kind of expression in the usage of Christians generally: ' . . . the elements pass into the divine substance' (Gelasius); ' . . . they are understood to be what they have become' (Theodoret).[36]

In time the language of symbolism was to be eclipsed by the shifting influences of history. The hesitations discovered above in Theodore and Cyril of Alexandria were the first cracks in a synthesis ultimately destined to dissolve.[37] In the East this came about especially during the reaction against Iconoclasm. While the Iconoclasts claimed that the Eucharist was the only acceptable *eikōn* or *typos* of Christ, the orthodox insisted that such symbolic language did not do justice to Eucharistic realism.[38] In the West symbolism was one of the casualties of the collapse of the ancient world. With the passing of Rome went much of its world-view, inevitably giving way, as we shall see, to the rising medieval tide.[39]

AMBROSE AND AUGUSTINE

Much of what we have considered so far of the patristic Eucharist concerned the writings of the Christian East. For a comprehensive view of the subject we need to see more of patristic theology in the West, and this brings us to two outstanding figures, whose writings shaped so much of the theology of the subsequent centuries. In Ambrose and Augustine we meet two writers whose works contain within themselves in embryo not only the teachings but the controversies which are to mark the history of the Western Eucharist. Though this influence affected the understanding of the Eucharistic Change in particular, it will be necessary to preface our treatment of each of them by saying something about the context of sacrificial understanding within which they approached the mystery.

Ambrose and Eucharistic sacrifice

For Ambrose salvation history is particularly relevant as the context within which the Eucharist is to be understood.[40] Following on Origen, he often presents the Eucharist against the background of a three-part scheme as follows:

| the Law | – the Gospel | – Heaven |
| shadow | – image | – truth. |

Coming events, we say, cast their shadows before them, and that is how Ambrose, in the wake of the Letter to the Hebrews (Heb 10:1), understands the signs and rituals of the Jews. In our scheme above, the Law designates the Old Testament. Its signs and rituals are but a shadow (*umbra*) of the reality or truth which is to come. They are not that reality itself. Their symbolism is shadowy and preliminary.

When we come to the order of things established by the New Testament, the situation is less straightforward. Here the ultimate truth and reality of salvation still lie in the future, in heaven, but they are anticipated here below in the reality of Christ. Since he is the image of the Father, it is the language of 'image' which is used to describe this intermediate stage between shadow and reality, participating in both. The truth of God is present in Christ but in a veiled way. Consequently the realities of the New Law share in that double quality. They are signs of an ultimate reality which they do not manifest openly, but at the same time they do contain the reality which under the Old Law was only prefigured in a preliminary way. This is the framework which gives us the key to that new sacramentality by which Christ fulfilled the empty shadows of the Old Law.[41] The following passage will illustrate how this framework fills out for us our appreciation of Ambrose's notion of the Eucharistic action:

At present we see the good things of God through the Image, and we possess the good things of the Image. We have seen the Prince of Priests coming to us, we have seen and heard him offering his blood for us. We priests, we follow him as best we can, in order to offer sacrifices for the people. Although we are weak in personal merit, nevertheless, in virtue of the sacrifice, we are worthy of some respect. Although at present Christ does not seem to be offering, nevertheless he himself is being offered up on earth when his body is being offered. Indeed he is made manifest as actively offering in us, for it is his word which consecrates the sacrifice which is being offered.[42]

Some scholars, on taking up Ambrose, have misread his use of symbolic language, not appreciating the change signified by the passage from the Old Law to the New. *Figura*, for instance, is taken by some simply in the sense of an empty sign, a meaning which in this scheme of things would apply, if anywhere, only to the Old Testament.[43] This misreading has some basis in Ambrose himself in so far as sometimes, as well as using a three-part scheme, he foreshortens it into a two-part scheme of 'figure' as opposed to 'truth'. In this way the same terms, such as 'figure' or 'species', can sometimes be used of the Old Law and sometimes of the New, depending on which scheme is in the background; but that does not mean that the same absence of reality, characteristic of the first dispensation, is being predicated of the second. Thurian puts it well:

One must not give to this patristic term 'figura' an over-spiritualistic meaning. Like *similitudo* it certainly underlines the difference between the sacrifice of the cross and the sacrament, but it also underlines the actuality of the sacrifice and the reality of the presence of Christ.[44]

The ultimate reason why it is so easy for us to misread these terms lies in the contrasting world-views behind Ambrose's use of language and ours. In Ambrose's case his framework is grounded in that profound biblical belief in God's lordship over history which was discussed in a previous chapter. This comes to Ambrose through his use of biblical typology according to which the mystery of salvation is the true, if hidden, meaning of the events of the Old Testament. This mystery is what begins to come into its own in the events of the New Testament as history moves towards fulfilment at the end of time. In this perspective the divisions of the centuries become irrelevant and there is a certain identity between the events of the Old Testament and those of the New. Our liturgy is drawn into this movement, and so the notion of a certain identity between the Eucharist and the sacrifice of Christ is here completely at home. This is why Ambrose can write of the sacraments with such striking realism: 'Face to face you have shown yourself to me, O Christ. I find you in your sacraments',[45] but that does not mean, as Thurian has pointed out, that the sacraments do not, at the same time, embody the difference between the historical and the sacramental. It is these different levels of meaning that the three-part scheme outlined above helps to keep in place.

Augustine and Eucharistic sacrifice

As we might expect, Ambrose's great convert, St Augustine, is not unfamiliar with the Ambrosian scheme of things, but he presents it in an even more profound and comprehensive way. In the bishop of Hippo the Platonic heritage, and specifically the notion of participation, intensifies the significance of the symbolism involved. As well as the horizontal scheme of salvation history, there is the vertical dimension of symbolic participation. Augustine seems to have been drawn to Platonism because it nourished and reinforced his fundamental desire for union with God in another world. In this philosophy the ideal world, the world of the really real, of *veritas*, is set above the world of sense, with the latter drawing from the former whatever reality it enjoys. Here below we live in a world of disharmony, dissimilitude and unreality, and so we must always be looking beyond this world and striving towards the Really Real, the Beautiful and the True.

For Augustine material beings are composed of similitude to God and dissimilitude to him. The more 'similitude' they have, the higher they are in the hierarchy of beings. 'To approach him is to become like him; to withdraw from him is to become unlike him', he writes in his commentary on the Psalms.[46] In the *Confessions* we find it more eloquently in a moving passage of personal history:

I discovered that I was far from you, my God, in the region of dissimilitude, as though I heard your voice from on high, 'I am the food of the strong; grow and you will eat me. You will not change me into yourself like the food for your flesh, but you will be changed into me' . . . And you cried out from afar, 'I am who am', and I heard you as one hears in the heart, and I could never doubt again.[47]

This gives us the context within which to understand Augustine's approach to sacramental symbolism. It is essentially a two-tiered approach, the duality being designated by different pairs of terms as different aspects are highlighted: sign and reality; sensible and intelligible; visible and invisible; carnal and spiritual; rites and fruits; in Latin *sacramentum* and *res sacramenti*. Augustine is one of the most consequential witnesses of the general symbolic mentality of the ancient world. The key point is that the sign cannot be adequately distinguished from the reality but participates 'in some way' in that which is symbolized.[48] It is what de Lubac called, in a memorable phrase, 'ontological symbolism', where the reality is always in some sense given with the sign.[49]

What Augustine is primarily interested in is the reality behind our rituals. He is a man for the great vision and the broad view. Indeed his attention is so fixed on the fruit of our celebrations that he sometimes does not do full justice to what is involved in getting there. Aspects which should be distinguished are easily run together, but his overall vision will always bring us to the heart of the reality, as in the famous passage on our worship in *The City of God*:

Thus is it brought about that the entire redeemed city itself, namely the congregation and society of the saints, is offered to God as a universal sacrifice through the great priest who also offered himself for us in his Passion, that we might be the body of so great a head, and that in the form of a servant. This he offered; in this he himself was offered, because thus is he mediator, in this is he priest, in this is he sacrifice . . . This is the sacrifice of Christians, 'many one body in Christ'. This is the practice of the Church in the sacrament of the altar familiar to the faithful, where it is clear to her that she herself is a victim in the victim she offers.[50]

In this text Augustine brings before us the ultimate reality of our celebration, the *res sacramenti*. The key to the whole thing for Augustine is our unity in the body of Christ, that unity into which the celebration of the Eucharist incorporates us ever more deeply: 'The one Christ, the full Christ, the whole Christ'.[51] True sacrifice is that of the whole city of God, the whole body of Christ, gathered in breathless adoration before the Father; and the point of our quotation in the preceding paragraph is that all this does not take place at a distance but is the very reality of what we ourselves do in our Eucharist. It is the whole invisible reality behind the sacramental 'similitude'.[52]

Ambrose and Eucharistic Change

The identity between the heavenly liturgy and that of the Church on earth, such as we have seen both in Ambrose and in Augustine, sets the scene for their view of the identity between the gifts we offer and the one offering of the New Law, the body and blood of Christ. On this point, however, there is a certain contrast in the language of the two saints. As well as speaking symbolically, Ambrose is very forthright in using the language of change, whereas Augustine tends to be content with the language of symbolism. As a result a contrast is sometimes instituted by scholars between 'Ambrosian transformism' and 'Augustinian symbolism'.[53] Where Ambrose gives us the most influential statement from the Western Fathers on the classical teaching on Eucharistic Change, his friend of Hippo was destined to be one of the main sources of difficulty with that teaching in Western theology. A typical passage of the bishop of Milan would be the following:

Now if the word of Elias was powerful enough to bring down fire from heaven, will not the words of Christ be powerful enough to change the nature of the [Eucharistic] elements? Concerning the fashioning of the whole of creation you have read, 'For he spoke, and they were made; he commanded, and they were created' (Ps 32:9). The word of Christ, then, which could make out of nothing that which was not, can it not change the things that are into that which they are not? For no less power is needed to give new natures to things than to change their natures . . . And this body which we bring about is that which was born of the Virgin. Why do you seek here the order of nature in the body of Christ, seeing that the Lord Jesus himself was born of a virgin, outside the ordinary course of nature? It was certainly the true body of Christ which was crucified and buried, and so this is truly the sacrament of his flesh.[54]

The theological reason why Ambrose can be so emphatic in his statement of the Eucharistic Change seems to be that, in the forefront of his mind, the Eucharistic body is seen as a *divinized* body. In this he stands in a line of Greek tradition going back through Gregory of Nyssa to Origen.[55] According to this tradition the Eucharistic body is a 'spiritual' body, by which the authors refer to its glorified, divinized state.[56] As a result, it is no longer subject to the ordinary laws of quantity, as when the risen Christ passes through closed doors (John 20:19). While this notion does not solve all the problems that can be raised against the Eucharistic Change, it does help people in thinking of the sacrament. It also lies behind one of the terms by which Ambrose refers to the Eucharistic Change, namely 'transfiguration'.[57]

Augustine and Eucharistic Change

Augustine is Ambrose's greatest convert. He participated in his liturgy and benefited from his teaching. This in itself should induce caution in anyone who would wish to see a fundamental difference in the Eucharistic faith of the two men. One illustration can be found in a favourite passage of the manualists, where Augustine speaks of adoring the sacrament before receiving it. In this he seems to be simply repeating a piece of exegesis which he took over from Ambrose, a reflection on the figurative meaning of Ps 98(99):5 where it speaks of 'worshipping the footstool' of the Lord.[58]

To approach Augustine with the questions of the dogmatic theologian is already to be out of sympathy with his own approach to the sacrament and so to be in danger of misreading him. Eucharistic spirituality rather than Eucharistic theology provides a more congenial point of entry into the concerns of this great saint, because basic for him, in this as in all things, is the love of God as the gateway to truth. 'Show me a lover, and he knows what I am saying.'[59]

Augustine has a number of favourite themes in his reflections on this sacrament, especially life, unity and sacrificial love. It is in the context of the last of these that his sense of the ordinary Eucharistic realism of the Church comes most clearly to expression. The basic point is that the sacrament is a great revelation to us of the love which poured itself out on the cross, and so it is an immediate challenge to us, not just to imitate the historical Christ, but to imitate the Eucharistic Christ:

The Jews came to him to crucify him. We come to him to receive his flesh and blood. By the Crucified One the Jews were cast into darkness. By eating and drinking the Crucified One we are filled with light.[60]

Those who above all others have understood what the Eucharist is saying to us and put it into practice are the martyrs. St Laurence in particular, deacon and martyr, learnt it from administering the Eucharistic blood:

The blessed apostle John explained the mystery of the Lord's Supper when he said: As Christ laid down his life for us, so must we lay down our lives for the brothers. Saint Laurence understood this, brothers. He understood it and he did it.[61]

It is the reality of Christ's gift of himself in the Eucharist which brings this home:

Great is the table where the food is the Lord of the table himself. No one feeds his guests with himself, but this is what Christ the Lord does. He it is who invites us, but he himself is the food and the drink. The martyrs recognized what they ate and drank, so that they paid him back in a similar way.[62]

The grace of martyrdom is not given to all of us, but all of us can learn from the Eucharist the lesson of a self-effacing love:

In his flesh and blood Our Lord has taught us humility, for when he entrusted his flesh and blood to us, he entrusted to us his humility.[63]

Augustine speaks with warmth of the Eucharistic humility of Christ in a way we associate rather with Francis and Bonaventure:

In his flesh and blood Christ wished to be salvation for us. How did he commend his flesh and blood to us? By his lowliness (*humilitas*). If Christ had not become lowly, he could not have been eaten or drunk.[64]

In this way it is important for Augustine to leave us before the truth of the Eucharist in all its stark immediacy:

You know the price that was paid out for you. You know to what you draw near, what you eat and what you drink; or better, whom you eat and whom you drink.[65]

These texts show us how Augustine the preacher presents the Eucharist to his congregation. This enables us to apply to him a distinction which was made in the case of Origen earlier on in the chapter, namely that between the witness to the faith and the speculative thinker. The texts we have just considered illustrate the former; and of course many others could be cited.[66] Even the language of change is not absent, though it is rare.[67] Nevertheless there remains another series of texts where Augustine's language is undoubtedly a source of embarrassment to scholastic writers in particular.[68]

The fundamental and sufficient answer to these difficulties lies in that 'ontological symbolism' which Augustine always takes for granted. For him the sign of the body of Christ will always in some sense be that body, whatever the obscurities this gives rise to. As one commentator put it, 'His Eucharistic theology is neither symbolist nor realist in the modern sense of these terms; it is sacramentalist'.[69]

However the fact of so much ambiguity in the statements of Augustine is itself something which needs explanation. De Lubac suggests that Augustine was more consequential than others in his Platonism, and in the dualism at its heart. For Platonists, matter remains irreducible and eternal. Christ's risen body, for instance, even in heaven, is considered 'to be in one place'.[70] In this way the spatial aspects of the sacrament remain a problem. Augustine's habitual way of focusing on the ecclesial body of Christ rather than on the physical in fact helps to take our attention off the issue. The Church is Christ, the whole Christ, and this Christ is our food and drink. This food is not changed into us, but we are changed into it!⁷¹ This appeal to the whole Christ may not be a deliberate attempt to get around the problem, but it certainly is no solution. Perhaps the difficulty we are dealing with helps to illustrate an appropriateness in the Church's eventually moving to another philosophy and theology on which to ground its teaching on this sacrament.

NOTES

1 Ignatius of Antioch, *Letter to the Smyrnaeans* 7, 1 (PG 5, 713).
2 Justin, I *Apology* 66 (PG 6, 428–429; RJ 128).
3 Ibid.
4 Commentators diverge in interpreting the phrase here translated as 'the word of prayer'. It may simply designate the whole Eucharistic Prayer (Ligier). J. Betz understands it as a prayer for the coming of the Word: *Die Eucharistie in der Zeit der griechischen Väter*, I/1 (Freiburg–Basel–Vienna: Herder, 1955), p. 270.
5 Justin, I *Apology* 66, 1 (PG 6, 428B).
6 I *Apology* 65 (PG 6, 428).
7 Irenaeus, *Against the Heresies* IV, 18, 5 (Har 2, 205–7). Notice that in the edition for *Sources chrétiennes*, the word 'spirit' here is written with a capital letter: SC 100, vol. II, p. 610.
8 *Against the Heresies* V, 2, 2–3 (Har 2, 319–23; SC 153, 30–40).
9 References in this paragraph to *Against the Heresies* IV, 20, 4 (Har 2 214–15; SC 100, 634–5). On the two aspects in Christ, see *Against the Heresies* III, 16, 6 (Har 2, 87–8; SC 211, 310–14).
10 In fact I think these phrases refer to what we now call the natural and supernatural orders, and probably specifically to the humanity and divinity of Christ present in the Eucharist.
11 See Harvey, op. cit., vol. 2, p. 502, note 8; also p. 205, note 3; p. 318, note 2.
12 M. Schmaus, *Dogma 5: The Church as Sacrament* (London: Sheed & Ward 1975), p. 97, commenting on Irenaeus, *Against the Heresies* V, 2 (Har 2, 317–24; SC 153, 34–40; RJ 249). 'Concomitance' is explained below (p. 124).
13 In reply to Schmaus one might point out that concomitance in the sense of the union of the divinity with the sacrament is certainly not absent from Irenaeus, and that as regards the union of flesh and blood, he does not seem to think in terms of a clinical separation of the two. We must be careful not to attribute to these early writers our own anatomical anthropology. See for instance the more existential anthropology in Clement of Alexandria's *Paedagogus* I, 6, according to which blood is not only 'the substance (*ousia*) of the soul' (PG 8, 296C) but it is also 'the substance of the human body' (PG 8, 308B). Indeed blood, he tells us, is 'a kind of liquid flesh' (PG 8, 297A). Blood in some sense implies the flesh.

The opposite is also true for Tertullian, who says 'Only a living body of flesh has blood': *Against Marcion* IV, 40 (PL 2, 461). Irenaeus describes blood as 'the link between soul and body' in *Against the Heresies* V, 3, 2 (Har 2, 326; SC 153, 48).

14 'Epiclesis' is the technical term for that part of the Eucharistic Prayer where the Church calls down (Greek: *epikalein*) the Holy Spirit or the Word of God on the celebration, with the intention either that the bread and wine may become the body and blood of Christ, or that the celebration may be fruitful, or for both intentions together.

15 *Ginetai* in Greek: *Against the Heresies* V, 2, 2–3 (Har 2, 320 and 323; SC 153, 34–7). For examples in the epiclesis see A. Hänggi and I. Pahl (eds), *Prex eucharistica* (Fribourg: Editions Universitaires, 1968), pp. 263, 280, 352.

16 Har 2, 502–3. This is the terminology found in the epiclesis in the Apostolic Constitutions VIII, 39 (*Prex eucharistica*, p. 92), in the Anaphora of Isaac (ibid., p. 335), in the First Anaphora of Eustathius of Antioch (ibid., p. 308) and in the Anaphora of the Twelve Apostles (ibid., p. 267) etc.

17 Ibid., p. 131.

18 Ibid., p. 353.

19 Ibid., p. 227.

20 For a further study of the epiclesis, see J. McKenna, *Eucharist and Holy Spirit* (London: SPCK, 1975).

21 Clement, *Paedagogus* II, 2, 29 (PG 8, 424B); I, 6, 49 (PG 8, 309A).

22 W. Barclay, *The Lord's Supper* (London: SCM, 1967), p. 12.

23 Origen, *Commentary on Matthew* 11, 14 (GCS X, 58, 8–9; PG 13, 948; RJ 504).

24 L. Lies, *Wort und Eucharistie bei Origenes* (Innsbruck: Tyrolia, 1978), p. 348.

25 Origen, *Homily on Exodus* 13, 3 (PG 12, 391).

26 Origen, *Commentary on John* 32, 24 (16) (PG 14, 809B).

27 Some modern scholars, following a number of manuscripts, have preferred to attribute these sermons to Cyril's successor, Bishop John of Jerusalem (386–417), e.g. Betz, op. cit. note 4 above, I/1, p. 101; E. Schillebeeckx, *Die Sakramentele Heilseconomie* (Antwerp: 'T Groeit, 1952), p. 76, note 104. More recently there has been a swing in favour of Cyrillan authorship, a discussion summed up in F. Young, *From Nicaea to Chalcedon* (London: SCM, 1983), pp. 128–30.

28 Cyril of Jerusalem, *Mystagogical Catechesis* IV, 3–6 (PG 33, 1100–1101).

29 A valuable instance is that of Gregory of Nyssa, *The Catechetical Oration* 37 (PG 45, 93; RJ 1035).

30 Gregory, loc. cit.; Chrysostom, *Homily on the Betrayal by Judas* I, 6 (PG 49, 380; RJ 1157).

31 I translate this from the Greek in a fragment preserved in PG 66, 26 (RJ

1113e). The original context will be found in *Homily* 15, 10 in R. Tonneau and R. Devreesse (eds), *Les homélies catéchétiques de Théodore de Mopsueste* (Studi e testi 145; Rome: Biblioteca Apostolica Vaticana, 1949), p. 475. The translation in the latter edition is done from the Syriac. The doctrine of Eucharistic Change seems to me clear in Theodore; see also E. Mazza, *Mystagogy: A Theology of Liturgy in the Patristic Age* (New York: Pueblo, 1989), pp. 88–90. J. T. O'Connor, *The Hidden Manna: A Theology of the Eucharist* (San Francisco: Ignatius Press, 1988), p. 71 is surprisingly unsure.

32 Cyril of Alexandria, *Commentary on Matthew* 26, 27 (PG 72, 452; RJ 2101).

33 Theodoret of Cyr, *Eranistes* 2 (PG 83, 168). One of the fullest discussions of these texts in English is still that of Darwell Stone, *A History of the Doctrine of the Holy Eucharist*, vol. I (London: Longmans, 1908), pp. 98–102.

34 A strong reaction against this latter deviation helps to explain the language of consubstantiation in Pope Gelasius, *Treatise on the Two Natures Against Eutyches and Nestorius* 14 (PLS 3, 773–774).

35 Darwell Stone could easily be read in this sense: op. cit., p. 98.

36 Gelasius, loc. cit.; Theodoret, loc. cit.

37 For a useful but different account of this change see Mazza, *Mystagogy*, pp. 102 and 167–74. It seems to me that Mazza puts the fundamental *cultural* change too early.

38 E.g., St John Damascene, *On the Orthodox Faith* 4, 13 (PG 94, 1144; RJ 2371); Nicephoros, *Antirrheticus* (PG 100, 336B–C). On the whole question see S. Gero, 'The Eucharistic doctrine of the Byzantine Iconoclasts and its sources', *Byzantinische Zeitschrift* 68 (1975), pp. 4–22. A brief but useful discussion will be found in A. Nichols, *The Holy Eucharist* (Dublin: Veritas, 1991), pp. 41–3.

39 The study of this change in the West is the achievement of H. de Lubac's great work *Corpus mysticum: l'eucharistie et l'église au moyen-âge* (Paris: Aubier, 1944).

40 On this see R. Johanny, *L'Eucharistie centre de l'histoire du salut chez saint Ambroise de Milan* (Paris: Beauchesne, 1968); E. Mazza, *Mystagogy*, pp. 14–44.

41 Ambrose, *On the Office of Ministers* I, 238 (PL 16, 94).

42 Ambrose, *Explanation of Ps 38* (PL 14, 1051–1052).

43 E.g., Hitchcock, *Church Quarterly Review* (1945), pp. 127–53.

44 M. Thurian, *L'Eucharistie: mémorial du Seigneur, sacrifice d'action de grâce et d'intercession* (Paris–Neuchâtel: Delachaux et Niestlé, 1959), p. 60, n. 19. For *similitudo* see Ambrose, *De sacramentis* V, 20.

45 Ambrose, *Apologia prophetae David* 12 (PL 14, 875).

46 Augustine, *Enarrationes in Psalmos* 34, sermon 2, 6 (PL 36, 337); see also *Confessions* XII, 28, 38 (PL 32, 842).

47 Augustine, *Confessions* VII, 10, 16 (PL 32, 742).

48 The expression 'in some way' can be illustrated by *Letter* 98, 9 (PL 33, 363; RJ 1424).

49 H. de Lubac, *Corpus mysticum*, p. 260.

50 Augustine, *The City of God* X, 6 (PL 41, 284).

51 *Christus unus, Christus plenus, Christus totus*: Augustine, *On the Merits of Sinners* I, 1, 36, 60 (PL 44, 145).

52 In the passage quoted from Augustine, *The City of God*, the aspect of Christ's immolation in the Eucharist is not emphasized, but this aspect is brought out more clearly in other passages, such as *Letter* 55, 2 (PL 33, 205); *Letter* 98, 9 (PL 33, 363); *Against Faustus the Manichee* 20, 21 (PL 42, 385).

53 E.g., K. Rahner, *Theological Investigations*, vol. IV (London: Darton, Longman & Todd, 1966), p. 310.

54 Ambrose, *On the Mysteries* 52–53 (PL 16, 406); word in brackets added.

55 De Lubac, *Corpus mysticum*, pp. 148–50.

56 Ambrose, *On the Mysteries* 58 (PL 16, 408–409).

57 Ambrose, *On the Faith* IV, 124 (PL 16, 641). On the frequency of this term in Hiberno-Latin sources and also on its peculiar inverse use see M. McNamara, 'The inverted Eucharistic formula "Conversio corporis Christi in panem et sanguinis in vinum": the exegetical and liturgical background in Irish usage', PRIA 87/C, no. 10 (Dublin, 1987), pp. 573–93.

58 Augustine, *Enarrationes in Psalmos* 9, 9 (PL 37, 1264); Ambrose, *De Spiritu Sancto* III, 11, 79 (PL 16, 828).

59 Augustine, *Treatises on John* 26, 4 (PL 35, 1608; RJ 1822). See also the phrase just cited in the text: 'Non intratur in veritatem nisi per caritatem', *Against Faustus* 32, 18 (PL 42, 507).

60 Augustine, *Enarrationes in Psalmos* 33, s. 2, 10 (PL 36, 313). On the general point being made in this and the following quotations see T. J. van Bavel, 'Das Sakrament der Eucharistie bei Augustinus', *Cor Unum* 39 (1981), pp. 121–35.

61 Augustine, *Sermon* 304, 2 (PL 38, 1395). This text is the Patristic Reading in the Divine Office for 10 August.

62 Augustine, *Sermon* 329, 1 (PL 38, 1454); Patristic Reading in the Divine Office in the Common for a single martyr.

63 Augustine, *Enarrationes in Psalmos* 33, s. 2, 4 (PL 36, 309).

64 Augustine, *Enarrationes in Psalmos* 33, s. 1, 6 (PL 36, 303).

65 Augustine, *Sermon* 9, 10, 14 (PL 38, 85).

66 E.g., Augustine, *Enarrationes in Psalmos* 98, 9 (PL 37, 1264); *The City of God* XVII, 20, 2 (PL 41, 556); *On Baptism* V, 8, 9 (PL 43, 181); *On the Merits of Sinners* I, 24, 34 (PL 44, 128); *Letter* 54, 3 and 6 (PL 33, 201 and 203); *Sermon* 329 (PL 38, 1454–1455).

67 E.g., Augustine, *Sermon* 234, 2 (PL 38, 1116). See also *Sermon* (Guelf) 7, 1 (PLS 2, 254).

68 E.g., Augustine, *Treatises on John* 25, 12 (PL 35, 1602), where eating by
    faith seems to take precedence over eating the sacrament. See also *Sermons*
    227 and 272, where the symbolism of the Church seems to eclipse the
    reality of the sacramental body (PL 38, 1099 and 1246).

69 P. Camelot, 'Réalisme et symbolisme dans la doctrine eucharistique de
    S. Augustin', RSPT 31 (1947), pp. 394–410, at p. 410.

70 Augustine, *Treatises on John* 30, 1 (PL 35, 1632), cited by de Lubac, op.
    cit., p. 153, n. 54; see discussion, ibid., pp. 150–3. My colleague, Fr
    Gervase Corcoran OSA, has pointed out to me against de Lubac that the
    text just quoted says only that the risen body of Christ *can* be in a place,
    and he argues that elsewhere Augustine counsels against enquiry into the
    risen state of Christ's body in heaven: *On Faith and Symbol* 6, 13 (PL 40,
    187–8).

71 Augustine, *Confessions* VII, 10, 16 (PL 32, 742), cited above at note 47 in
    this chapter. This phrase of Augustine had a particular fascination for de
    Lubac since he saw it as the epitome of the consummation of the mystical
    life in heaven: see discussion in *Corpus mysticum*, pp. 202–7. In Augustine
    the phrase refers to his relationship to the Word in general, but de Lubac
    always understood it Eucharistically, since the Eucharist is what prepares
    us for the next life. The matter is discussed in P. McPartlan, *The Eucharist
    Makes the Church* (Edinburgh: T. & T. Clark, 1993), pp. 67–74.

8

⊠ *The early medieval Eucharist*

When Pope Hadrian I acceded to the request of Charlemagne and despatched to him for use in Gaul a copy of the Roman sacramentary, the gesture was a symbol of the movement of history from the ancient Mediterranean world of classical civilization to the emergent nations of medieval Europe. With this change a whole new climate of thought begins to pervade the schools and cloisters of the Western Church. While this development affects the entire range of liturgy and theology, its import on the understanding of the Eucharist touches on two points in particular.

First of all, the Eucharist was destined to become a focal point for faith and piety in a new way. When the writers of the patristic period had thought about this sacrament, their attention was principally on the total work of our redemption which this ritual actualizes and renews amongst us. In the Middle Ages people began to pay more attention to the extraordinary means which the sacrament itself represents as the Lord's chosen vehicle for bringing his redemption home to us.

Secondly, and more fundamentally, the change from the classical to the medieval world brought with it the loss of that ancient sense of 'ontological symbolism' which, in the previous chapter, we saw underlay the mentality of the classical past. With the advent of the Middle Ages, a new empiricism takes its place. The people of the new age had lost the key to the sacramental synthesis of the ancient Church. As a result, they were soon in trouble, and the Eucharist became a matter of significant controversy for the first time.

Paschase and Ratramn

Towards the end of the seventh century a group of monks from the Colomban foundation at Luxeuil established at Corbie on the Somme a monastery which was destined to achieve renown in Eucharistic theology. By the ninth century Corbie had passed over to the Benedictine rule and was to have as its abbot a man renowned for his learning and holiness, Paschase Radbert. Around the year 831 he became the author of what is considered the first monograph on Eucharistic doctrine, *De corpore et sanguine Domini*.[1]

Paschase's work was a comprehensive one. It would be a pity to see it only from the point of view of its well-known Eucharistic realism since, in fact, it deals with all the main aspects which were seen as significant for the sacrament at that time. His insistence on the immediacy of Christ in the sacrament is but part of a larger concern with the wonder of the divine life and of how it is maintained within us. In this his master is Hilary of Poitiers. Hilary was insistent on the fact that the life of grace is more than a merely moral union. His word for it is a 'natural' union between ourselves and Christ, and the Eucharist he sees as essential for maintaining this union.[2]

It is in this context that Paschase takes up a chance remark of Ambrose and gives it a central place in the tradition of Eucharistic theology: that the flesh of the sacrament is the same as that which was born of Mary, suffered on the cross and rose from the grave.[3] This observation, of course, is not so much erroneous as unnuanced. That Paschase himself was not unaware of a certain distinction between the historical and the sacramental is indicated by his application of the word 'mystical' to the Eucharistic body and his insistence that all is to be understood in a 'spiritual' and not in a 'carnal' way.[4] What really gave a pretext to those who would accuse him of a crass realism was his naïve appeal to stories of miraculous appearances of Christ in the sacrament.[5]

In Corbie at this time there was another monk, Ratramn by name, who was destined to become something of a symbol of opposition to Paschase's physicalism. Whether there actually was an open conflict between the two monks is not entirely clear. Certainly where Paschase wished to start from the truth of Christ's flesh in the Eucharist, Ratramn's starting point was the aspect of figure and mystery. Later Ratramn was adopted by Berengar and, by association with the latter, condemned at the Council of Vercelli in 1050. Later still, in the sixteenth century, he was taken up by many Protestants as a forerunner of their denial of transubstantiation. The Protestant martyr, Nicholas Ridley (*c.* 1500–55), once said that Ratramn 'was the first that pulled me by the ear and that brought me from the common error of the Romish Church'.[6]

The difference of opinion at Corbie came about in the following way. In response to an invitation from his king, Charles the Bald, Ratramn took up his pen and composed a work on the Eucharist with the same title as that of Paschase.[7] It was not a total consideration of the subject but a response to two specific questions put to him by Charles. First, is Christ present in the Eucharist in mystery or in truth (*in mysterio an in veritate*)? Secondly, is the body of Christ in the Eucharist the same as that born of Mary?

Ratramn was much looser than Paschase in his language on the truth of the sacrament. To the first question he opted for the view 'in mystery' or 'in figure'. He seems unable to assert unequivocally that Christ exists in the sacrament 'in truth'. Consequently his reply to Charles' second question was also in the negative. Christ, he said, is in the sacrament the way the Church is there.[8]

Was Ratramn orthodox? This is an issue which scholars have debated without being able to come to a consensus. While some have called his orthodoxy into question, others have thought they can defend him, for instance by appealing to the underlying Platonism of his views.[9] Certainly, the differences between abbot and monk do bear witness to the difficulties which were inevitable once the heritage of the ancient world passed into the hands of those who no longer understood its language. Central to these differences was the meaning of truth (*veritas*) as applied to the sacraments. Both Paschase and Ratramn take it as referring to concrete reality rather than to the aspect of fulfilment. Both would claim to follow Augustine and Ambrose, but clearly this is not Augustine and Ambrose as we know them.

From this dispute, if dispute it was,[10] tradition has retained the image of Paschase as the epitome of literalism in Eucharistic doctrine. He was accused by Rhabanus Maurus of holding that Christ is put to death in the Mass. Though some of his expressions do tend in that direction, even he seems to wish to stop short of such a conclusion.[11] However Paschase remains the prototype of a phenomenon in the Eucharistic tradition by which intensity of devotion easily falls prey to exaggerations on the side of realism.

The ninth century marked a new beginning in more ways than one. It has been described as 'a watershed' in the history of our liturgy, with an increasing clericalism and a growing emphasis on the sacredness of the rite.[12] It is the time when hand communion begins to be excluded, the chalice begins to be withheld from the laity, and unleavened bread comes into use. In all these developments Paschasian literalism must have played a part, preparing the ground for later controversies.

The tenth century was a time of little development in Eucharistic theology. The only two significant works of the period on the sacrament both bear witness to the predominant influence of Paschase.[13] It was only in the eleventh century that the difficulties inherent in the Paschasian position came out into the open. The name at the centre of this new controversy was one destined to taunt and intrigue Eucharistic theologians ever since: Berengar of Tours.

The Berengarian controversy

Berengar's was a long life (*c.* 1000–88). In that time his views on the Eucharist brought him to the centre of attention in the theological world of his day, meriting eventually no less than two solemn condemnations by the Church at Rome. If Paschase was the epitome of literalism in Eucharistic theology, Berengar became the paradigm of the opposite. One of the remarkable aspects of these early controversies is the way issues which we associate with a later stage of the tradition are already anticipated by the people of the Middle Ages. Berengar was a Luther before his time. His basic position was a denial of the Eucharistic Change: after the consecration you may refer to the Eucharistic gifts as Christ's body and blood, but in reality they remain bread and wine.[14]

There were a number of influences bringing the teacher of Tours to this view. The most obvious was his reaction against the exaggerations of Paschasian realism. More fundamental was the new philosophical climate which was beginning to form in European thought. De Lubac sets Berengar at the beginning of that dialectical theology which, through Abelard and Anselm, would develop into Scholasticism.

Our new dialecticians can now only pull asunder a reality which one might have thought had been knit together for ever by those geniuses of ontological symbolism which the Fathers of the Church were. In the hands of Berengar the sacramental synthesis falls apart.[15]

One of the agents of this change was Aristotle. Up to this time symbolism and Platonism had gone together. Now the influence of the Stagirite was ushering in a more empirical approach to reality. In some ways it was the beginning of the modern world with its empiricism and its individualism. In the eleventh century, however, scholars had not yet got much further than the use of Aristotelian terms. They still had a long way to go in appropriating Aristotle's notion of reality. Basically Berengar seems to have been a naïve realist in his philosophy.[16] In such an approach the sensible qualities of a thing cannot easily be distinguished from its substance, and since in the Eucharist there is no change in the sensible qualities of the gifts, there can, for Berengar, be no change in what they ultimately are.

Berengar himself was clever in argument, and at this remove it is difficult to pin down his own precise position.[17] He may not have been the pure symbolist he is sometimes thought to have been, but we can certainly trace to the Berengarian side in this controversy the notion that in the consecrated gifts there is a coexistence of bread and wine with the body and blood of Christ. This view is significant in that it implies a separation of the notion of presence from that of change, and it is worth bearing in mind that its emergence coincides with that of the naïve realism which we have just uncovered.

Part of the difficulty in the eleventh century was the inability of the theology of the day to handle the issues which Berengar was raising. If Berengar's position was unacceptable, so too was the kind of crude realism with which he was commonly confronted. This latter approach had its hour of triumph in the text of an oath which Berengar was required to take by the Synod of Rome in 1059 in the reign of Pope Nicholas II:

... the bread and wine, which are placed on the altar, are after the consecration not only a sacramental sign but also the true body and blood of Our Lord Jesus Christ, and not only in sacramental sign but in all truth are empirically (*sensualiter*) handled and broken by the hands of the priest and crushed by the teeth of the faithful.[18]

One of the most important results of the controversy surrounding Berengar was the way it breathed life into theological reflection
on the problems he was raising. Berengar had put his finger on real
weaknesses in the Paschasian orthodoxy of his day, especially on
its failure to do justice to the distinction between what happens to
the consecrated species and what happens to Christ's body and
blood. This movement of reflection would come to fruition only
two centuries later, but in Berengar's day it begins in his own work
and in that of formidable adversaries of his such as Lanfranc of Bec
(*c.* 1005–89) and Guitmund of Aversa (*c.* 1015–*c.* 1085).[19]

Familiar with Aristotle's writings on logic, Berengar had used
the term *substantia* to refer to the Eucharistic gifts, but for him the
term meant 'concrete reality', including that of the perceptible
qualities. Lanfranc and Guitmund take up the challenge of this
Aristotelian vocabulary, but turn it against their opponent. It is
Lanfranc who finds the language for a solution to Paschase's
problem concerning the sacramental body and the historical body
of Christ: in one way they are the same, in another not so, for they
are the same 'in essence', but differ on the level of appearances.[20]
As later theology puts it, they are the same in substance but differ
in the mode of their existence.

Guitmund carries the matter forward. He is the first to put the
notion of 'substantial change' to the forefront of Eucharistic
theology. He seems closer than was Berengar to the Aristotelian
context of the term in so far as he distinguishes *substantia* from
accidentia.[21] He describes the Eucharistic Change as not a creation,
but a 'substantial transmutation' (*substantialiter transmutari*).[22]
However he remains particularly unsatisfactory in his account of
what happens to the body of Christ when the consecrated species
are subjected to change or putrefaction. Guitmund is content to
say that any such change, as affecting the body of Christ, is only an
illusion.[23]

Twenty years after his first appearance at Rome, Berengar was
summoned to defend himself once again, this time before the
redoubtable Pope Gregory VII. The defendant drew up his own
profession of faith, couched in the language of identity, and at first
the Pope was satisfied with this, but when the question came for
decision in the Lent of 1079, the phrase *substantialiter converti* was
introduced into the final text.[24] Pope Gregory, apparently, was
quite sympathetic to Berengar, but nonetheless insisted on the key
adverb 'substantially', feeling that only such a term would suffice

to dispel the ambiguities of Berengar's traditional language. This is an experience which surely has some relevance today for ecumenical discussion of agreed statements on doctrine.

The text of this oath marks the first occasion on which the Magisterium turns to the language of the philosophers for the expression of its Eucharistic faith. As we have already pointed out, though the background of this language lies ultimately in Aristotle, the notion of 'substance' involved is still very far from that of his philosophy. It is simply a way of underlining that the Eucharistic Change is a concrete reality. As often happens in the Church, once a difficulty is raised, it can be answered only in the terms of the objectors. In fact, scholars will point out that, far from committing the Church to Hellenistic influences, this choice of language is actually a way of defending Church teaching from such rationalism.[25] The rationalism of the day was really on the side of Berengar.

Of the two oaths required of Berengar, that of 1079 was the more reasonable and, in the long run, the more significant. It had doubtless benefited from the advances made in the intervening years by theologians like Lanfranc and Guitmund, and it continues to exercise an influence in our own day, having been cited, for instance, as recently as 1965 by Paul VI in his encyclical *Mysterium fidei*.[26] At the time, however, the difference between the two oaths was not always appreciated, and the formula of Nicholas II continued to be referred to, even turning up in the sixteenth century to receive the unlikely approbation of Luther.

In conclusion to this episode we can say that the Berengarian controversy was of some lasting significance in theology. Though the movement in support of Berengar did not outlast his lifetime, his position had raised questions for theological reflection which would continue to engage some of the best minds of Europe for the next two centuries. This would mean that, centuries before Luther would return to the same problems, a theology of the Eucharistic Change had been worked out in advance. At the same time it must be admitted that this development contributed to a certain imbalance in Eucharistic theology. The concentration of theologians' minds on questions of change was not accompanied by an equal interest in the notion of Eucharistic sacrifice. A style of theology was developing which, right up to our own day, has tried to face questions of Eucharistic presence independently of, and often prior to, questions of Eucharistic sacrifice. The weaknesses

122   *Problems in theology: the Eucharist*

created by this approach will be indicated later in this book, in Chapters 10 and 14 especially.

THE TWELFTH CENTURY

The twelfth century is one of the most fundamental moments of change in the history of the Eucharist in the Western Church. As a recent historian of the doctrine put it, sometime between the death of Berengar (1088) and the Fourth Lateran Council (1215), a whole new attitude came to the fore in Western spirituality, one centred on the corporal presence of Christ in the sacrament.[27]

One could perhaps characterize the new development as a change from the dynamic to the static. In the patristic view of the Eucharist the primary emphasis was always on the sacred action in the liturgy, Christ's great act of worship consummated by holy communion. While this of course continued to be held in honour, it was now complemented by the more static attitude to which we refer. In time this new attitude would call into being a whole new set of Eucharistic practices. It struck a chord in the profound contemplative spirit of the day, and in some cases led to remarkable gifts of Eucharistic mysticism.[28]

The causes of this change are inevitably complex, and scholars will differ in the way they present them. The most obvious factor, and the one closest to our interest in this book, is the emphasis left in theology by the controversies that had gone before. The very tendency of devotion to separate the reserved sacrament from its primary context in the Mass parallels the way Lanfranc and his followers neglected the theology of the sacred action in order to deal with questions of presence.

Then there was the desire to emphasize among the faithful such points as heresy had called into question. Though this factor was less obvious in the first half of the century than in the second, when aspects of Eucharistic doctrine were being denied by the Cathars and Waldensians,[29] it must have been an influence ever since the time of Berengar. It cannot be mere coincidence that the first procession with the Blessed Sacrament which we know of was arranged by Lanfranc, the great adversary of Berengar.[30] There is also the fact that it is from the monasteries of Bec and Cluny around this time that we hear of a movement to have the reserved sacrament located on the altar of the church.

Finally there was the growing devotion to the humanity of Christ.[31] Certainly this is one of the most characteristic developments of the whole medieval period. It was well described by G. L. Prestige as follows:

During the twelfth century a revolutionary change passed over the devotion of the Western Church. Attention came to be concentrated less exclusively on the miracle of redemption and more deliberately on the wonder of its method. The man Christ Jesus is regarded with a mystical rather than a historical adoration. He is contemplated now not only as deliverer and illuminator, bringing heaven down to earth; not only as pattern, guide and judge, raising earth to the radiant majesty of heaven; but still more as companion, friend and brother, though divine, as husband and lover of devoted souls, as the most intimate associate of Christian hearts and the object of a passionate spiritual affection. He is sought not so much as the temporal revelation of the Father as for the sake of His own perfect human qualities; and not so much by way of saturation with His Holy Spirit as by direct mystical union with His earthly experiences, and especially with the events of His passion.[32]

Given the mentality of the day, it was inevitable that the movement in the one area of devotion should have its impact on the other. Though the influence between the two developments was reciprocal, it seems that the more fundamental one was the christological rather than the sacramental. Thus we note that St Bernard of Clairvaux was a leading figure in devotion to the humanity of Christ, but his writings, dating from the first half of the century, seem as yet relatively untouched by the new Eucharistic piety. St Francis of Assisi, on the other hand, coming at the end of the century, shows us how his devotion to the humanity of Christ has found in the Blessed Sacrament the Lord's incarnation renewed.[33]

The language of presence in theology

Consequently we come to one of the principal features which mark off medieval theology of the Eucharist from that of the preceding centuries, namely the language of presence. For the ancient Church 'the corporal presence of Christ' was a phrase to describe the state that came to an end with the Ascension.[34] When his presence in the Church was spoken of, it was understood as a presence in a different mode, a spiritual presence.[35]

The signal of a change, which is eventually to take over Eucharistic language in the West, comes with Paschase and his insistence on the sacramental body as the 'true' body of Christ. As we have seen, Paschase himself was not unaware of a difference between the sacramental mode and the historical mode of Our Lord's bodily existence. But those that came after him, especially those involved in opposing Berengar, were destined to speak in such a way that this difference of mode became overshadowed by the affirmation of the substantial identity of the body in both cases.[36]

To this principle the reaction against Berengar added yet a second one which, when translated into preaching and devotion, would be fundamental to the new attitude which was emerging. Berengar had taunted Lanfranc that in the Eucharist he seemed to think that we eat little portions of Christ's flesh.[37] Clearly the orthodox could not let such a charge stand, and soon we see the point being made that under either species we have the whole Christ, body, blood, soul and divinity. This is what we mean by the principle of concomitance, and we find it being put forward already by John of Mantua, writing around 1080.[38] It is surely not a coincidence that it is around this time that we first find evidence of the custom of addressing Christ directly in the Eucharistic species.[39] During the twelfth century this principle of concomitance becomes common, though not yet universal, teaching, once it is taken up by the founders of the school of Laon.[40]

With the principle of concomitance established, and the growing sense of an identity between the historical body and the sacramental body, the stage is set for the development of the new Eucharistic movement. The initial impetus then came from the eleventh century, and the thirteenth will see its full development in liturgy and spirituality, but the theology on which it is based is largely the achievement of the twelfth. An indication of the new mentality will be found in the way Hugh of St Victor (*c.* 1096–1141) reinterprets the ancient distinction of corporal presence from spiritual presence, with the former phrase now being applied to the body and blood of Christ in the sacrament.[41] More and more we see a tendency to regard Christ's existence in the Eucharist as a kind of re-edition of his historical existence on earth. The reception of his body in holy communion is understood on the analogy of receiving a guest into one's house, like the centurion in Matthew 8:8 or Zacchaeus in Luke 19:5–6.[42] The classical text about Christ's presence in the Church, Matthew 28:20, comes to be applied by many to his presence in the Eucharistic gifts.

In their account of the origins of this movement, scholars sometimes place too much emphasis on the second of those causes we have listed above. In other words, they try to explain the rise of this movement as simply a reaction against heresy. While this factor, as we have said, must have played its part, it does not seem right that the purely negative attitude of countering a heresy should be given the credit for calling into being a spirituality which was so rich and profound in itself.

Nor does such an explanation quite fit the facts. Even prior to the disputes with Berengar there was evidence of a growing reverence for the reserved sacrament.[43] In the first half of the twelfth century there was little support for Berengar, and the movements of the Cathars and Waldensians had not yet got under way; yet right in this period we find the theology of presence clearly stated in, for instance, the theologian to whom we have just referred, Hugh of St Victor.[44] A truer explanation seems to be that this devotion corresponded to something deep within the people, and that it is a case of theology and liturgy answering the needs of the time.

This greater clarity with regard to Christ's presence in host and cup is well illustrated by a terminological refinement which emerged at this time. In the previous chapter we have seen how Augustine thought of the sacrament according to a two-tiered framework:

sacramentum – res sacramenti.

This had the benefit of holding the various realities in the sacramental mystery in a close synthesis, but it must be admitted that sometimes it left aspects of the sacrament, and in particular the objective actuality of Christ's body and blood, in some obscurity. In the first quarter of the twelfth century – we can trace it first in Alger of Liège (d. *c.* 1132)[45] – theologians began to think in a three-tiered framework. While this received various formulations, one of the clearest was as follows:

sacramentum tantum – sacramentum et res – res tantum.[46]

The advantage of this framework lay in that it set out clearly the level on which Christ's body and blood are contained in the sacrament. This was the level on which so much of the theological reflection of this century would take place. Its disadvantage lay in leaving a certain distance between the ritual itself and some of the effects previously seen as intimate to it. In this way it illustrates that sundering of the patristic synthesis of which de Lubac spoke.[47]

Spiritual communion

In his study of the Eucharist in the early scholastic period, Gary Macy is anxious to underline the diversity that reigned among the schoolmen, but at the same time he endeavours to introduce some order into this welter of opinions by reducing the diversity down to certain basic models. The first model is that of the tradition stemming from Paschase and taken up with vigour in the controversy with Berengar. In this approach the insistence on Eucharistic realism is but part of a larger emphasis on the objective necessity of the Eucharist as a means of salvation. While Paschase stopped short of seeing this necessity as an absolute,[48] he and his followers tended to take texts like John 6:53 fairly literally. This tendency must have remained an influence in the new ritualism of the Middle Ages. It certainly was a factor in the medieval custom of communicating infants from the chalice on the occasion of their baptism.[49]

In the twelfth century a different model is formed in the school of Laon.[50] Beginning with Anselm of Laon (d. 1117) – not to be confused with the Anselm of Bec and Canterbury – a new generation emerges, whose greater sense of spirituality, and of the role of the subject, is in line with the progress of medieval thought generally. For them the key to salvation lies in the individual's faith and love. Consequently the fruit of the Eucharist must lie in a growth in those key qualities of the spiritual life.

The role of faith in our worship is one of the recurrent problems of sacramental theology. From the time of Paschase it had arisen in the discussion of questions like unworthy communion.[51] Paschase had replied by simply calling down on unworthy recipients the judgement spoken of in 1 Corinthians 11:29. In the eleventh century some tried a more nuanced approach, speculating, for instance, that in such circumstances the sacrament would revert to being bread and wine.[52] Twelfth-century theologians distinguished two kinds of reception, variously described as 'sacramental eating' on the one hand and 'spiritual eating' on the other, or 'sacramental' as distinct from 'real' eating, or 'corporal' as distinct from 'spiritual' eating. In each case the point was that only the proper dispositions gave one access to the fruits of the sacrament.[53]

In this usage we notice that the term 'spiritual communion' refers to an actual reception of the sacrament and that a fruitful one. But in the meantime the school of Laon came up with the idea that not only was the Eucharist not absolutely necessary for salvation, but the fruits of the Eucharist could be received even apart from the actual reception of holy communion. To readers of Augustine this idea was not totally strange, given the famous remark 'Believe, and you have eaten'.[54] For the school of Laon our union with God in faith and love is what the sacrament is all about. Consequently, wherever that union is achieved in our faith and love, whether through actual reception of holy communion or not, there we have the reality (*res*) of the sacrament in its crucial sense.

This is the origin of the custom of spiritual communion, in our sense of the term, which became widespread from this time on.[55] In itself the custom could be adjudged positively in so far as it can lend depth and significance to devotion to the reserved sacrament. But unfortunately it is a custom which easily develops a life of its own, and instead of being complementary to holy communion becomes a substitute for it. This seems to be what actually happened in the Middle Ages, at a time when the level of actual reception of the sacrament was extremely low.[56] To many people at this time it seemed more important to *see* the sacrament than to receive it. It is remarkable that a practice which had its origin in such valuable theological ideas should end up in a manner so detrimental to liturgy.

Eucharist and Church

Another area of Eucharistic theology where the passage from the patristic to the medieval world in the West was not made without significant loss concerns the connection between the Eucharist and the Church. The most influential study in this field has been that of de Lubac in which he traced how the term *corpus mysticum* moved over from designating the Eucharist to designating the Church. That this transition was possible at all is itself already an indication of how tradition had viewed Eucharist and Church as intrinsically correlative aspects within the one mystery. By the end of the

Middle Ages, in this as in other spheres, this vision of the patristic writers lay in pieces.

De Lubac summed up the mentality of the ancients in a famous phrase: the Eucharist makes the Church.[57] Indeed it is only in so far as one is a member of the Church that one can *truly* – for which we must read *fruitfully* – receive the body of Christ; and the fruit of that receiving is the love and unity of Christians.[58] Eucharist and Church were united in the one sacramental mystery, and reference to this ritual mystery was precisely the meaning of the word 'mystical' at this time.

In the Middle Ages this 'mystical' and symbolical kind of thinking, as we have seen, gave way before the advance of dialectic. On the one hand, the meaning of 'body' in the Eucharist came to be focused in a more exclusive way on the 'body born of Mary'. On the other hand, the sense of the mysteriousness of the Church was being diminished by the rise of canonists and bureaucrats. The Papacy was coming to the height of its temporal power, and 'Church' would now mean something rather different from the *societas sanctorum* of which Augustine wrote.

One of the positive features of the Middle Ages was a growing appreciation of the value of the individual. This was reflected among the theologians of Laon and St Victor in their stress on personal faith and love as dispositions for fruitful reception of the sacrament. This is not to say that the social aspect of Christianity was being denied. In that world it could not but be taken for granted. However it may be that some felt that this new tendency needed to be qualified. With Gilbert of La Porrée, in what looks at first like a rediscovery of ancient tradition, a new emphasis in Eucharistic theology emerges by which the unity of the Church is stressed as the ultimate fruit of the Eucharist. The point is taken up by Peter Lombard (c. 1100–60), and so passes into thirteenth-century theology.

This new emphasis was in fact less traditional than would at first appear. With the undermining of the ancient sense of symbolism, the immediacy of the link between Eucharist and Church had been weakened. This development affected the understanding of both Church and Eucharist. The very sense of the Church as mystery, whether within the liturgy or otherwise, now began to yield to a more sociological and juridical approach, with the Papacy being given an ever more central role. This was paralleled on the level of theology by the weakening of the word 'mystical'. Once this epithet began to be applied to the ecclesial body in contrast to the sacramental body, the latter drew to itself the sense of the real and the true, so that 'mystical' was felt to refer to something which was not fully real.[59] For Peter Lombard the unity of the Church is a reality 'not contained' in the sacrament.[60]

In the Eucharist itself, questions of Christ's presence in the sacramental gifts became more and more central, and the more juridical climate of the time was reflected in the way the dispositions for receiving the sacrament were discussed. One began to speak less and less with the Laon and Victorine schools of the primacy of faith and love, but more bluntly of 'being free from sin',[61] while the weakening of the sense of the actuality of the Church in the celebration left more room for the general growth of individualism in the approach to the sacrament.

Speculative questions

The history of the Eucharist in the twelfth century is a story on two levels. The most obvious and far-reaching level is the one we have just described, that of spirituality and devotion. Underpinning this was the level of theological reflection, out of which some of the key ideas for the movement of spirituality emerged. However theology has its own questions and its own dynamic. Its agenda had been set for it by the controversies of the time of Berengar, and the dynamic, which had been put in train, would come to a head only in the subsequent century. In itself, therefore, the Eucharistic theology of the twelfth century represents a phase which is important mainly for that influence on the spirituality of the time which we have just seen, but also as a stage in the emergence of the achievements of high scholasticism.

With the benefit of hindsight, the problem left to theology by the controversies of the eleventh century could be described as follows. The issues which Berengar had raised were ultimately ontological in character, so that theology found itself before the laborious process, first, of establishing a metaphysics and, secondly, of applying it to the sacrament. The situation of the theology of the sacrament could be described as a dilemma between the exaggerated realism of Paschase on the one hand and the exaggerated symbolism of the Berengarians on the other. The problem lay in identifying a level of being on which a position between the two extremes could be established. The level which was eventually marked out was that of metaphysics; and here we might notice, as often in theology, that recourse to metaphysics comes about, not as a result of idle speculation, but in order to find a radical answer to concrete questions.

Already Guitmund of Aversa had cast the problem in the language of substance and accident, but we must not conclude that his readers would have immediately understood these terms in their proper Aristotelian sense. Matter and form, substance and accident, became the standard armoury of the medieval scholar, but it would be many a long day before the concepts behind these terms were genuinely those of the master.

In the twelfth century three opinions in particular were commonly cited as relevant to the understanding of the Eucharist. Two of them came under the general heading of the substantial change of bread and wine, whereas the third held for a denial of such change. The first and most common opinion took the notion of 'change' strictly, which it interpreted as a change of the substance of bread and wine into Christ's body and blood. The significance of this view is brought out by contrasting it with its main rival, the theory of annihilation / succession. According to this second theory there is a substantial change in the Eucharist only in a loose sense. Strictly speaking, the substance of bread and wine is annihilated, to be succeeded by the substance of Christ's body and blood.

The third opinion commonly mentioned in this context is that which denies any substantial change in the Eucharist. This opinion had its origin, of course, in the Berengarian controversy, and by the twelfth century it had few, if any, defenders in the schools. We should notice, however, that we speak of this opinion in terms of substance, but the notion of substance at this time was still a very confused one, as we will see. This fact was not sufficient to win supporters for this third opinion, but it does help explain the hesitation of some in repudiating it as contrary to the faith.[62]

The difficulties in this whole question throughout the twelfth century focus on how 'form' is to be understood on the one hand, and on how 'matter' is to be understood on the other. One could highlight the problem area by considering two different approaches to the meaning of the word 'substance': *substantia* from *substando*, or *substantia* from *subsistendo*. The first of these notions located substance on the side of matter as that which *stands under* the formal principles of the thing. This was the general view of the twelfth-century writers. In this view matter was seen as a determinate, or relatively determinate, physical substrate of ordinary change.

The second notion of substance, the properly Aristotelian one, was not discovered until the thirteenth century. Before this could happen two basic insights had to come about. First of all, matter had to be seen as pure potency. This was first put forward by Gilbert of La Porrée and Poitiers (d. 1154) before the middle of the century. It took a considerable time for this viewpoint to be accepted. The second insight concerned form, and this was arrived at only in the next century in the work of William of Auxerre (d. 1231), when he came to the notion of substantial form as a single principle. It was only when these two insights had been gained that a properly Aristotelian notion of substance as a composite of substantial form and prime matter could be proposed.

From this history two important points emerge for our topic. In the first place it makes clear that the word 'transubstantiation' is not a term with a single meaning. It seems that it came into use sometime before the middle of the twelfth century as a designation of the annihilation / succession theory. Between that time and its classical formulation by Aquinas, some hundred years later, the term had to cover a wide diversity of philosophical and theological viewpoints.

Three main usages may be distinguished. Firstly there was the meaning for which the term was first devised, the annihilation / succession theory.[63] Secondly there was what seems to us its most appropriate meaning, namely to designate the theory of 'change' in the strict sense. Thirdly the word is used simply as a synonym for *mutatio* and *conversio*, and so it is used in a non-technical sense as a term for the ordinary teaching of the Church.[64] Added to this diversity one should also take into account the differences of interpretation within the first two of these approaches, as theologians struggled with different views of matter and form, essential and non-essential properties, and so on.[65]

In the second place, this history surely throws some light on the point raised by some writers today concerning a certain lack of clarity, if not hesitation, on the part of the theologians of this time in censuring the denial of substantial change in the Eucharist.[66] To an extent this whole question is a false one, since it implies a kind of clarity about the nature of theology and the relationship of Scripture, faith and dogma which did not exist for a considerable time after this period.[67] The further use of this research for denominational reasons today – to reduce the content of the doctrine to one of presence rather than of change – does not do justice to the basic fact that throughout the twelfth century the denial of the change of bread and wine had no significant support in the schools of Catholic theology.

The problem arises once one moves from the ordinary language of the faith – that bread and wine are changed into the body and blood of Christ – into the language of the schools: substance, matter and form, transubstantiation. Given the confusion of the time concerning the metaphysical composition of reality, it is understandable that scholars would be slow to place dogmatic censures on positions expressed in terms of an uncertain philosophy.[68]

A suitable conclusion to a review of twelfth-century theology comes with the work of Pope Innocent III, whose pontificate bridged the passage from one century to the next (1198–1216). Before he became Pope he had already written a study entitled *The Sacred Mystery of the Altar*, in which the new devotion to the corporal presence of Christ finds expression.[69] In the speculative order, however, this work has not got beyond the imperfect metaphysics of the day, where substance is placed on the side of matter. His own view favours understanding the change in the Eucharist in the strict sense, namely as the change of this material substrate in the bread and wine into that of Christ's body and blood. The theory of annihilation / succession is dealt with only to be rejected, but it is noteworthy that he is prepared to include this latter view under the term 'transubstantiation'.[70]

The key event of Innocent's pontificate for the doctrine of the Eucharist was the Fourth Lateran Council of 1215. In the creed of this Council we have the first use of the language of 'transubstantiation' in a conciliar document (DS 802). Some authors have tended to exaggerate the force of this teaching, referring to it as a 'formal definition' of the notion.[71] Undoubtedly some distinctions are called for.

The situation of this Council makes it clear that this statement was the culmination of the struggles of the Church throughout the latter half of the twelfth century against the Cathars' denial of the actuality of Christ's body and blood in the Eucharist. Clearly the statement is an affirmation of the Eucharistic Change and not just of Eucharistic presence,[72] but there is nothing, either in the text of the decree or in the position of the Cathars, to suggest a need to canonize a mere theological opinion. If it were, whose opinion would it be? Surely not that of Innocent III, whose philosophy and theology were soon to be surpassed.

The significance of the document, therefore, lies in adding the weight of conciliar authority to the general teaching of the Church on the matter. As regards content, it does not add anything to the *substantialiter converti* of 1079. On the latter occasion the Magisterium had taken its first cautious step in the direction of nascent scholasticism with the use of the word *substantialiter*. In 1215, when scholasticism was approaching its zenith, the Magisterium took a step back from the schools and contented itself with expressing its doctrine in what was for that time a loose use of scholastic language. Such, and nothing more, was the 'definition' of Lateran IV.

NOTES

1 Paschase, *De corpore et sanguine Domini*: PL 120, 1267–1350. Modern edition by Bede Paulus, *Corpus Christianorum, continuatio medievalis*, vol. 16 (Turnhout: Brepols, 1969).

2 See Hilary, *On the Trinity* 8, 14 (PL 10, 247). One might consult the excerpt from Hilary in English in A. Hamman (ed.), *The Mass: Ancient Liturgies and Patristic Texts* (Staten Island: Alba House, 1967), pp. 198–201.

3 Paschase, *De corpore* 1, 2 (PL 120, 1269B), citing Ambrose, *De Mysteriis* 53 (PL 16, 407).

4 Paschase, PL 120, 1355A. For 'mystical body' in Paschase, see PL 120, 1273A and 1285A. He probably also uses the word 'spiritual' for the Eucharistic body as H. de Lubac notes *Corpus mysticum: l'eucharistie et l'église au moyen-âge* (Paris: Aubier, 1944), p. 147, citing PL 120, 1281C. His sense of a difference of the historical from the sacramental body is also indicated by his expression *medium corpus* for the latter: *Expositio in Matt.* 12, 26 (PL 120, 896C), thus distinguishing it within the triad of senses of 'body', *De corp.* 7 (PL 120, 1284–1286).

5 As de Lubac remarks, Paschase made it worse by increasing the number of such stories in his second edition: op. cit., p. 183.

6 Cited by J. Pelikan, *The Christian Tradition: A History of the Development of Doctrine*, vol. 4 (Chicago–London: University of Chicago Press, 1984), p. 199.

7 Ratramn, *De corpore et sanguine Domini*: PL 121, 125–170. The modern edition is by J. N. Bakhuizen van den Brink, *Ratramnus, De corpore et sanguine Domini: Texte original et notice bibliographique* (Amsterdam:

North Holland Publishing Co., 1974). A recent study is that by J.-P. Bouhot, *Ratramn de Corbie: histoire littéraire et controverses doctrinales* (Paris: Etudes Augustiniennes, 1976).

8 Ratramn, *De corpore et sanguine Domini* 96.

9 Thus J. F. Fahey, *The Eucharistic Teaching of Ratramn of Corbie* (Mundelein: St Mary of the Lake Seminary, 1951). Other ways of defending him are found in P. F. Palmer, *Sacraments and Worship* (London: Longmans, 1957), p. 224, n. 1; Bouhot, op. cit., pp. 157–8. Critical are J. R. Geiselmann, 'Abendmahlstreit', LThK I, 33, and H. Peltier, 'Ratramne', DTC XIII, col. 1784. J. T. O'Connor remains undecided in *The Hidden Manna* (San Francisco: Ignatius Press, 1988), pp. 90–3. It seems to me that ch. 77 of Ratramn's work substantiates Bouhot's argument.

10 It is integral to Bouhot's interpretation of Ratramn that there was no disagreement between Paschase and Ratramn on essentials: Bouhot, op. cit., pp. 85–8.

11 Rhabanus, *Letter to Frudegard* (PL 120, 1355A), though he had said, of Christ in the Mass, *iterum patitur* (PL 120, 1302B). The remark of Rhabanus is in *Letter* 2 to Egiles, 6 (PL 112, 1516) cited by P. F. Palmer, op. cit., pp. 226–7.

12 N. Mitchell, *Cult and Controversy* (New York: Pueblo, 1982), p. 96.

13 Gezo of Tortona, *De corpore et sanguine Christi* (PL 137, 371–406), and Heriger of Lobbes, *Sicut ante nos dixit* (PL 139, 179–188). The latter work has sometimes been attributed to Gerbert of Auvergne, later Pope Sylvester II.

14 J. de Montclos, *Lanfranc et Berenger: La controverse eucharistique du XIe siècle* (Louvain: Spicilegium Sacrum Lovaniense, 1971), pp. 142–8. Nathan Mitchell attributes to Berengar an affirmation of the real presence of Christ's body and blood in the sacrament (*Cult and Controversy*, p. 141), but this is contradicted by Montclos, whom Mitchell frequently cites. Montclos states that Berengar's views on presence 'have nothing to do with what the authentic faith calls real presence' (op. cit., p. 147). For a summary in English of Montclos on Berengar see O'Connor, *The Hidden Manna*, pp. 96–112.

15 De Lubac, op. cit., p. 260.

16 He is one of those for whom, as Bernard Lonergan would say, the real is 'the already-out-there-now-real'. See B. Lonergan, *Insight* (London: Longmans, 1967), pp. 251–2.

17 Part of the difficulty lies in that much of our knowledge of the Berengarian side is only indirect, based on remarks in the works of adversaries such as Guitmund of Aversa. The latter's terms for his opponents are *umbratici* and *impanatores*. The *umbratici* would be supporters of an empty symbolism. The best term for the second position would be one he uses once, 'companation' (PL 149, 1482C) rather than 'impanation'. This

helps to suggest that he does not seem to mean an entitative relationship between the bread and the substance of Christ, as in the usual meaning of 'impanation', found shortly after, for instance, in Alger of Liège (PL 180, 754). Though an analogy with the hypostatic union is mentioned once (PL 149, 1482C), the relationship of the bread and the substance of Christ's body attributed to his adversaries seems to be only one of coexistence, for instance in PL 149, 1485A, similar to that found in the notion later called 'consubstantiation'.

18 DS 690.

19 Lanfranc, *De corpore et sanguine Domini* (PL 150, 407–442); Guitmund, *De corporis et sanguinis Christi veritate in Eucharistia* (PL 149, 1427–1494).

20 Lanfranc, *De corpore* 18 (PL 150, 430).

21 Guitmund, PL 149, 1481B.

22 Idem, PL 149, 1467B.

23 We already find in him the standard medieval comparison: the illusion is like that of a bent stick in water – Guitmund, *De corp.* 2 (PL 149, 1438D).

24 The final text is given in DS 700. The text of Berengar's proposal, made before the Pope and his advisers the previous All Saints, will be found in Montclos, op. cit. note 14 above, p. 222.

25 A more famous instance of this paradox will be found in Christology, as described by B. Lonergan, 'The dehellenization of dogma' in *A Second Collection* (London: Darton, Longman & Todd, 1974), pp. 11–32. This way of interpreting Berengar's oath is found in P. Gy, *La Maison-Dieu* no. 137 (1979), p. 95.

26 Paul VI, AAS 57 (1965), p. 768.

27 G. Macy, *The Theologies of the Eucharist in the Early Scholastic Period* (Oxford: Clarendon, 1984), p. 86.

28 E. Longpré, 'Eucharistie et expérience mystique: moyen âge', *Dictionnaire de spiritualité*, vol. 4, cols 1592–1604.

29 The Cathars were a medieval sect who held the visible world to be evil and rejected the Old Testament. Although they accepted the New Testament, they denied the sacraments. Originating in the East, they became widespread in the West only from about 1150 on. The Waldensians were a group of radical Christians, followers of a merchant of Lyons called Valdes. Their movement began in the 1170s. Unlike the Cathars, they held to the Eucharist, but some of them denied the necessity of ordained priests to celebrate it or questioned the validity of celebration by unworthy priests.

30 Mitchell, *Cult and Controversy*, pp. 130–1. B. Neunheuser, citing P. Browe, notes that the first mention of genuflecting before the sacrament and incensing it comes from Bec and Cluny at this time: *Eucharistie in Mittelalter und Neuzeit* (Freiburg: Herder, 1963), p. 37.

31 Thus Macy, op. cit., p. 41. See also J. Jungmann, *Missarum sollemnia* (Vienna–Freiburg–Basel: Herder, 1962), I, p. 156.

32 G. L. Prestige, *Fathers and Heretics* (London: SPCK, 1940), p. 185.

33 St Francis of Assisi, 'Admonitions I', *Writings and Early Biographies: English Omnibus of the Sources for the Life of St Francis*, ed. M. A. Habig (London: SPCK, 1973), pp. 77–9. In this text Francis applies the notion of presence in Matt 28:20 to the Eucharist.

34 Leo, *Second Sermon on the Ascension* 2 (PL 54, 398A). For Augustine and Cyril of Jerusalem, see references in de Lubac, *Corpus mysticum*, p. 179.

35 De Lubac notes an instance from the Gelasian Sacramentary where 'corporal presence' is applied to Christ's presence in the Church, but such a mode of expression is altogether exceptional for its time: *Corpus mysticum*, p. 178.

36 *Christus substantialiter semper idem*: Guitmund, *De corp.* 2 (PL 149, 1461C). See also Lanfranc, *De corp.* 18 (PL 150, 430C); Durandus of Troarn, *De corp.* part IV, 9 (PL 149, 1387B).

37 Berengar, *De sacra coena* 9 (Beekenkamp, p. 14); 30 (ibid., p. 66); 35 (ibid., p. 94).

38 Text in Macy, op. cit., p. 165, n. 152.

39 Mitchell, *Cult and Controversy*, pp. 164–5.

40 E.g. William of Champeaux, texts cited in Macy, op. cit., p. 176, n. 17. See also Jungmann, *Missarum sollemnia*, I, p. 156. That it was not yet universal teaching is shown by the resistance to the view of Peter the Singer (d. 1197) concerning the need for a double consecration: on this see Mitchell, *Cult and Controversy*, pp. 151–9. Eventually the classic scholastic formulation of the doctrine is adopted by the Magisterium in the third chapter of Trent's Decree on the Eucharist (DS 1640–41).

41 De Lubac, *Corpus mysticum*, pp. 177–82.

42 This analogy was not unknown among the ancient writers. It began to be found in the liturgy with the use of the words of Matt 8:8 before communion from the tenth century on: Jungmann, *Missarum sollemnia*, vol. II, pp. 441, 443.

43 For instance, ever since the ninth century the custom had been spreading of reserving the sacrament on the altar rather than in the sacristy, though, as we have already noted, this custom was promoted in a special way by Bec and Cluny in the eleventh century. The use of sanctuary lamps is mentioned from the eleventh century on.

44 Hugh of St Victor, *De sacramentis* 2, 8, 13 (PL 176, 470B).

45 Alger, *Liber de misericordia et justitia* I, 62 (PL 180, 884D); *De sacramentis* I, 5 (PL 180, 752–754).

46 *Sacrament only – sacrament and reality – reality only*. Macy traces this formulation to an anonymous *Summa sententiarum* from the school of Hugh of St Victor, dated roughly in the second quarter of the century: Macy, op. cit., pp. 84–5. In the following century (1202) this framework is adopted on the level of the Magisterium in a letter of Innocent III, *Cum Marthae circa* (DS 783).

47 De Lubac, *Corpus mysticum*, p. 260. See note 4 above.

48 Paschase, *De corpore* 19, 4 (PL 120, 1328C).

49 For instance, William of Champeaux, *Fragmentum de sacramento altaris* (PL 163, 1039). This custom dropped out from the twelfth century on, when the withholding of the chalice from the laity became more general: see C. Crawford, 'Infant communion: past tradition and present practice', *Theological Studies* 31 (1970), pp. 523–36. On the general question of the necessity of the Eucharist one might read Aquinas, ST III, q. 73, a. 3, and the useful discussion in O'Connor, op. cit. note 9 above, pp. 316–20.

50 Historically the school of theology at Laon had been founded in the ninth century by Scotus Eriugena, but here the term is used for convenience to designate, following Macy, a particular current in twelfth-century theology. It should be noted, however, that there is some discussion as to whether one can really speak of a 'school' of Laon in this sense: see Macy, op. cit., ch. III, especially p. 75.

51 Paschase, *De corpore* 6 (PL 120, 1282–1283).

52 This view is discussed and rejected by Guitmund, PL 149, 1491–1494.

53 Macy, op. cit., pp. 76, 77, 79 and notes; see also de Lubac, *Corpus mysticum*, pp. 175–82.

54 Augustine, *Treatises on John* 25, 12 (PL 35, 1602).

55 Macy finds it first in a sentence-collection attributed to Anselm of Laon: op. cit., p. 77.

56 The twelfth to the fourteenth centuries were marked by a serious decline in the frequency of holy communion: thus Macy, op. cit., p. 119, citing P. Browe and J. Duhr. P. Gy remarks that, with the exception of Rome, where weekly communion was common until the eighth century, the norm for the average Christian, from the fourth century until St Pius X, was three or four communions a year: *La Maison-Dieu* no. 137 (1979), p. 82. Interesting evidence is also provided by D. Power, *The Eucharistic Mystery* (Dublin: Gill & Macmillan, 1992), pp. 184–7.

57 De Lubac, *Corpus mysticum*, p. 103; see also ch. 5 ibid.

58 Augustine, *The City of God* XXI, 25, 2 (PL 41, 741).

59 See the anonymous *Treatise on the Sacraments* cited by de Lubac, *Corpus mysticum*, p. 287, n. 12.

60 Peter Lombard, *Commentary on First Corinthians* 11, 23–24 (PL 191, 1642A). De Lubac contrasts this with earlier usage: *Corpus mysticum*, pp. 282–3. He also points out that when the first treatise on the Church comes to be written by James of Viterbo in the first years of the fourteenth century, it will be produced without reference to the Eucharist: ibid., p. 131.

61 Macy finds this first in the sentence-collection entitled *Sententie divinitatis* of the mid-twelfth century: op. cit., p. 111; see also pp. 129–30.

62 The theological qualification of this opinion in the writings of the time is studied by H. Jorissen, *Die Entfaltung der Transsubstantiationslehre bis zum Beginn der Hochscholastik* (Münster: Aschendorff, 1965), chapter 2.

63 Various candidates for the honour have been put forward. At the moment the favourite is Master Roland of Bologna in his sentence-collection published before 1150: thus Neunheuser, op. cit., pp. 27–8; also Jorissen, op. cit., p. 7. Some doubt has now been cast on whether this Roland is the Roland Bandinelli who eventually became Pope Alexander III. Other instances of the use of the term in this sense are Gaufried of Poitiers and Pope Innocent III: Jorissen, op. cit., pp. 34–5.

64 For instance, Baldwin of Ford (d. 1190), *Tractatus de sacramento altaris* (SC 93, 148; PL 204, 662B) as found in Jorissen, op. cit., p. 17, n. 24.

65 These diverse concepts are well documented by Jorissen, op. cit., chs 3 and 4.

66 The principal study of this topic is Jorissen, op. cit., ch. 2. This work is then used in a Lutheran perspective by J. F. McCue, 'The doctrine of transubstantiation from Berengar through the Council of Trent' in P. Empie and T. A. Murphy (eds), *Lutherans and Catholics in Dialogue I–III* (Minneapolis: Augsburg, n.d.), pp. 89–124.

67 Jorissen himself cites the work of A. Lang on this issue (op. cit., p. 12), but if his own invaluable work is open to criticism, it is on this very point of judging one period with the clarity of another.

68 Examples to illustrate this point would be theologians like Robert Courson (d. 1219) and Gaufried of Poitiers (d. *c.* 1235) who held that the *forma substantialis*, the *paneitas*, did not change. For the theologians of high Scholasticism this would smack of a denial of substantial change, but that is not so absolutely clear when the issue is viewed according to the notion of form prevailing in the twelfth century.

69 Innocent III, *De sacro altaris mysterio* IV, 44 (PL 217, 885C). Some of Innocent's formulation of this perspective is taken up by Urban IV in his Bull *Transiturus* (1264), by which he established the Feast of Corpus Christi: see P. Gy in J. Doré (ed.), *Sacrements de Jésus-Christ* (Paris: Desclée, 1983), p. 86.

70 Jorissen, op. cit., pp. 34–5, citing *De sacro altaris mysterio* IV, 20 (PL 217, 870C–D).

71 McCue, art. cit., p. 94.

72 In the phrase of this document, 'under the appearances of bread and wine', Aquinas sees expressed the exclusion of the substance of the bread and the wine: 'In decretalem 1a expositio ad archidiaconum tridentinum', *Opuscula omnia*, ed. P. Mandonnet (Paris, 1927), vol. 5, p. 339.

9

⊠ *The Eucharist in Aquinas*

When in 1264 St Thomas Aquinas was invited to draw up the divine office for the Feast of Corpus Christi, it was not only a recognition of the pre-eminent place of the great Dominican among the Eucharistic theologians of the day, but also an acknowledgement of the depths of his devotion. There is even a tradition that on Holy Thursday of that same year he had already been selected to preach before the Papal court on the subject of the sacrament.[1] However that may be, there is certainly in the hymns, readings and antiphons of his office of Corpus Christi a fervour which the reader of the *Summa Theologica* could easily miss:

O most precious and wondrous banquet, bringing us salvation and filled with all goodness! What can be more precious than this feast in which, not the flesh of calves and kids, as in the Old Law, but Christ, the true God, is set before us to be eaten! What can be more wonderful than this sacrament, for in it bread and wine are substantially changed into Christ's body and blood . . . No one can put into words the goodness of this sacrament, in which spiritual sweetness is tasted at its source, and the memory of that all-surpassing love is brought to mind which Christ showed in his passion.[2]

Before writing of Aquinas as theologian of the Eucharist, it is only right to see him first in the role of preacher and man of prayer. For Thomas the Eucharist was never simply a theological problem. Clearly his dedication to expounding its mysteries had its roots in his own personal spirituality and in his deep sense of the role of the Eucharist in the pastoral life of the Church.

Thomas's writing on the Eucharist inevitably comes out of the previous tradition of faith and theology. It is, as de Lubac put it, a very reservoir of the riches of the patristic Church. As for the Middle Ages, there was, first of all, the influence on him of his teacher, Albert the Great. Of Albert's treatise *De corpore Domini*,

Grabmann declared that it was 'a book of great depth of thought and spirituality, ranking as the most beautiful ever written on its sublime subject', and one 'that had an influence on the Eucharistic teaching of German mysticism'.[3]

Thomas is a beneficiary not only of scholastic but of monastic theology. One of those who influenced his teaching on the Eucharist was the saintly and learned Cistercian Baldwin of Ford. It is from him, we are told, that Thomas grew to appreciate the centrality of divine love in the theology of the sacrament.[4] This view fitted easily into the general approach to Eucharistic sacrifice which Thomas, like so many before him, had inherited from St Augustine.

THE EUCHARIST AS SACRIFICE

Up to the time of the Reformation, Church teaching on the Eucharist as sacrifice was never seriously called into question. This meant that reflection on this aspect was much less systematized than that on the great area of Eucharistic theology which had figured in the disputes of the ninth and eleventh centuries. St Thomas is no exception in this. There is no one section of his *Summa* which gives us his total treatment of the matter. It is scattered through a number of places and really pervades his entire treatment of the sacrament.[5] Those who approach him today, expecting to be met with neat definition and comprehensive speculation on this question, will be disappointed. At times it is hard to be sure of the precise import of what he says, and the force of his argument seems to slip through one's fingers. The reason for this, I believe, is symbolism. Thomas held to the sacramental principle in a way that is no longer ours. This principle is the mainspring of his entire thinking on the Eucharistic sacrifice.

First comes his view of the sacrifice of the cross, and inevitably the question it poses as to the nature of sacrifice. For Thomas, as for Augustine, the spiritual sacrifice is the key. Once the inner attitude is one of love, surrender, oblation, then the external act will be in some sense a sacrifice, even if it is only an ordinary act of love and mercy. This approach yields a readily intelligible answer as to how Calvary is a sacrifice. Indeed, for this line of thought, Christ's death is immediately the greatest of all sacrifices, since it embodies the highest instance of the sacrificial attitude ever found in a human heart.

When we come to the Eucharist, its sacrificial nature is plain, once one sees it as the sacramental sign of the cross. For Thomas there is only one sacrifice in the New Law. On Calvary it happened as an historical event on the stage of human history. In the time of the Church that one sacrifice becomes actual from day to day on the stage of the sacraments. The key to this approach is the sacramental principle: sacraments bring about that which they signify.[6] If the Eucharist is the sacramental sign of the sacrifice of the cross, then it must in some sense contain that sacrifice and bring its effects about in our own time.[7]

Is this a way of saying that the Mass is a repetition of Calvary? This charge has been levelled against Catholic doctrine, and it may well be that many of the faithful, especially in the Middle Ages, have actually understood the Mass in that way. But like other theologians of the time, Thomas is at pains to point out that that cannot be so. Christ is not crucified in the Mass. The Mass is the presence of 'the one who suffered', not of the suffering of Christ; that is to say, Christ's death is present, not in all its historical concreteness, but through its effects.[8]

If it is through signifying Christ's sacrifice that the Eucharist brings it about, a final question might be: how does the Eucharist signify the cross? Clearly it does so by the words of consecration, which are all about the cross.[9] But as well as the words, there are the species, and Thomas is one of those who finds a reference to Christ's death in the separation of the species in the sacrament.[10] There is also the breaking of the host, and then the many signs of the cross in the liturgy of the day.[11] There is an interesting statement of Thomas which sees the commemoration of the Passion in the gesture of eating and drinking at holy communion, but this must not be seen to take from the centrality of the consecration in the constitution of the sacrifice.[12]

TRANSUBSTANTIATION

Given this context of Eucharistic sacrifice, we are in a better position to appreciate Thomas's account of transubstantiation. This is a connection which many exponents of his teaching fail to make. It is true that, such is the inner logic of Thomas's complex theory, one can seem to do it justice without referring to sacrifice, but if one leaves out this context, it easily becomes an abstract language-game. For Thomas himself transubstantiation was the unique masterpiece of Christ's sacrificial love.

In his approach to transubstantiation Thomas was of course the beneficiary of those who had gone before him, not just of his own teacher, Albert the Great, but of all those who for two centuries had been grappling with the problems raised by Berengar.[13] We have already described the situation as a search for a level of reality that will be sufficiently spiritual to avoid the literalism of Paschase, and sufficiently objective to avoid the weaknesses associated with Berengar.

The level that was eventually identified was that designated by the term 'substance'. This term had a long history in the exposition of the faith. Originally it was associated with the problems of Christology, but ever since the fifth century it had been used of the Eucharist.[14] In this context it even had a biblical ring to it because of Jerome's phrase 'supersubstantial bread' in his translation of Matthew's version of the Our Father. Clearly the term has had different meanings in accordance with the philosophical sophistication of its users. For Thomas the meaning is metaphysical, not physical, as the following quotation points out:

Substance cannot be seen by the bodily eye, nor is it the object of any sense, nor can it be imagined.[15]

Because this level of being is perceived by the understanding, not by the senses, it avoids a crude Paschasianism. Because its objectivity is that proper to a true affirmation, it is not to be dissolved into a vague symbolism.

Aquinas' response to this issue is a complex piece of technical systematics. It is the kind of thought which is somewhat alien to many people today, not least because the grasp of its presuppositions has been so seriously weakened in recent times. One of the main presuppositions is the faith itself. This kind of thinking comes to us from an age of faith, in which the sense that all things are under the hand of God was part of the air they breathed. Crucial also is the belief that we are talking about Christ in the context of what is sometimes called a high Christology. Transubstantiation makes no sense except where the substance at its heart is that of Christ himself, the God–man, in whom everything is under the dominance of divine personhood and nature. While the effort at systematic presentation seems to state things in the terms of a general philosophy, it must also be borne in mind that in the case of Christ these categories are found in a situation that is altogether unique.

Before examining Thomas's exposition of the matter, one could express it in a less technical way through an analogy. What is at issue is a question of presence. Ordinarily material realities become present to each other through the contact of quantity with quantity (*per modum quantitatis*). In the case of the presence of Christ's body in the Eucharist, though his body is of course a quantity, it is not present in that quantified way. It is present more like the way the soul is present in the body (*per modum substantiae*). This mode of presence is not quantitative but spiritual. For example, the soul is said to be present in each and every part of the body, but if the finger is broken off, one does not break off a part of one's soul. The presence of Christ's body in the Eucharist can be said to be spiritual in a somewhat similar way.[16] In biting the host, I do not bite Christ!

Thomas's more technical account of transubstantiation[17] begins appropriately with the question: How does Christ come to exist in the sacrament in the first place? Is it by local motion, namely by Christ's moving from heaven to earth? Behind this second, seemingly strange, question we can detect the unresolved issue in Augustine about the location of the heavenly Christ. As de Lubac observes, 'For many Augustinians the localization of the body of Christ will constitute for centuries the principal difficulty against sacramental realism'.[18] Thomas however has no difficulty. It is not by local motion, because Christ is not in the Eucharist as in a place. Localization is a matter of the contact of quantity with quantity, but that is not how Christ exists in the sacrament. If Christ does not come to be in the Eucharist by local motion, then it can only be by the change of what is there into himself.

The strangeness of the article in St Thomas from which these ideas are taken is a measure of that gulf between Aquinas and ourselves on which we have just been reflecting. The irony of this is deepened by the fact that this article embodies the fundamental shift in St Thomas's thought on the Eucharist to a plane different to that on which the majority today are thinking. By this article Aquinas is trying to move us out of imaginative categories into intellectual ones. The Eucharistic Change can only be a matter of the understanding, not of the imagination. Since his rejection of the very notion of a localization of Christ within the species is here the key to his postulating a substantial change, by that very fact he has denied any validity to the notion of Christ as present in the species apart from the change of bread and wine into Christ. For Aquinas the existence of Christ in the sacrament is the result of the change, not its prior condition. This is why for him change is as much a part of the faith as presence. It is part of the meaning of the very words of Christ.[19]

By what kind of change, then, does Christ come to exist in the sacrament? The only possibilities Aquinas considers are an ordinary substantial change and a change 'of the total substance'. An ordinary substantial change is one by which a new substantial form is brought about in the material substrate common to starting-point and end-point in any such change. But in the case of the Eucharist this cannot be, since here there is no common substrate, or subject, of the change. Indeed in this case the end-point of the change, which is Christ himself, exists as fully individuated even prior to the change. All that can be said to be common to both starting-point and end-point in the Eucharist is the fact that both realities share in the common nature of being.

Furthermore there is no correlation between the quantity of the bread at the starting-point and the quantity of Christ's physical being at the term. Consequently there can be no question here of educing the substantial form of the term from any material substrate. This unique situation is what Aquinas has in mind when he insists that in the sacrament it is 'the total substance' which is changed, namely substantial form, prime matter and the existential act of being, the *esse*.[20] We can only add that all this is very far from anything which Aristotle ever dreamt of. Apart from revelation, it makes no sense, and that is surely one good reason why the twelfth century coined a special name for it – not 'transformation' but 'transubstantiation'.[21]

What then happens to the accidents of the bread and wine once their entire substantial reality has been changed? Clearly the accidents remain unchanged, as our senses make abundantly manifest, but in a unique situation. Ordinarily accidents inhere in a subject. In this case the previous subject exists no more. Does this mean that the accidents inhere in the substance of Christ? The answer must be negative, since that would expose Christ's body to material change in a way that would contradict his glorified state. Thomas's account of this obscure point maintains that the accidents exist without a subject, but that the accident of quantity acts as a 'quasi-subject' for the rest. Consequently, when I bite the host, it is this 'quasi-subject' which is bitten, not, strictly speaking, the body of Christ.

A question remains about the being of these accidents, including that of the relevant quantity. What maintains them in being? Previously they had been maintained in being by their respective substances. In scholastic philosophy there is a kind of action always exercised by a substance on its accidents, holding them in being. Indeed this activity can be described as a condition of this presence of the substance to the accidents and through them to the world about. What happens in the case of the consecrated species?

Once one reaches this degree of refinement, the person unfamiliar with scholastic philosophy will probably withdraw in despair or derision, but the convinced scholastic presses on relentlessly. For Thomas the role previously exercised by the respective substances is now taken over by the power of God working through the original miracle of transubstantiation.[22] The accidents are maintained in being and activity through the divine action itself. The principal cause is God, but this action is mediated through the substance of Christ into which the previous substances have been changed by the original miracle.

Such is the classical account of transubstantiation. Whatever one might think of its usefulness for the Church, especially today, it remains as an outstanding piece of human reflection and ingenuity. If thought about the structure of matter can issue in something as arcane as Einstein's theory of relativity, then it is hardly surprising that reflection on divine intervention in the material world should challenge our intellects in a comparable way. Generally today people do not get to this point at all, since the basic presuppositions are no longer shared. In the Middle Ages, on the other hand, they were taken for granted, but few could follow them through in the case of the Eucharist with the rigour that marks this achievement of Aquinas.

SUBSEQUENT DISCUSSIONS

The truth of our last remark is borne out by the subsequent history of theology. We must never assume that Aquinas' account of transubstantiation, even though we describe it as 'classical', was the only one in the field. Medieval theology was no monolith, as the following quotation from Congar underlines:

In the second half of the thirteenth century, with perhaps one or two exceptions, all of them thought in Aristotelian terms. But we must beware, and not believe that under this terminology we will really find Aristotle's thought and his conception of things. Under a literary and perhaps psychological unity, the schools preserved a profound diversity in their philosophical thought and their systems of the world . . . The categories of matter and form, of hylemorphic composition, for example, in these different authors cover very different notions, and examples could be multiplied.[23]

If authors differ in their notions of matter and form and being, they will differ in their notion of transubstantiation. This is soon seen to be true in the contrast that emerges between Thomists and Scotists. Thomists follow St Thomas in presenting the doctrine of Eucharistic Change as the meaning of Scripture. Scotists do not see this position as required by the biblical narrative, but they accept it as a requirement of Church teaching, citing in particular the profession of faith of the Fourth Lateran Council.[24] Left to themselves, they would have preferred the position which came to be known as consubstantiation, according to which the bread and wine after the consecration remain in their natural substances but coexist with the body and blood of Christ. Here we find that distinction between presence and change which we already saw emerging with the naïve realism of Berengar.

At first sight this difference looks like a merely incidental dispute among schoolmen, but on closer analysis one finds that the difference is a fundamental one. If Bernard Lonergan is correct, it is ultimately a question of how you understand the real. According to him, the real for Scotus is the already-out-there-now-real of naïve realism, and the act of knowing is understood by Scotus on the analogy of seeing. In such a view the meaning of substance, and so of transubstantiation, is fundamentally different. Metaphysical substance is understood as a kind of paper-thin substance underlying the physical. This is why it can be imagined to be present independently of the question of change. For this school of thought, the emphasis shifts from change to presence, and so one might detect an influence of Scotism, or of its off-shoot, nomina-lism,[25] in the way the term 'Real Presence' eventually entered into usage as the most common language in which the mystery is expressed.[26]

There is one further new development at this time, which points to another significant question. Scotus's appeal to the teaching of Lateran IV on transubstantiation was destined to become a commonplace among his followers. The curious thing is that all through the thirteenth century theologians did not cite this Council in quite this way. This contrast can be explained by the fact that it is only as a result of the work of high scholasticism that the Aristotelian notion of substance came to dominate in the schools. This advance in theology brought a new clarity, not only to the formulation of the dogma, but even to the formulation of the heresy being rejected, eventually destined to be called con-substantiation. To read any significance into the 'silence' of the thirteenth-century Eucharistic theologians about Lateran IV is to project the clarity of a later time into an earlier period.[27]

The division between Thomists and Scotists also affects their approaches to the Eucharistic sacrifice. Central to the Thomist view is the unicity of the sacrifice. Every Mass is the one sacrifice of Christ, in which he remains the immediate and primary offerer. For Scotists, on the other hand, the Mass is 'the sacrifice of the Church'. In this view there are really many sacrifices, and the immediate offerer is the Church, not Christ. In this the Church is acting by deputation from Our Lord, who for Scotists can be described as the mediate offerer of the Mass.[28] For Thomists, of course, the Church also offers the Mass, but mediately and secondarily.

Behind such a contrast a philosophical theology can discern the same influences at work which we have seen already in the case of transubstantiation. The naïve realism which we detected there is the result of a particular interpretation of human knowing which Lonergan describes as conceptualism: 'Conceptualism places conception before understanding and things before their orders.'[29] Thomism puts first the total order within which the individual entities – in our case each Mass – have their meaning. Scotism puts first the individual Masses, which it then draws into a total order by means of the moral causality of 'deputation'. This Scotist approach has certain advantages from the liturgical point of view, but the Thomist approach is a better instrument for dealing with theological difficulties, in particular those raised by the Reformers concerning the uniqueness and sufficiency of the cross.

NOTES

1 An extant text of a sermon for this occasion, *Hodiernae festivitatis*, is acknowledged as authentic by P. Mandonnet and I. T. Eschmann but

rejected by P. Gy, 'L'Office du Corpus Christi et la théologie des accidents eucharistiques', RSPT 66 (1982), pp. 81–6, reference at p. 84, n. 18.

2 Readings 2 and 3 of the office *Sacerdos in aeternum*, still read in part in the current office, *Miserator Dominus*. The authenticity of the attribution of this text to Aquinas is defended by P. Gy, 'L'Office du Corpus Christi et S. Thomas d'Aquin: état d'une recherche', RSPT 64 (1980), pp. 491–507.

3 M. Grabmann, *Der Einfluss Alberts d. Gr. auf das mittelalterliche Geistesleben*, cited by B. Neunheuser, *Eucharistie in Mittelalter und Neuzeit* (Freiburg–Basel–Vienna: Herder, 1963), p. 39.

4 M. Lepin, *L'idée du sacrifice de la Messe d'après les théologiens depuis l'origine jusqu'à nos jours* (Paris: Beauchesne, 1926), p. 160.

5 The principal treatment comes in the Third Part of the *Summa* within the presentation of the Eucharist as sacrament: III, qq. 73ff.; see also III, qq. 22 and 46–50. The subject is also treated in the Second Part, second half, within the treatment of the virtue of religion: II–II, qq. 81ff. Liam Walsh points out, following Lepin, that the post-Tridentine theologians tended to concentrate on the latter treatment and to neglect the former: L. Walsh, *The Sacraments of Initiation* (London: Geoffrey Chapman, 1988), pp. 256–7.

6 ST III, q. 83, a. 1. We might remark how Thomas expresses the sacramental principle for the sacraments of the New Law: *efficiunt quod figurant; simul sunt causae et signa; non solum significant sed causant gratiam* – III, q. 62, a. 1. These expressions, especially the first, seem to me only verbally different from the phrase of the manuals *significando causant*. For another view see D. Power, *The Eucharistic Mystery* (Dublin: Gill & Macmillan, 1992), pp. 233–5.

7 We might notice also how Aquinas has not fallen into the later common severance of sacrament from sacrifice, as when he says *Hoc sacramentum est simul sacrificium et sacramentum*: ST III, q. 79, a. 5, c. The most influential exponent of this sacramental doctrine of sacrifice in modern theology was Anscar Vonier, whose work will be discussed in Chapter 11 below.

8 ST III, q. 22, a. 5, ad 2; cf. III, q. 62, a. 5; q. 73, a. 3, ad 3.

9 ST III, q. 78, a. 2, ad 2. Thomas even finds significance in the verb's being in the indicative and not in the imperative (loc. cit.).

10 ST III, q. 76, a. 2, ad 1. While it is disputed to what extent this notion is scriptural, it is certainly patristic teaching, for instance Gregory of Nazianzen, *Letter* 171 (PG 37, 280).

11 ST III, q. 83, a. 5, ad 7 and 3.

12 ST III, q. 74, a. 1, c. On the constitutive role of the consecration see III, q. 82, a. 10. This last reference should be contrasted with the sequence *oblation – consecration – reception* in III, q. 83, a. 4, c. This sequence is simply a liturgical description, not an assertion that the offering of the sacrifice precedes the consecration of the gifts in principle. The latter is

the view of T. Talley in K. Stevenson (ed.), *Liturgy Reshaped* (London: SPCK, 1982), p. 60.

13 In his book on this topic Gary Macy insists that we must not reduce early scholasticism to being simply 'an incubation period' for the emergence of the classical teaching on transubstantiation: *The Theologies of the Eucharist in the Early Scholastic Period* (Oxford: Clarendon, 1984), p. 2.

14 Probably the first extant instance is in a homily known by its first word, *Magnitudo*, now attributed to the Breton monk Faustus of Riez, but formerly placed among the works of Caesarius of Arles (PL 67, 1052–1056), English text in A. Hamman (ed.), *The Mass* (Staten Island: Alba House, 1967), pp. 233–9.

15 ST III, q. 76, a. 7.

16 Thomas actually applies the term 'spiritual' to the mode of Christ's presence in the Eucharist in ST III, q. 75, a. 1, ad 1 and 4.

17 ST III, q. 75, a. 2.

18 H. de Lubac, *Corpus mysticum: l'eucharistie et l'église au moyen-âge* (Paris: Aubier, 1944), p. 153.

19 See how Aquinas argues from Scripture in the article on transubstantiation, especially from the fact that the form is not '*Hic* est corpus meum': ST III, q. 75, a. 2, c. Unlike the metaphysical account of transubstantiation, the notion of Eucharistic Change is not a mere theologoumenon for Aquinas. In *The Eucharist* (London: Sheed & Ward, 1968), pp. 63–4, Schillebeeckx argues from 'the concrete structure of his treatise' that Thomas deduced change from presence in so far as this article 2 on change in question 75 of the Third Part *follows* on article 1 on presence. In reply I would say that one could also interpret the sequence of topics as simply passing from the more general to the more specific. It is also noteworthy that some of the elements of the discussion of presence in his *Commentary on the Sentences: In IV Sent.* d. 10, aa. 2–4 are moved in the *Summa Theologica* to question 76 of the Third Part, i.e. *after* the exposition of transubstantiation.

20 ST III, q. 75, a. 4, c.

21 P. Gy detects an increasing reserve on the part of Aquinas as regards this term; he prefers to speak of 'substantial conversion'. In his *Commentary on the Sentences* 'transubstantiation' occurs 88 times; in the *Summa* it occurs only four times: *La Maison-Dieu* no. 137 (1979), p. 96, n. 38. Perhaps in his mind the latter term was tainted by its origins in the twelfth-century notion of substance as basically material, but this can only be conjecture.

22 ST III, q. 77, a. 5, c.

23 Y. Congar, *A History of Theology* (New York: Doubleday, 1968), p. 108.

24 DS 802.

25 Nominalism was that movement in late medieval philosophy and theology which tended to treat universal concepts and the natures to which they

refer as mere names (*nomina*). Its presuppositions were widespread among theologians, both Catholic and Protestant, in the sixteenth century.

26 One of the first significant occurrences of the phrase 'real presence' is in the Bull *Transiturus* (1264) of Urban IV establishing the Feast of Corpus Christi for the universal Church. Not only does Aquinas not use the phrase, but he is reluctant even to speak of 'corporal presence'. This is because, strictly speaking, it is the accidents of bread and wine, not the substance of Christ, which are present by quantified contact with a place. Probably for the same reason he avoids the example of contemporaries like Bonaventure in using Matt 28:20 in a Eucharistic sense – to preserve the realism of the accidents of bread and wine, as P. Gy puts it in J. Doré (ed.), *Sacrements de Jésus-Christ* (Paris: Desclée, 1983), p. 77 and p. 100, n. 41.

27 This is the only serious criticism one can make against the invaluable work of Jorissen. In particular one must regret his habit of applying the term 'consubstantiation' to the denial of change, not only in the thirteenth century but even in the twelfth. To import a term from a later time in this fashion inevitably leads to a falsification of horizons.

28 See F. Clark, *Eucharistic Sacrifice and the Reformation* (London: Darton, Longman & Todd, 1960), pp. 249–67, 328–38.

29 B. Lonergan, *Insight* (London: Longmans, 1967), p. 695. The connection between naïve realism and the way the process of abstraction is understood in rational psychology is best explained by Lonergan in his book *Verbum: Word and Idea in Aquinas* (London: Darton, Longman & Todd, 1968).

10

⊠ *The sixteenth century*

With the century of the Reformation we open up some of the saddest pages in our story of the Eucharist. The sacrament of unity now becomes a sign of deep divisions, which have remained in Christianity down to our own day. However, the first step in trying to overcome such wounds is to understand them, and this will be our aim in the chapter now beginning.

Historians will have no difficulty in listing the many abuses which had plagued the Western Church in the preceding century. Liturgy was one of the areas where abuses were rife, and, of course, at the centre of the liturgy was the Mass. A study of these abuses lies outside the scope of this work, but some knowledge of them from established authors is a necessary precondition for appreciating the many legitimate concerns of those seeking change at that time. 'In arguing over doctrine', wrote David Power, 'both sides were simultaneously arguing for a practice or for its abolition.'[1]

Stipends, benefices, Masses for the dead, the vernacular, the chalice for the laity, such issues loomed large in the propaganda of the time in a manner that made it difficult to separate legitimate reform from theological error. One can sometimes seek the right things for the wrong reasons, or, as Newman put it, 'If you attempt at a wrong time what in itself is right, you perhaps become a heretic or a schismatic'.[2] The 'right things' included many of the liturgical reforms for which responsible Catholics were already pressing well before the Council of Trent.[3] The 'wrong reasons' were the theological principles which pitted the Reformers against the tradition.

THE REFORMERS AND THE MASS

The two theological principles which constituted the core of the Reformation were 'Scripture alone' and 'Justification by faith alone'. Of these the second was immediately relevant to the sacrifice of the Mass. The crucial term in the Reformation slogan was that little word 'alone'. 'Justification by faith' was a clear Pauline principle, but when the Reformers added the word 'alone', they meant to exclude all that they would call 'works', namely the whole aspect of human co-operation in the economy of grace. The work of justification, they insisted, is totally a divine work. We can *do* nothing except receive the fruits of what God has done in Christ. In such a context the Mass as offering, since it is something we *do*, becomes a central issue.

The Eucharist, said Luther, 'is something we receive, but a sacrifice is something we offer'.[4] Consequently there is little room for Eucharistic sacrifice in Luther's theology. Where he does accept the term for the Eucharist, it is only in a metaphorical sense, as in the usage in Romans 12:1, or in the sacrifice of praise in Psalm 49(50).[5] The very notion of Eucharistic sacrifice was the epitome of the whole execrated doctrine of works, which probably explains what Dix has called 'the puzzling violence of the Reformers against the Mass'.[6] A sample of that polemic can be found in the following text: 'Yea, I declare that all the brothels (though God has reproved these severely), all manslaughters, murders, thefts and adulteries have wrought less evil than the abomination of the popish mass.'[7]

The same theological stance can be recognized in the milder writings of Melanchthon:

There are two kinds of sacrifice: one is propitiatory sacrifice, that is the work of meriting for others the remission of guilt and eternal punishment, or the work of reconciling God and placating the divine anger on behalf of others, and satisfying for guilt and eternal punishment. The second kind is a sacrifice of thanksgiving, which does not merit the forgiveness of sins nor reconciliation, but is carried out by those already reconciled so that, for the forgiveness of sins already received and for other benefits, we give thanks or acknowledge our debt by this very obedience.[8]

For the Reformers, the active role in redemption is entirely God's, and was carried out on the cross. The propitiatory work which saved us belongs entirely to the past, and that is why for us today worship can only be to receive, not to give. The most we might offer to God is our praise:

Prayer for other people is not as with works. It does not offer to God any work which would pay a price on their behalf, but it only desires to *receive* from God.[9]

Now if the Mass is not a sacrifice, what is it? It is a banquet, the Supper of the Lord, which has no meaning unless the participants go to holy communion. This is the origin of the Reformers' bitter opposition to the notion of a private Mass, which for them meant a Eucharist in which only the priest communicated.[10]

But how is the efficacy of the Lord's Supper to be understood? In Luther's first response to this question the sacrament is seen as a promise, an assurance of salvation, with the elements as 'visible words' bringing home to us the saving message of the cross. In 1520 he put it like this:

For unless we firmly hold that the mass is the promise or testament of Christ, as the words clearly say, we shall lose the whole gospel and all its comfort. Let us permit nothing to prevail against these words – even though an angel from heaven should teach otherwise (Gal 1:8) – for they contain nothing about a work or sacrifice. Moreover, we also have the example of Christ on our side. When he instituted this sacrament and established this testament at the Last Supper, Christ did not offer himself to God the Father, nor did he perform a good work on behalf of others, but, sitting at the table, he set this same testament before each one and proffered to him the sign. Now, the more closely our mass resembles that first mass of all, which Christ performed at the Last Supper, the more Christian it will be.[11]

In this passage there are two points worthy of comment. First of all we should notice the implied separation of the Last Supper from the sacrifice on the following day. Here the Last Supper is interpreted as simply something Christ did there and then for those present. Secondly we should notice how the whole direction of worship is from God to human beings. The aspect of ascent from the human to the divine is mentioned only to be dismissed. This is in line with the remark of the Anglican scholar Gregory Dix on the purpose of religion for the Reformers: religion is 'not for the worship of God but for the comfort of men'.[12] The whole efficacy of the sacraments, said Luther, consists in faith, and not in the doing of a work.[13]

A second approach to the Eucharist among the Reformers, and one which was common among them, was to regard the celebration as a simple commemoration of the sacrifice of the cross. By this we mean a nostalgic evocation of that green hill long ago where Christ had redeemed us once and for all. Behind this approach lay the tradition of medieval piety, which had loved to see the Mass as an allegory of the Passion, but the difference was that for the Reformers all this was simply an exercise of faith on the part of the worshippers, a reassurance of salvation by thinking of the cross. The medieval sense of actuality was denied as implying a pointless repetition of what had happened once and for all.

The Eucharistic Change

The two chief roots of popery, wrote Cranmer, are 'the popish doctrine of transubstantiation' and that of 'the sacrifice and oblation of Christ made by the priest for the salvation of the quick and the dead'.[14] The second of these points we have just seen, and on this there was a general consensus in the new movement. The rejection of transubstantiation was a much more complex issue, and here the Reformers found it much more difficult to agree. 'It is very important', wrote Calvin to Melanchthon, 'that no suspicion of the divisions among us be conveyed to future generations, for it is more ridiculous than anyone can imagine that, after having broken with everyone, we should, ever since the beginning of the Reform, agree so little among ourselves.'[15]

On one aspect of the question there was agreement, namely that in the Eucharist bread remains bread and wine remains wine, but after that their paths diverged. Transubstantiation was rejected by them on two main grounds: firstly, it was considered a medieval invention, and secondly, it was held to be contrary to Scripture, where the sacrament is referred to as 'bread':

Sacred Scripture, in fact, gives us to understand that the bread remains present, since St Paul mentions it when he says ' . . . the bread that we break' (1 Cor 10:16), and again, ' . . . and let him eat of that bread' (1 Cor 11:28) . . . We do not concern ourselves with the sophistical subtlety of transubstantiation, according to which they imagine that the bread and wine lose their substance, and there remains only the appearance and colour of bread, not true bread.[16]

There is an initial attraction about Luther when he speaks as the plain blunt man. He is as impatient with the subtleties of Zwingli and Calvin as he is with those of the medievals. For him the word of Scripture in its obvious sense is enough, and so while dismissing the doctrine of transubstantiation, he holds, through thick and thin, to a true presence of Christ in the sacrament:

Enough for me the following: 'This is my body.' I confess that the body is in heaven. I confess as well that it is in the sacrament. I don't care whether this be against nature as long as it is not against faith.[17]

This is the teaching which is eventually formulated in common Lutheran usage as Christ's being truly present 'in, with and under' the bread and wine.[18]

In rejecting transubstantiation Luther is, to an extent, speaking simply for himself. He considers that it would be 'a superfluous miracle'.[19] He makes a distinction between the fact of Christ's presence and its mode, and maintains that no explanation of its mode can be of obligation; but having rejected the notion of a more philosophical theology, he has set aside the very instrument that might have helped him to see that his own unexamined assumption of a distinction between presence and change itself implies a particular philosophical presupposition which is not beyond question.[20] That there was a large measure of naïve realism built into his position is surely made clear by the following surprising statement:

That in and with the bread the body of Christ is truly partaken of, that accordingly all that takes place actively and passively in the bread takes place actively and passively in the body of Christ, that the latter is distributed, eaten and masticated with the teeth.[21]

Luther however was not always the plain blunt man. Zwingli and Calvin raised objection to his notion of true presence on the good Augustinian principle of the localization of Christ's body in heaven. Luther countered this argument with an appeal to the divine ubiquity: the body of Christ can be everywhere through sharing in the omnipresence of the divine person. This view, which verges on impanation, was rejected by the other main Reformers, because they rejected the notion of the interchange of predicates on which it was based.[22] The theory was never received into the Lutheran confessions of faith.

The other extreme from Luther among the Reformers was the position of the Sacramentarians, Zwingli, Carlstadt and their followers. This was the division highlighted by the famous Colloquy of Marburg (1529), with Luther and Melanchthon on one side, and Zwingli and Oecolampadius on the other. Zwingli insisted that Christ's body, being finite, must exist in a place, and since that can only be in heaven, then there is no true presence of Christ's body in the sacrament. The only meaning of presence he will allow is that of a presence in the soul of believers through their faith. The bread and wine are called 'body' and 'blood' only in so far as they are signs of this presence. His viewpoint is well captured in the following quotation:

When a father of a family must go on a journey, he gives to his wife a ring, on which he has engraved his portrait, and he says to her: 'Here I am, myself, your husband; I am not leaving you at all; even during my absence you will be able to rejoice in me.' This father represents well Our Lord Jesus Christ. In going away He has left to His Church, His spouse, an image of Himself in the sacrament of the Supper.[23]

Calvin's position is an intermediate one between the Lutherans and the Sacramentarians, sometimes referred to as a theory of 'virtual presence'. He shared Zwingli's view about the localization of Christ's body in heaven, 'things severed and removed from one another by the whole space between heaven and earth',[24] but he considered that Zwingli neglected the fact that the bread and wine 'are signs in such a way that the truth is joined with them'.[25] The link between the substance of Christ's flesh and blood and the elements is the power of the Holy Spirit, in virtue of which the bread and wine, much like the water in Baptism, become objectively 'effectual means of grace'.[26] Calvin put it this way: 'We say that Christ descends to us by the outward symbol and by His Spirit, that He may truly quicken our souls by the substance of His flesh and blood.'[27]

There was one other problem between the Catholics and the Reformers in the question of presence which deserves mention, and that is the reservation of the Blessed Sacrament. This custom gave particular offence to the Reformers, not only because it contradicted their insistence on the Eucharist as a banquet, but also because it embodied the Catholic belief in the objective and permanent presence of Christ. Even the notion of reserving the host for the communion of the sick was repugnant to many of them, though not to Luther himself. It implied a meaning of presence outside the context of the word of God in the celebration, and so the view that came to predominate was that of Melanchthon, according to which whatever notion of presence was affirmed of the sacrament was held to be verified only within the context of the actual celebration, and for many that meant only at the moment of reception.[28]

THE COUNCIL OF TRENT

The Catholic response to the difficulties raised by the Reformers eventually took shape in the great Council which gathered in the little town of Trent in the year 1545. It opened with a stirring speech from Cardinal Pole:

Before the tribunal of God's mercy we, the shepherds, should make ourselves responsible for all the evils now burdening the flock of Christ, not in generosity but in justice . . . Let us come to what are called abuses . . . It will be found that it is our ambition, our avarice, our cupidity that have wrought all the evils on the people of God.[29]

These bold and honest words bring home to us that concern for reform in the Church was no monopoly of any one side in the sixteenth-century dispute. They also serve to underline the gravity of the abuses which the Council was called upon to remedy; but such was the confusion of the period, that reform of abuses alone would not be a sufficient answer to the needs of the time. The central task of this Council would be a dogmatic one: to sift the wheat from the chaff in the welter of opinions and theories from which the demands for reform drew their inspiration.

There are five decrees of this Council which deal directly with questions of the Eucharist. They are as follows:

(a) The Decree on the Most Holy Eucharist (11 October 1551)
(b) The Decree on Holy Communion (16 July 1562)
(c) The Decree on the Sacrifice of the Mass (17 September 1562)
(d) The Decree on Abuses in the Celebration of Mass (17 September 1562)
(e) The Decree on the Petition for the Chalice (18 September 1562).

The first three of these will be familiar from the standard collections of Church documents. The fourth one is often neglected, though it contains important indications of the position of the Council. In the fifth decree, which dealt with the discipline to be followed concerning communion in both kinds, the Council declined to decide the matter and left the issue of the chalice for the laity to the discretion of the Pope.[30]

To appreciate these decrees, especially the theological significance of their sequence in time and their division of the material, it is necessary to bear in mind the history of the Council and of how the discussion of these matters fits into the progress of the sessions.

The Council took place in three sets of sessions or periods, in each of which discussion of the Eucharist took place.

In the first period, there was a discussion, in committee and in council, both of a decree 'on the Eucharist', as they put it, and of a decree on the Mass (3 February–31 May 1547). From the beginning these two aspects were separated, reflecting how the sacrament had been approached since medieval times. The views of Luther and the other Reformers were examined through studies of *The Babylonian Captivity of the Church*, the Confession of Augsburg, and the works of Oecolampadius and Zwingli. A document 'on the Eucharist', namely on the aspect of sacramental presence, was approved but never defined. A separate discussion on the Mass as sacrifice of propitiation was begun but then deferred until the consideration of the other sacraments should be completed.

The subject was taken up again in September 1551 and a completely new text for a decree 'on the Eucharist' was drawn up (3 September–11 October 1551). The treatment of holy communion was deferred until they should return to the question of the Mass, but on 11 October 1551 the thirteenth solemn assembly of the Council gathered to define the decree on the Eucharist. There were about 100 members of the Council present, only 50 of them bishops. In the following December they took up again the discussion of the Mass, focusing this time on how the Mass had its efficacy precisely as an application of the cross; but this discussion was never completed, and the Council was soon suspended.

In the third period of the Council, on 6 June 1562, they began with discussion in committee and general assembly on holy communion, with special reference to questions of communion in one kind and the necessity of communion for children. These discussions bore fruit in the 21st plenary session of the Council, on 16 July 1562, when the Decree on Holy Communion was solemnly defined. Three days later they formed two committees, one to deal with the doctrine of the Mass and the other with abuses in its celebration. Completely new texts were drawn up, and, after discussion in committee and council, these led to the two documents on the Mass which we now possess being solemnly passed and defined in the 22nd plenary session on 17 September of that year. On the following day the passing of the decree on the chalice brought the treatment of the Eucharist to a conclusion.

Interpreting the conciliar documents

With these five documents in our hands, the question now arises as to their interpretation. Conciliar hermeneutics is not any more straightforward than the interpretation of Scripture. Two different questions have to be distinguished. Firstly one has to establish the meaning of the texts, trying to approach as closely as possible the mind of the authors who composed them. The second question concerns the force of these documents in today's Church, a question which returns to one of interpreting the mind of the original authors as to the force with which they wished to convey their teaching. Four general principles of hermeneutics will be found useful in trying to answer these questions.

In the first place one should consider the adversaries against which the documents were directed. It is a commonplace of Church history that usually it is only when called on to refute an error that the Magisterium clarifies a point of teaching. Certainly this is true at the Council of Trent, and so a preliminary to interpreting a text of the Council is to know what was being said by those whom the Council wished to confront. This is why this present discussion was preceded by the opening section of this chapter on the teaching of the Reformers.

Secondly, one has to take account of speeches and other statements made during the Council and preserved in the records or 'Acts' of the proceedings. These are an invaluable indication of how the participants actually understood what they were saying and doing. For instance, Cardinal Crescenzi, the Papal Legate, remarked in 1551, 'The Council has enough to do if it wishes to condemn heretics; it is not for it to take sides in the disputes among different schools'.[31] In the context of the Eucharist this would refer to such disputes as those between Thomists and Scotists, for instance on the connection between transubstantiation and the teaching of Scripture.[32]

A third basic principle is clearly that of attention to what the texts say, and to the kind of language in which they are couched. As we will see in a moment, what the documents themselves actually say as to their intention is especially crucial in assessing them. As regards the kind of language used, it is important not to be misled by the systematic style which such documents often assume. Church teaching often draws on philosophical discussion for the sake of clarity in its expression, but that does not mean that it is taking up a position on such a systematic or philosophic plane. As one scholar remarked in another context, 'It is not the task of councils to produce metaphysics, but to serve the Church's proclamation of revelation'.[33] Bernard Lonergan put it well when he made a distinction between systematic and post-systematic language.[34] In fact the Magisterium may sometimes take up a position on a systematic level, if the situation requires it – the teaching of the Council of Constance (1415) on the Eucharist is a case in point – but it must not be concluded as self-evident from the systematic-sounding language of Trent's decree on the Eucharist that the sixteenth-century Council intended a similar approach.

Fourthly there is that question of the force of the documents to which we have already referred. We will be familiar with the well-known premise of the Second Vatican Council which disclaimed all intention to define new doctrine. Can the same thing be said of the Council of Trent? It is the whole situation of the Church at that time which enables us to answer that question. Already we have seen the attitude of the Reformers for whom points of doctrine were central to their dissent. Then there was the feeling of the Catholics of the period that these denials were striking at the very existence of the Church. This is the kind of situation in which nothing less than the highest exercise of the Magisterium and an absolute commitment on the central points at issue would seem to meet the needs of the time.

That this in fact was what occurred is confirmed by reading the introductions to the relevant documents. There we see how the Council felt that things revealed by Christ were in question. What the Church wished to make clear was not just points of philosophy or theology but elements of the truth revealed by Christ, elements central to the ordinary preaching of the faith.[35]

From this it follows that in the Tridentine Magisterium one may expect to find defined doctrine, but this does not mean that everything taught by this Council is on that level. The documents we are concerned with are divided into chapters and canons. While the chapters are a key source for the interpretation of the related canons, it is also clear from the Acts of the Council that the participants understood these two sections to have differing force. Thus Peter de Soto denies the sacrificial nature of the Last Supper, but he accepts that it may be taught in a chapter.[36] The canons are something else, and it is there that one may expect to find solemn definitions of the Church's faith.

At the same time, not everything in the canons is precisely on that level. The primary notion of a canon is that it embodies 'the maximum penalty of the Church'.[37] This penalty is applied to the defence not only of revealed faith, but of points the rejection of which would be understood to endanger that faith. As a result, some of the points in these canons can be clearly matters of ecclesiastical discipline, such as, for instance, the requirement of paschal communion.[38] However, once the issue contained in the canon is seen as a point of revealed doctrine, then to attach to its denial the maximum penalty of the Church is a way of conveying an absolute commitment of the Church to its truth.

From all this there results a better view of the scope of the Council's teaching. The dominant intention is clear. It is not a matter of philosophical refinements or medieval inventions, but to set before Christians the faith revealed by Christ and that which was always taught in the Church of God.[39] This view of the Council's intention will itself become a norm of interpretation for us as we go on to bring out the main points in the documents with which we are concerned.

The Decree on the Eucharist

The first of these documents to be passed by the Council, the *Decree on the Most Holy Eucharist*, took up that aspect of the sacrament which the Council was best equipped to tackle, the theology of Eucharistic presence, which had been scrutinized and debated ever since the disputes of the Middle Ages. This, together with the fact that it was one of the most characteristic points on the agenda of the Reformers, made it an obvious choice for their first response. The document was not intended as a total treatment of the subject, but concentrated on the main questions in dispute. In eight chapters it surveyed the issues, basing the Council's position on an emphatic presentation of Scripture, and leaving no doubt that they felt it was ultimately a matter of divine revelation.

The document concludes with a series of eleven canons, of which the first two are the most important dogmatically. The first of these is clearly directed against the Sacramentarians: the integral Christ is 'contained' in the sacrament. It is noteworthy that both the canons and the chapters in Trent do not use the phrase 'Real Presence', this expression occurring only in the heading to chapter 1. The word *virtute* in this canon is sometimes held to refer to the position of Calvin. This is not totally certain, but if Calvin is not condemned by canon 1, he is certainly condemned by canon 2.

The second canon of this decree is one of the most important statements of the whole Council, both for those times and for today. The position directly in mind is the Lutheran one, and here the Church attaches its maximum penalty to any denial of the substantial change of the bread and wine in the Eucharist. The differences between Luther and the Swiss Reformers were notorious, so that, despite the contrary view of one or two of their number, the members of the Council were clear that the full truth about Eucharistic presence was not sufficiently vindicated by the first canon alone.[40] In this sacrament, presence without change is not enough. It can never be enough to say that Christ is truly present in, with and under the bread and wine. Canon 2 should be read in conjunction with chapter 4 of the same decree, where this teaching is presented as that to which Scripture refers in the Institution Narrative, without specifying how immediately this truth is contained in Scripture – the point in dispute between Thomists and Scotists.

This second canon speaks of 'substance' and of 'transubstantiation'. Does this use of terms mean that the Church here commits itself to a particular philosophy of being? The question has been much discussed in our own day, and good reasons have been brought forward in favour of an affirmative reply. For one thing, there is the precedent of the condemnation of Wyclif by the Council of Constance, where the Magisterium took up a position within a definite philosophical framework.[41] Then there is the fact that when Trent's chapter on the subject comes to explain this canon, it expresses itself in the terms of Aquinas, terms which he certainly would have understood by reference to his own philosophy.[42]

Despite such indications, the majority of scholars today do not accept that this Tridentine definition commits the Church to a particular philosophy. The principal reason for this negative view is the clear intention of the Council not to enter into scholastic disputes but to set forth the ancient faith as revealed by Christ, taught by the Fathers and preached by the Church to all. It is true that its choice of language is coloured by scholastic usage, but to use the expressions of an author such as Aquinas does not mean that one commits oneself to all that the author meant by them.

Though the notion of substance is a pivotal concept in Aristotelian philosophy, there is a looser and vaguer understanding of reality associated with the term.[43] Indeed a certain notion of substance – whatever term, if any, is used – is a prior condition of all human thinking. When water is changed into wine at Cana, some notion of substance is implicit in grasping that event as a miracle. 'Substance' designates the fundamental reality of a thing. It is that in the bread which makes it to be bread, and not flesh nor wood nor stone. In virtue of this pre-philosophical notion of substance, the actual term came to find its place in the Eucharistic tradition from the fifth century on.[44] Another influence was the Vulgate translation of the petition in the Lord's Prayer for *panis supersubstantialis*, which many of the patristic commentaries connected with the Eucharist. We also recall that for Gregory VII the insertion of *substantialiter* into Berengar's text was the key point for ensuring Eucharistic orthodoxy at the Synod of Rome in 1079.[45]

In interpreting the text of Trent there are three possible meanings of the term 'substance' which we need to bear in mind:

(a) 'substance' in the pre-philosophical sense, as explained above;
(b) 'substance' in the metaphysical sense of Aristotle and the scholastics;
(c) physical substance, as understood in contemporary physics.

Clearly Trent was not using the term in the third sense, for on that level there is no change in the Eucharist. Nor was it using it in the second sense, which entered the theology of the Eucharist only in the high Middle Ages. Trent was quite consciously appealing to ancient tradition, as the quotations from the Fathers of the Church in the Acts of the Council show.

That this was the mind of the Council is also borne out by internal evidence. The Introduction to the Decree has already made clear the intention of the Council to speak on the level of faith and tradition. Then there is the interesting fact that nowhere does the text employ the Aristotelian correlative of 'substance' to designate the properties which remain unchanged. It never speaks of 'accidents' but of 'species', appearances, a word which comes from patristic and liturgical tradition. Furthermore some would argue that the phrases 'substance of the body', 'substance of the blood', into which the elements are said to be changed, suggest that body and blood are each conceived as separate substantial realities. This might be the language of common sense, but it does not represent the main line of the Aristotelian tradition.[46]

This pre-philosophical approach to 'substance' also provides the key for interpreting the term 'transubstantiation' in the Council's teaching. The two terms are correlative to each other. Just as we have distinguished at least two different levels on which the term 'substance' can be understood, so must we distinguish two different levels for interpreting transubstantiation. The most obvious level is that of philosophical theology in which the term was first formed, but if one should choose to take the Tridentine text on this level, then one is left with the question: to which of the various interpretations which the term covered in its chequered history is one committed? In particular, is it to the Thomist or to the Scotist view?

One will be saved from such a dilemma if one acknowledges that Trent wished to avoid such choices and took its stand on some pre-philosophical level of meaning; but, in the case of transubstantiation, what could this be? What else if not the notion of the Eucharistic event which we have been calling 'Eucharistic Change' from the beginning of this book? It is true that the term 'transubstantiation' comes from philosophical theology. It is also probably true that the majority at Trent would have invoked Aristotle in their personal speculations on the matter, even though many of these had more a nominalist idea of substance than a strictly Aristotelian one. But in determining the conceptual content to which the Church committed itself at this point, the pastoral intention of the Council, as outlined above, must be held to have predominated over the speculative associations of the term.[47]

As we have seen, the Council wished only to expound the ancient faith revealed by Christ and handed down in previous tradition. The only notion of the Eucharistic event which satisfies such criteria and to which a term like transubstantiation could refer is that which we have all along called 'Eucharistic Change'. To express this belief we do not need Aristotle. It must be possible to put such a familiar part of our faith into words of one or two syllables, and that is precisely what we did on the first occasion when this matter was treated in this book.[48] Consequently it is the whole context of the teaching of the second canon and the different levels of meaning for the term 'transubstantiation' which enable us to say that the point to which we are committed by this canon is not a mere theologoumenon, but an article of the faith.

Finally there is a problem raised by the concluding phrase of the canon, which concerns the aptness of 'transubstantiation' not just as a notion but as a term. To deal with this, we introduce yet another distinction. Meaning is one thing; formulation of meaning is another. On the level of meaning, there are two notions to which the term 'transubstantiation' can refer. The first is the dogmatic notion to which the Church is committed by this second canon – what we have been calling 'Eucharistic Change' all along. The second is the theological notion of the schools, intimately related to a particular philosophy, which many will find helpful, even if it cannot be required of all.

Our dogmatic notion can be named in various ways. Trent chose to call it 'transubstantiation', but all it said was that this term was 'most appropriate'. That is not the language of an absolute commitment. The same notion could be covered by different terms, as patristic usage illustrates. The absolute commitment of Trent in this canon has to be seen to rest on the notion rather than on the term. Given this concluding statement of the canon, this term must always have an honoured place in Catholic thought, but it is not ruled out that in certain circumstances other terms might be used to cover the same dogmatic notion, or even to draw it into a higher synthesis.

One further significant teaching in this decree concerns the permanence of Christ's existence in host and cup until the species are consumed. This point was important as being the basis of devotion to the reserved sacrament, and so its status in Catholic doctrine is clarified in two chapters (nos 5 and 6) and in three canons (nos 4, 6 and 7). The central point of the permanence of Christ's presence is defined in canon 4. Here the Council has Melanchthon principally in mind. Luther, as noted in the preceding section, was exceptional among the Reformers in allowing that communion be brought to the sick without further celebration of a service. However he was as adamantly opposed as the other Reformers to the veneration of the reserved sacrament.

In the period after the Council such veneration was destined to become one of the most public and obvious features to distinguish Catholics from Protestants, and a Catholic church from a Protestant one. The location of the tabernacle on the high altar became general practice only from this time on.[49] Processions of the

Blessed Sacrament, especially on Corpus Christi, became one of the major ways of asserting one's confessional, and at times even one's national, identity.

In this context, then, it is somewhat surprising to find the restrained terms in which Trent treats of the doctrine on which all these later, often flamboyant, demonstrations were based. In chapter 5 of the decree it accepts the point made by the Reformers that this sacrament was instituted in order to be taken in holy communion.[50] This must belong to the primary purpose of the sacrament. However for Trent this purpose does not exclude the secondary one of adoration, just as the Son of God was adored by the angels, the Magi and the apostles.[51] It must be admitted that in the subsequent period this secondary purpose often, in practice, overshadowed the first, an imbalance which the contemporary Magisterium is trying to correct.[52]

The decrees on the Mass

At the centre of the tragedy of the sixteenth century there was the Mass. Like an electrical storm around a mountain-top, the fire and crackle of controversy had descended on what had always been regarded as the most serene and sacred institution in the life of the ordinary Christian. The decree on the abuses in celebrating the Mass gives a good idea of the mood of the Council members. They see themselves as approaching something majestic and awesome – *hoc ipsum tremendum mysterium*, this awesome mystery, is how they put it. They feel that they are like the Lord himself coming to the cleansing of the Temple.

As we mentioned already, the question of the Mass had been under discussion from the beginning of the Council, but on 7 March 1547 Cardinal Cervino, the president of the session, had proposed that its discussion be postponed until after the sacraments had been treated. This delay for purely practical reasons – to lighten an overloaded agenda – had important implications. It reinforced the tendency to separate the treatment of Eucharistic Change from other aspects and to give it a greater prominence. It underlined how the Council did not intend to give a total treatment of the Eucharist, and so it meant that the Mass was dealt with in a rather piecemeal manner.

There is a striking contrast between the way the Council takes up this issue and the way it had taken up that of transubstantiation and associated questions. In the latter case it had a whole tradition of theology to draw on. In this case the relevant theology will be the result of the Council rather than its presupposition. This is yet a further reason why the Council concentrates on rebutting the main difficulties of the Reformers rather than on presenting a satisfying synthesis.[53]

If, as has been pointed out, arguments over doctrine at that time were simultaneously arguments over practice,[54] the principal practice over which they were divided was the offering of Mass 'for the quick and the dead'.[55] The Reformers particularly took exception to the notion that the Mass could benefit people, whether present or absent, who did not participate in the banquet. What was really at issue for the Catholics, of course, was the belief that the Mass is more than a banquet. It is a propitiatory offering calling down God's grace and mercy on all for whom it is offered. The Reformers' polemic against the system of Mass-stipends is well known. Luther, says Power, regarded the private Mass as the fundamental abuse.[56] But with all these attacks the underlying issue was the notion of the Mass as propitiatory sacrifice.

The dogmatic canons on the Mass

Given this situation, it is not surprising that the vindication of the Mass as propitiatory sacrifice is the central point of the whole dogmatic decree on the Mass. The kernel of the Council's teaching on the matter is contained in the first three of the nine canons of the document. In the first of these we are told that in the Mass 'a true and proper sacrifice' is offered to God.[57] The meaning of this sentence is illustrated by considering a question submitted for consideration when the Council resumed the discussion of the Mass in July 1562:

Is the Mass a mere commemoration of the sacrifice carried out in the Supper but not a true sacrifice?[58]

This question shows how 'true sacrifice' was opposed to the notion of a purely subjective memorial of the sacrifice of Christ. By this first canon, therefore, it is defined that the Mass is not simply a calling to mind of something done long ago. The alternative, in the minds of both Catholics and Reformers, was that the Mass is propitiatory. Implicit in canon 1, this point is made explicit and definitive in canon 3.

It is remarkable that, in giving this teaching, the Council never reached an agreed position as to what constitutes sacrifice as such, nor even as to how exactly propitiation works.[59] Nevertheless the Council is clear that the position of the Reformers cannot do justice to the tradition of the Church. From the earliest times the Mass had been an offering for the living and the dead. That is what they mean by propitiatory sacrifice, placing their primary emphasis on its power to obtain mercy and repentance for sinners. In the second chapter of the decree they go some way towards meeting the objections of the Reformers by pointing out that its efficacy can reach only those already disposed by faith and repentance to receive it. The Mass is not magic. Nowhere does the document use the easily misleading phrase *ex opere operato*.

The second canon of the decree raises a number of points which go beyond the precise issue of propitiatory sacrifice. It is one of the rare cases where the Church exercises its prerogative of defining the meaning of a text of Scripture. This touches on a number of delicate issues for the theologian and the exegete.

In facing these issues it is useful to bear in mind a standard point of theological hermeneutics, namely that, in any teaching of Popes or Councils, we are bound by what they say, but not necessarily by the reasons for which they say it. In the case before us, two assumptions of the theologians of Trent are to be noted. First, they take for granted that all priesthood is essentially cultic, so that the cultic powers of offering and consecrating the Eucharist are central to the definition of the sacrament of Orders, as they understood it. This assumption helps explain why the question of priesthood has to be raised at all at this point,[60] but it is not a view of the priesthood to which we are irrevocably committed by this text. A further factor, of course, was that the role of the priest was central to the complex Mass-system which Trent was out to vindicate. The view of priesthood operative in all this would have to be considerably nuanced today in the light of the teaching on Orders in the Second Vatican Council.

Secondly, they assume that Christ actually said these words at the Last Supper. In fact the relevant sentence is found in only two of our four Institution Narratives, and its historicity must remain an open question in contemporary exegesis. However that does not undermine the Tridentine definition. It only helps to determine its scope.[61] The minimum meaning of this definition of Trent is twofold: firstly, that Our Lord's institution of the Eucharist, as referred to in this text of Scripture, implied the institution of the apostles in their role of responsibility for the continuing celebration of the Eucharist; secondly, that it implied the communication to them of whatever priestly powers were needed for such a role. In fact a number of exegetes will agree that the Greek word *poiein* in the phrase 'Do this in memory of me' has as one of its meanings 'appointment to a cultic role'.[62] We should notice, however, that the canon does not require us to hold that all the apostles' powers of ordination are communicated at this point, as Trent itself implies elsewhere (DS 1670). In tradition, Pentecost is also understood as involved in the 'ordination' of the apostles.

The chapters on the Mass

Besides the issue of propitiatory sacrifice, the decree raised a number of other points of some significance. As well as its nine canons, the document comprises nine chapters, of which the first two are of particular interest. In the first of these we have an impressive scriptural presentation of the Mass and the Last Supper, comparable in quality to the Council's masterpiece, the document on justification. We notice in particular the following fine piece of biblical theology brought together by the Council into one eloquent Latin period:

After celebrating the ancient Passover, which the multitude of the children of Israel used to immolate as a memorial of their coming out from Egypt, he established himself as the new Passover, to be immolated by the Church through its priests under visible signs, in order to celebrate the memorial of his own passing from this world to the Father, when he redeemed us by the shedding of his blood, rescued us from the power of darkness and brought us into his kingdom.[63]

One of the hotly debated points in this chapter was whether the Last Supper was to be regarded as a sacrifice. The affirmative view seemed to many to take from the propitiatory function of the cross. The negative view seemed to create a dichotomy between the Last Supper and the sacrifice of the Mass. From the perspective of present-day theology we can interpret this dispute as a conflict between notions of natural sacrifice and sacramental sacrifice, which were not yet fully worked out at that time. Fortunately the Council did not decide the issue in a fundamental way. They were content to teach in the first chapter of the decree that in the Last

Supper Christ offered himself, but they left open how this was related to the other aspects of Christ's sacrifice.[64]

The second chapter dwells on the relationship between the Eucharist and the cross. The theories that would deal with this issue in subsequent times would be legion, but in this text all this speculation is given a basic doctrinal framework. The chapter teaches at once a certain identity and a certain difference between the cross and the Mass. They are the same in so far as in both we have the same Victim, the same Offerer and the same effects. They differ in the manner of offering, Calvary being carried out by Christ individually and that in his own blood, the Eucharist being carried out through the instrumentality of priests and that in an unbloody manner. What is remarkable in this, as in the entire decree, is the way the Council, in avoiding the wrangling of the schools, manages to set out points of doctrine which transcend so much of the controversies of their day as of ours.

Looking back over the documents of the Council on the Eucharist, one can see that the basic thrust of the Council Fathers was for a vindication of the tradition as they knew it. They reinforced the cult of the Blessed Sacrament, which had come to dominate since the Middle Ages, and they defended the Mass as an institution with its system of stipends, its view of the priest and the associated system of benefices. In both cases they grounded practice in a resolute exposition of doctrine. The policy was to draw a clear line between truth and error, but its effect was to make permanent the divide that had already emerged between Catholics and Reformers. This means that, despite real achievements in the doctrinal field, they failed in one of the main tasks of the Council, namely to heal the divisions of Christendom and to win the Reformers back to the old allegiance. The sacrament of the Eucharist, founded for the unity of Christians, would remain one of the main sources of division for the succeeding centuries.

The story of the sixteenth-century dispute is not an encouraging one. Each side so resolutely execrated the positions of its opponents that at first there seems no room for a middle ground; and as long as one remains within the perspective of the sixteenth century, that dilemma remains. It is only when one moves to another viewpoint, such as we can assume today, that things begin to look different. Contemporary ecumenical discussion has set itself the task of getting behind the bristling array of mutual anathemas to explore the misapprehensions of the other side on which the condemnations were based. Through this strategy positions which once seemed to be mutually exclusive begin to seem less so, and a possibility of hope is created which once would have seemed a chimera.[65] The next chapter will include a summary review of the main points of these discussions in so far as they concern the Eucharist.

NOTES

1 D. Power, *The Sacrifice We Offer: The Tridentine Dogma and Its Reinterpretation* (Edinburgh: T. & T. Clark, 1987), p. 29.
2 J. H. Newman, *Letters and Diaries*, vol. XIX (London: Nelson, 1969), p. 179.
3 The humanist Georg Witzel (1501–73) would be an example.
4 J. Dillenberger (ed.), *Martin Luther: Selections from His Writings* (New York: Doubleday, 1961), p. 287.
5 B. Neunheuser, *Eucharistie in Mittelalter und Neuzeit* (Freiburg–Basel–Vienna: Herder, 1963), p. 53.
6 G. Dix, *The Shape of the Liturgy* (Westminster: Dacre Press, 1945), p. 629. Luther does sometimes accept the notion of sacrifice of praise or thanksgiving, but the term 'sacrifice' here is not used in the strict sense of objective offering. It is a metaphorical use of the term, as in the offering of prayers of one kind or another.
7 Luther as cited by Dix, op. cit., p. 634, from *Werke* XV, 773–4.
8 P. Melanchthon, *Loci praecipui theologici, ad editionem Lipsiense A. MDLIX* (Berlin, 1856), p. 112.
9 Ibid., p. 114 (emphasis added).
10 See Power, op. cit., p. 51.
11 M. Luther, *The Babylonian Captivity of the Church*, as translated in *Luther's Works*, vol. 36 (Philadelphia: Fortress, 1959), pp. 51–2.
12 Dix, op. cit., p. 635.
13 *The Babylonian Captivity of the Church*, ed. cit., pp. 65–6.
14 T. Cranmer, *Writings and Disputations Relative to the Sacrament of the Lord's Supper* (The Parker Society; Cambridge: The University Press, 1844), p. 6.
15 Cited by L. Godefroy, DTC, vol. V, col. 1342.
16 Luther, *Articles of Schmalkalde*. This argument from Scripture is found already in Berengar: see J. de Montclos, *Lanfranc et Berenger: la controverse eucharistique du XIe siècle* (Louvain, 1971), pp. 135–7.
17 Luther at the Colloquy of Marburg, cited by P. F. Palmer, *Sacraments and Worship: Liturgy and Doctrinal Development of Baptism, Confirmation and the Eucharist* (London: Longmans, 1957), p. 244.

18 The first usage of the three prepositions together is attributed to Willibald Pirckheimer (1470–1530), as cited in McNeill's edition of Calvin's *Institutes* (London: SCM, 1961), vol. 2, p. 1383, n. 66.

19 The phrase is from a remark in *The Babylonian Captivity of the Church*: *Luther's Works*, vol. 36, p. 29. In his later writings Luther's rejection of transubstantiation becomes more absolute.

20 See the discussion of Berengar in Chapter 8 above.

21 Luther to Melanchthon (1534), cited A. Harnack, *The History of Dogma* (New York: Russell & Russell, 1958), vol. 7, p. 264. Luther, as cited by Harnack, ibid., is the unlikely supporter of the 1059 formula of the oath required of Berengar; for text see also *Luther's Works*, vol. 37 (Philadelphia: Fortress, 1959), pp. 300–1.

22 Luther held for an interchange of predicates between the two natures in Christ. Calvin shared the traditional view which limited such interchange to one between nature and *person*. Though with this view Luther comes close to a theory of impanation, impanation in the strict sense was more the view of Osiander than of Luther.

23 Zwingli, *De vera et falsa religione*, II, as cited by L. Godefroy in DTC, vol. V, col. 1342.

24 Calvin, *Institutes*, IV, 17, 24, p. 1390.

25 Calvin, 'Petit traité sur la Sainte Cène', *Opera selecta* (Munich: Christian Kaiser, 1926), vol. I, p. 529.

26 The phrase is that of the Calvin scholar John Barkley, formerly of Assembly's College, Belfast, in a workshop in the Irish School of Ecumenics. Compare Calvin, 'Petit traité . . . ', *Opera selecta*, vol. I, p. 508.

27 Calvin, *Institutes*, IV, 17, 24, p. 1390. We notice that Calvin is not afraid of the word 'substance', a feature that is a help in ecumenical discussion today with the Reformed tradition.

28 The focusing of the presence on the reception rather than on the consecration is due especially to Calvin and has been called Receptionism. According to Bicknell it was at one time the predominant view in the Church of England: E. J. Bicknell, *A Theological Introduction to the 39 Articles of the Church of England* (London: Longmans, 1961), p. 391.

29 CT, tome IV, part I, pp. 549–50, as cited by P. Hughes, *The Church in Crisis: A History of the Twenty Great Councils* (London: Burns & Oates, 1961), p. 281.

30 Decree dated 18 September 1562: DS 1760. For a commentary on the Council's treatment of this whole question see J. M. Huels, 'Trent and the chalice: forerunner of Vatican II?', *Worship* 56 (1982), pp. 386–400.

31 CT, tome VII, part IV, vol. I, p. 143.

32 The differences between Scotists and Thomists on the Eucharist are outlined in the final section of Chapter 9 above.

33 A. Grillmeier, *Christ in Christian Tradition*, vol. I (Mowbray, 1965), p.486.

34 B. Lonergan, *Method in Theology* (London: Darton, Longman & Todd, 1972), pp. 311–12; also p. 304. See also K. Rahner, *Theological Investigations*, vol. 14 (London: Darton, Longman & Todd, 1976), p. 79.

35 See especially the introduction to the Decree on the Eucharist (DS 1635).

36 CT, tome XIII, vol. I, pp. 730–1.

37 Cardinal Crucis, ibid., tome VI, vol. I, p. 166. Notice also the remark of Alyphius, 'He who dissents from what is established here is a heretic, because when the Church condemns something, the person holding that view is a heretic, *especially* when it is a matter of faith' (my italics): CT, tome VI, vol. I, p. 139.

38 Council of Trent, Decree on the Eucharist, canon 9 (DS 1659).

39 Such phrases will be found in the Introduction to the Decree on the Eucharist (DS 1635). Note also: ' . . . what was always held in the Church of God', ibid., ch. 4 (DS 1642); ' . . . these things to be preached to the faithful', Introduction to the Decree on the Mass (DS 1738).

40 This point is made against E. Schillebeeckx, *The Eucharist* (London: Sheed & Ward, 1968), pp. 44–8, who neglects the significance of the Council's implicit *rejection* of the view of Archbishops Nausea of Vienna and Campeggio of Feltre, who held that canon 2 was sufficiently contained in canon 1: CT, tome VII, vol. I, pp. 188 and 149 respectively.

41 DS 1151–1153: Errors 1–3 of John Wyclif.

42 In the Decree on the Eucharist, chapter 4, we read ' . . . conversionem fieri totius substantiae panis in substantiam corporis Christi . . . ' (DS 1642). In Aquinas we read 'Tota substantia panis convertitur in totam substantiam corporis Christi . . . ' (ST III, q. 75, a. 4, c). One important difference between these two texts is underlined in note 46 below.

43 This is what Bernard Lonergan would call 'the language of common sense'. See *Insight* (London: Longmans, 1967), pp. 176–8; *Method in Theology*, pp. 81–3.

44 As noted in Chapter 9 above, note 14, the earliest witness is in the homily *Magnitudo*, found among the works of St Caesarius of Arles and St Jerome but now attributed to the fifth-century Breton monk Faustus of Riez. Text in English in A. Hamman (ed.), *The Mass* (Staten Island: Alba House, 1967), pp. 233–9. See Rouet de Journel, *Enchiridion patristicum*, n. 2231.

45 Montclos, op. cit. note 16 above, p. 230.

46 Though the wording of ch. 4 of the Decree recalls that of Aquinas in ST III, q. 75, a. 4, one should notice the absence of the word *tota* in the Decree's description of the substance into which the bread and wine are changed. For Aquinas this word is crucial, since there is only one substance in a living being, even a material one. The way the Decree speaks of 'the substance of the body' and of the 'substance of the blood' smacks of a tendency within nominalism to identify substance and quantity, a tendency which would later find fuller and more explicit expression among the theologians influenced by Descartes.

47 'Although the term is of more recent date, the belief and reality (*fides et res*) is nonetheless very ancient', Acts of the Council: CT, tome V, p. 945.
48 See Chapter 4 above.
49 The practice was promoted especially by St Charles Borromeo (1538–84), and also by the Jesuits. It was taken up in the Roman Ritual of 1614 (tit. V, c. 1, n. 5).
50 DS 1643.
51 For these three references the Council cites Heb 1:6; Matt 2:11; Matt 28:17.
52 *De sacra Communione et de cultu mysterii eucharistici extra Missam*, nn. 80–81, *Notitiae* 9 (1973), pp. 317–18.
53 For instance, in ch. 5 of the Decree on the Eucharist (DS 1644), there is a fine statement of the relationship of the Mass to the resurrection which nowhere is integrated into the Council's teaching on propitiatory sacrifice.
54 D. Power, *The Sacrifice We Offer: The Tridentine Dogma and Its Reinterpretation* (Edinburgh: T. & T. Clark, 1987), p. 29.
55 Thirty-Nine Articles, art. 31; see also note 14 above.
56 Power, op. cit., p. 29. By 'private Mass' here was understood a Mass at which only the celebrant took communion.
57 The phrase 'in the Mass' indicates that this propitiatory sacrifice takes place somewhere within the complex of rites known as 'the Mass'. The phrase deliberately leaves undecided questions as to where exactly in the Mass this occurs.
58 CT, tome VIII, p. 719. The reference to the Last Supper in this text is surprising. Power, op. cit. note 54, p. 94, thinks that it is a copyist's error. The version finally incorporated into canon 3 of the decree refers rather to the cross, which was the form in which this point had been previously proposed in the parallel documents of 1547 and 1551: texts in Power, op. cit., pp. 189–90.
59 The discussion on how propitiation works is followed closely by Power, since it is so important for contemporary agreed statements on the Eucharist: op. cit. note 54, pp. 42, 121; 123; 131; 172.
60 A close association in theology between questions of the Eucharist and questions of the priesthood goes back to medieval discussions and controversies such as those at the time of Lateran IV. See Power, *The Eucharistic Mystery* (Dublin: Gill & Macmillan, 1992), pp. 245 and 177–8.
61 For an exegete on this issue, see R. Brown, *The Critical Meaning of the Bible* (London: Geoffrey Chapman, 1981), pp. 40–1. For the meaning of the text itself see X. Léon-Dufour, *Sharing the Eucharistic Bread* (New York: Paulist, 1987), pp. 130–8.
62 E.g., X. Léon-Dufour, *Sharing the Eucharistic Bread*, p. 109.
63 Council of Trent, Decree on the Mass, ch. 1 (DS 1741).
64 Power, *The Sacrifice We Offer*, pp. 105–16.
65 See for instance K. Lehmann and W. Pannenberg (eds), *The Condemna-*

tions of the Reformation Era: Do They Still Divide? (Minneapolis: Fortress, 1990).

11

⊠ *Modern developments*

The period after Trent in the Catholic Church was one of the most energetic and expansionary in its history, but at the centre of all this activity the cult of the Eucharist was an abiding source of stability and strength. Cleansed of the more obvious abuses and tightly controlled by the Holy See, this cult, in Mass and tabernacle, had a place without equal in the hearts of the faithful, but all according to the image of the Eucharist as outlined and structured by the Council Fathers. Sacrament tended to be separated from sacrifice. The Mass, Trent's 'awesome mystery', was isolated from the people as the sacred drama of the sanctuary, too holy to be anything but the preserve of the cultic priesthood. The centre-piece of Catholic piety was the Blessed Sacrament, enthroned on the main altar of the church, like a king in his court. Devotion to both sacrament and sacrifice was pervaded by the sense that these two mysteries identified the people as Catholics and separated them from the Churches of the Reform.

In the theological schools this same division of sacrament from sacrifice was reflected in the way the subject was treated in manual and lecture, and this continued right up to our own time. Concerning the theology of presence, little that was new was said until the middle of the twentieth century. The teaching of the medievals and the firm guidelines of Trent were seen as a sufficient basis on which to ground devotion within the Church and to defend it from criticism from without.

It was really only in the theology of the Mass that there was any movement. Melanchthon had taunted the Catholics that, with all their talk of sacrifice, they had no definition of the notion to offer.[1] This jibe had the effect of galvanizing his opponents. It started a whole line of development in Catholic theology, concentrating on two questions:

(a) What is the definition of sacrifice?
(b) How is this definition verified in the case of the Eucharist?

It is worth recording this approach, if only to explain how Catholic theologians eventually escaped from the dilemmas it created. For one thing, as we saw in Chapter 2 above, it has proved impossible to arrive at one universally accepted definition of sacrifice. But what is more important, it is the whole conceptualist and rationalistic method implicit in such an approach which theology today would wish to set aside. Sacrifice cannot be defined in the abstract. Its meaning is integral to the faith and worship in which it is found, and so it can be defined only *a posteriori*. Calvary is clearly a sacrifice for the New Testament, and for the Christian tradition it is in some sense actual in the Mass. In whatever sense, then, that Calvary was a sacrifice, this must be verified in the case of the Eucharist in a manner dependent on the sacrifice of the cross.

The theology of the Mass, from the post-Tridentine period until recent times, is a series of theories, one after the other, trying at once to answer the difficulties of the Protestants and to draw the points established by Scripture and Tradition into a coherent synthesis. In the twentieth century the two most influential theories were those of Maurice de la Taille and Anscar Vonier.[2] The first of these did theology the great service of helping it establish the oblationist approach to sacrifice, which we have described in Chapter 2 above. The second gave us one of the most influential formulations of the theory of sacramental sacrifice, an approach which grows out of the Thomistic tradition but which began to receive more attention in the twentieth century through the work of a number of scholars, such as L. Billot and O. Casel.

Central to Vonier's thesis was his notion of the world of the sacraments as 'a middle world' between Creator and creation. It is neither nature nor divinity, but partakes of both.[3] 'Sacraments have a mode of their own, a psychology of their own, a grace of their own.'[4] 'Sacraments are not substitutes for anything else, they are their own end and justification. They produce their own grace and produce it in a way entirely different from all other modes of participating in the divine life.'[5] 'Any effort we make in order to cultivate sacramental thoughts will be rewarded with precious fruits in our own spiritual life. It will make us into true mystics.'[6]

In virtue of this distinction of worlds, Vonier makes a sharp distinction between 'natural sacrifice' and 'sacramental sacrifice'. The sacrifices of the Old Law – and even the sacrifice of the cross, unique as it was – all come under the heading of 'natural sacrifice', for they are all human acts, carried out in human circumstances and natural events. The Mass and the Last Supper belong to a different realm altogether. This is why they are not sacrifices additional to that of the cross, nor, strictly speaking, do they complement the cross. The distinction of categories appropriate to natural sacrifice from those appropriate to sacramental sacrifice helps to vindicate the specific nature of the cross as a sacrifice in its own right, independent of Last Supper and Mass.[7]

Such an emphatic statement of the distinctiveness of the sacramental world might cause some problems today, where we are so conscious of the way the sacraments are rooted in the universal patterns of human rituals. However Vonier is here being strictly theological, and the distinctiveness of the sacraments is maintained in virtue of their intrinsic link with salvation history rather than with nature, that is to say, with the incarnation and redemption specifically, and ultimately with the distinctiveness of the supernatural life communicated to us by the Son of God.[8]

In this way a sacrament is at once sign and cause of the divine life within us. It is specific of a sacrament that it must be both sign and cause in one. If it were only sign, it would have nothing to connect it with the power of Christ's death.[9] Consequently it both signifies what it causes and causes what it signifies. Indeed the one aspect is the instrument of the other, so that it causes what it causes precisely by signifying it.[10] This gives us 'the sacramental principle', which is the cornerstone of this entire theory: sacraments effect that which they signify.

For Vonier, as for Aquinas, all the sacraments are implementations of Christ's death on the cross, for all grace is derived from the sacrifice of Christ. Consequently, through faith and sacraments, by which this grace is communicated to us, we are the beneficiaries of the cross of our Saviour. In itself this is enough to constitute the Eucharist as one of the seven sacraments, but it does not bring out that which is specific of the Eucharist as sacrifice. This latter point only emerges when Vonier observes that on the cross, as well as destroying sin, Our Lord was carrying out an act of worship, offering himself as an oblation and victim to God.[11] This is the aspect of the cross which is specifically signified in the Eucharist, and so being signified there, it is caused there, being made an actuality amongst us in the kernel of its reality.[12]

The sacrifice of the Mass, then, rests on an identity between the inward kernel of what happened on Calvary and the inward kernel of the sacramental rite. It does not rest on any change in the person of Christ nor even on any alteration to his body and blood:

> The essence of the sacrifice of the Mass ought to be completely stated . . . The Eucharistic sacrifice is not directly a mystery of Christ's Person, but it is directly a mystery of Christ's body and blood. Christ's body is offered up, Christ's blood is offered up; these are the inward kernel of the external sign in the sacramental rite; and beyond these – the Body and the Blood – the sacrament as sacrament does not go.[13]

The separation of the body and blood is seen by Vonier, following Aquinas, as constituting 'the inward kernel' of the sacramental symbolism, as it was at the heart of the events on the cross:

> Christ's death is Body and Blood separated; we do neither more nor less when we sacrifice at the altar . . . In the mystery of Christ's Body and Blood we must find the essence of the Eucharistic sacrifice.[14]

Quite fortuitously, this approach of Vonier to the Mass has acquired an added significance for reasons that have no direct connection with his theory. As we saw in Chapter 3, one of the great developments in Eucharistic theology in this century has been the growing appreciation of the meaning of 'memory'. We saw then that this perception has revolutionized the approach of scholars, both Catholic and Protestant, to the whole question of Eucharistic sacrifice. Here I would wish simply to underline the similarity between this discovery by exegetes and liturgists and the main lines of Vonier's theory.

Once one compares the two approaches, one can see that Vonier is really saying in a scholastic way what the exegetes are saying in a semitic way. As the sign of the cross, the Eucharist contains the cross. As the memorial of Christ's sacrifice, it in some sense contains that sacrifice. This approach may not answer all our questions, but it does give Vonier's theory a new significance as a scholastic underpinning for contemporary reflection on the Eucharistic memorial, which remains the principal movement of thought on the subject in scholarship today.

CONTEMPORARY THOUGHT ON EUCHARISTIC CHANGE

If the discussion of Eucharistic sacrifice was largely pursued in the tranquillity of scholarly interchange, the same cannot be said of the question of Eucharistic Change, at least in the 1960s. It was all part of the ferment surrounding the Second Vatican Council, when theological issues were widely reported in the media and discussed by the public at large. The Eucharistic Change was one of the major issues in these discussions, not only because of its ecumenical significance, but also because it became symptomatic of the general ferment in theology at that time.

However in Eucharistic theology the issue had been incubating ever since the 1940s. It was no passing fancy, but was arising from fundamental developments in the theological scene, of which three in particular might be mentioned. First of all, there was the patristic revival, which had been gathering pace in Catholic scholarship ever since the First World War. From this came a realization that symbolism was seen rather differently by patristic writers to the way we see it today; this in turn seemed to call for a reassessment of how some traditional positions with regard to the Eucharist were to be presented. These points were one of the elements in the 'New Theology', which was the occasion of the encyclical *Humani generis*, and explain the reference to the Eucharist in that encyclical.[15]

Secondly there were some developments in contemporary physics, which raised questions about how the notion of substance was employed in many formulations of Catholic doctrine. This situation led to a public controversy between F. Selvaggi, Professor of Cosmology at the Gregorian University, and Carlo Colombo of the Catholic Faculty of Milan. The controversy was not of lasting significance, since Colombo had no difficulty in pointing out that science deals with phenomena, and on that level there is no claim that the Eucharist involves a change.

In this context it is not irrelevant to add that the theologian of the Eucharist does not have to decide physical questions on the constitution of bread and wine. Is there a single 'substantial form' in the case of either bread or wine, or are these really conglomerates of different substances? That is a purely physical question. However the ultimate substance or substances in bread or wine be determined, there will always have to be some substantial form or forms, of whatever kind, giving reality to the physical entities, and that is enough for our purposes. From the point of view of metaphysics, physical questions about atoms or molecules are only incidental questions of detail.

The third source of movement in the theology of Eucharistic Change came from contemporary philosophy. With the opening out of Catholic schools to the more existentialist and personalist philosophies of our time, the Aristotelian presuppositions of much of our language on this truth became more and more problematical. Not only the notion of substance, but the very objectivist language in which the truth was traditionally expressed, were found to be a stumbling-block in contemporary communication and research.

What one scholar has called 'the first wave' of the public discussion of the issue was centred in France.[16] In Catholic circles, one of the instigators of the movement was J. de Baciocchi.[17] Among Protestants there was the work of F. Leenhardt and that of M. Thurian.[18] The basic insight of these theologians was the notion that the 'substance' of a thing is ultimately that which it is for the Creator. The role of the creative word of God, as expounded by St Ambrose in the context of the Eucharist, was invoked by them in support of their ideas. Consequently when Our Lord says 'This is my body', by that very fact the creative power of the word reaches down to the ultimate reality of the bread, so that it becomes the instrument of his presence for those who can look beyond the appearances. Empirically there is no change, but existentially the bread and wine are drawn into the one plan of the Creator to address us through these gifts. This is a real change, and Leenhardt even accepted the term 'transubstantiation' as a name for the change.

On the Catholic side terms like 'transfinalization' and 'transignification' had been in circulation privately since the time of the New Theology, but they began to enter into public use only from the end of the 1950s. Thurian went so far as to say that, after the Eucharistic celebration, Christ retains his relationship to the consecrated host, so that this monk of Taizé acknowledged a legitimate place for the reserved sacrament. These ideas formed the background for the important Agreed Statement on the Eucharist issued by Catholic and Reformed theologians at Les Dombes in 1972.

Since it is the contention of this book that an ultimate theological judgement on these new approaches to the Eucharistic

Change has not yet been made, it will be enough here just to make a few comments on the theories we have just described. One of the striking innovations for Catholic theologians in this kind of reflection lay in their being prepared to accept the expression of Protestant Christians as a genuine *locus theologicus*. The shift of emphasis in the work of Leenhardt suggested that with transubstantiation one should not start with its effect on *things*, namely on the bread and wine, but rather see it as a *consequence* of what Christ is doing in the Eucharist.

Those theologians who had reservations about the direction of this way of thinking feared its 'ontological voluntarism', to use a phrase of one of them, Charles Journet. While it is true that things are what God wants them to be, nevertheless the fact remains that he wills to work through the created order. The supernatural builds on the natural. This is why the notion of substance entered in the first place. Some theologians raised the question as to whether the new theories did not mean that the natural was being dissolved into the supernatural and not being allotted its due consistency.

The 'second wave' of the new theories, which developed principally in Holland, brought out into the open that which is the fundamental origin of all this ferment in theology. That ultimate source is philosophical. Ever since the time of Kant, there has been a radical shift in philosophy generally towards the human subject. It is what Bernard Lonergan called the shift from the realm of theory to that of interiority.[19] It has taken some time for this change in the climate of thought to reach Catholic theology, but this is what we have been witnessing in the area of the Eucharist, especially since the 1960s.

'Transignification' and 'transfinalization' are among the new names which have been applied to the Eucharistic Change in the light of this new approach. The first means literally a change of meaning and the second refers to a change of purpose, but one need not make too much of any difference between the two terms, since the meaning is ordinarily seen as part of the purpose of the Eucharistic gifts. At first such neologisms can sound very artificial, but they represent the continuation of a process which we saw already in the patristic Church, where writers coined their own terms in order to do justice to the uniqueness of the sacrament. 'Transignification' and 'transfinalization' are no more improbable as terms than the 'transrhythmization' of Chrysostom and the 'transelementation' of Gregory of Nyssa.

Another lesson from the past in facing the new ideas comes from the history of the term 'transubstantiation'. We saw how this medieval neologism took a whole century before it reached its most authoritative interpretation in the work of Aquinas, covering a number of different meanings on the way. Similarly we are now only at the beginning of the process of trying to think of the Eucharistic Change in the light of interiority. At this stage there is as yet no one accepted meaning of the new terms. Transignification theories are no monolith. Each theologian has to be examined on his or her merits, and probably some will be found acceptable, some not so. It may well take another hundred years before a universally acceptable interpretation of what is meant by transignification will be achieved. Given this limitation, the most one can attempt here is a certain description of the general lines of the new approach and of the pitfalls that go with it.

We live in a human world. As well as the world of the scientist or economist there is the world in which we live our ordinary lives. Things have their reality within a world. The things of the scientist are objects to be classified and analysed. The things of our human world are instruments of living and are enmeshed in levels of reality which the scientist can miss. 'The botanist's plants are not the flowers of the hedgerow; the source which the geographer establishes for a river is not the "springhead in the dale".'[20] This level of reality, then, is found only within a referential totality, of which we in our ordinary living are part.[21]

One of the problems with the traditional language in which the mystery of the Eucharist is expressed is that, rightly or wrongly, it very easily suggests that the bread and wine are being taken as simply physical objects. That there is another way of taking them is suggested by the liturgy itself, when it speaks of what 'earth has given and human hands have made'. Here the bread and wine are seen under the aspect of their human and religious significance, and it is precisely by trying to develop the notion of a change on this level of meaning that contemporary theologians are trying to make progress. Clearly not all are equally successful, and some are more respectful of Church tradition than others.

The risk in this approach is immediately evident. There is the danger that the 'change' does not get beyond the psychic level. To do justice to the teaching of the Church, it will never be enough simply to 'think differently' about the consecrated gifts. That 'thinking differently' must be correlative to a new meaning existing in the things of this world in some objective way. A seashell can become an ash-tray, or a piece of cloth a flag of surrender, without any change in the objects concerned. Though such comparisons have sometimes been used for the Eucharist, they cannot be sufficient. Transignification need not be reduced to such triviality.

At this point I will refrain from giving my own approach to this question, reserving that for the final section of the book. Instead I will go on to refer to Paul VI's encyclical *Mysterium fidei*, which represents the principal reaction of the Magisterium to the new theories. This encyclical appeared while the Second Vatican Council was still in session. The main burden of the encyclical was a word of warning, drawing the attention of theologians to points of doctrine to which the Church was committed. That this was necessary was clear, given the loose way in which some theologians had been approaching the issue in the preceding period. But perhaps the most significant point in the encyclical was the fact that it did not close off the new line of reflection which had been emerging in the schools.[22] Indeed Pope Paul himself uses some of the language of the new approaches in his own presentation of the mystery.[23]

While the encyclical was welcomed by the members of the Council, naturally it was criticized by those theologians who felt themselves condemned by its strictures. Charles Davis, writing at the time in a London newspaper, said that the Pope had failed to understand what the theologians he was criticizing were saying. For most people however the encyclical was a justified exercise by the supreme custodian of the faith of his responsibility for the Church's tradition. Transignification and transfinalization may open up possible lines of reflection for the future, but for Paul VI the dogmatic notion of transubstantiation remains the yardstick of any future developments.

At the same time the encyclical may be seen as theologically quite significant in pointing to a more flexible notion of presence than that generally prevalent in the Church even still. Taking his cue from the Council's Liturgy Constitution, which had been approved by the bishops two years previously, the Holy Father sets the traditional doctrine of Real Presence within the context of liturgical presence generally. He points out that the expression 'real presence' could be misleading, if it were taken to imply that the other modes of presence were not real. There is in fact a whole constellation of ways in which Christ is really present to his people, not only within the liturgy, but also in the life of the Church generally.

To many congregations it still comes as a surprise when you tell them that Christ is really present from the beginning of the Mass, whether there is a tabernacle in the church or not. We have been so used to the tinkling of the consecration-bell as the signal of Christ's coming that we are ill-prepared for this teaching on the manifold modes of his presence. The fundamental reality, through which the problem of distance between Christ and ourselves is overcome, lies in the mystery of the Church itself (cf. Matt 28:20). It is from Christ's presence in the Church that all the other modes of 'real presence' flow. The consequence of this for the understanding of these modes is surprising. It means that any one of these instances of presence, including that of the Eucharistic gifts, does not come about as though the problem to be solved were one of spatial distance. The problem they are designed to meet is one of what we might call moral distance, namely that of the weakness of our response to a presence already there.

In line with this approach the Mass can be described as a mounting mystery of presence, leading up to and away from its central moment where Christ gives himself to the Father under the signs of our gifts. Leading up to that centre we have, first of all, the way Christ is already present from the beginning of the Mass in the congregation gathering in his name. Then there is the way he becomes really present in the reading and preaching of the word. Through the sacrament of Orders he is present in another way in the priest acting in his person. Then we come to the central action of the Mass, where Christ offers himself to the Father and to us. Leading away from that centre we have the celebration of holy communion with Christ present in one way in the host and in another way in the cup, and he is present then in those who receive him at the altar. After the Mass he is present in the sacrament reserved in the tabernacle, and he is present in the people going out from the church. Finally, through these very people and through their Mass together, Christ is more fully present in our world.

In this encyclical the Pope does not develop the implications of this expanded notion of presence, but it is already clear that he has given a valuable lead to teachers and catechists. One of the advantages of this teaching is that it levels down the approach to the great truth that bread and wine become the body and blood of Christ. It, as it were, habituates us to the notion of Christ's being really present; and once he is present, we can expect him to renew among us something like the kind of signs he worked in Cana and at the multiplication of the loaves.

This teaching also sets a valuable headline for the reflections of theologians. Without saying as much, it signals a break with the spatial notion of presence, which has dominated Catholic attitudes in the past. It points rather to a notion of presence as a relationship between persons, for it is only the personal aspect which can make sense of why a single mode of real presence is not enough. Presence as a human reality admits of degrees, and this is why more than one mode of presence is required – to build up an appeal to the varied facets of the person. In Chapter 14 an attempt will be made to develop this more personalist notion of presence.

AGREED STATEMENTS

While discussion of transignification continues among theologians, there is one further area of progress in Eucharistic theology which deserves special mention. It is that of ecumenical agreed statements. Over the past thirty years or so, a number of such statements have been produced through dialogue between various Churches. These discussions grew out of the work of the World Council of Churches, but at a certain point the Roman Catholic Church became officially involved. The statements serve as a kind of mirror of the current state of Eucharistic theology, as well as being an important source of further theological development.

One of the main planks of these discussions has been the contemporary view of Eucharistic memorial described in Chapter 3 above. It was this perception which broke through the impasse created in the sixteenth century, and it has carried the whole discussion of the Eucharist beyond the limits of a purely subjective approach. At a meeting of the Fourth World Conference on Faith and Order in July 1963, this discovery of the scholars entered the arena of inter-Church dialogue, initiating a developing consensus, which reached a certain climax in the Faith and Order Paper accepted in Lima, Peru, in January 1982.[24] This paper is, strictly speaking, not so much an agreed statement between Churches as a description of a developing consensus offered to the Churches for reflection, indicating also areas of disagreement. Its text on the point we are considering reads as follows:

The eucharist is the memorial of the crucified and risen Christ, i.e. the living and effective sign of his sacrifice, accomplished once for all on the cross and still operative on behalf of all humankind. The biblical idea of memorial as applied to the eucharist refers to this present efficacy of God's work when it is celebrated by God's people in a liturgy . . . It is not only a calling to mind of what is past and its significance. It is the Church's effective proclamation of God's mighty acts and promises.[25]

As regards the doctrine of the Eucharistic Change, the various agreed statements manifest a greater diversity. The Lima Statement, reflecting, as it does, so many denominations, tries to steer a middle course:

Christ's mode of presence in the eucharist is unique. Jesus said over the bread and wine of the eucharist: 'This is my body . . . this is my blood . . . ' What Christ declared is true, and this truth is fulfilled every time the eucharist is celebrated. The Church confesses Christ's real, living and active presence in the eucharist. While Christ's real presence in the eucharist does not depend on the faith of the individual, all agree that to discern the body and blood of Christ, faith is required.[26]

The most striking formulation of this truth remains that agreed by Anglicans and Roman Catholics in the Windsor Statement of 1971:

The elements are not mere signs; Christ's body and blood become really present and are really given . . . the bread and wine become the body and blood of Christ by the action of the Holy Spirit, so that in communion we eat the flesh of Christ and drink his blood.[27]

To have reached the point where such statements can be formulated and accepted by inter-denominational groups is in itself a considerable achievement, but the crux of the matter lies in the extent to which these formulations are accepted officially by the various Churches as an adequate expression of their faith. The volumes of official responses to the Lima Statement illustrate in a striking way the gulf between agreed statements and agreed faith.[28]

For the purposes of this book the most important of such responses are those which emanate from the Holy See. There have been official responses both to the Lima Statement and to the statements of the Anglican–Roman Catholic International Commission known as ARCIC I.[29] These responses are too detailed to be described here, but the general position is clear and consistent. The Vatican statements express satisfaction at the degree of progress which has been achieved so far, and they highlight various expressions in the texts where this progress is to be found. But the Vatican documents tend to focus on the two main issues of Eucharistic sacrifice and Eucharistic Change, where, in varying degrees, they end up by finding the texts too ambiguous and so acceptable only as a basis for further dialogue, not as adequate expressions of Catholic faith.

If such a reply is disappointing for many, one should not underestimate the importance of such ongoing dialogue and reflection. One of the ways these agreed statements bear fruit is precisely in helping to change people as they reflect with openness on what others are saying. A study of the documents of the World Council of Churches from Montreal 1963 to Lima 1982 will certainly bear that out.

In the area of the Eucharist the following points for such an ongoing dialogue might be underlined. As regards the Eucharistic sacrifice, while much discussion tends to circle around terms like 'sacrifice' and 'memorial', there remains an underlying issue which is not always addressed. The biblical meaning of memorial has certainly moved the discussion beyond a purely subjective notion of the Eucharistic event, but this idea remains ambivalent as to whether it refers to a purely *downward* movement, or whether it includes an *upward* movement from the Church to God. For the Catholic side in any dialogue, this latter aspect will have to be expressed. This is the importance of the phrase in the Windsor Statement that we 'enter into the movement of his self-offering'. There is nothing similar in the Lima text. As will appear more clearly in Chapter 13 below, the issue here is related to the whole question of justification by faith, so that agreement on the latter point is directly relevant to agreement on the Eucharistic sacrifice.

As regards the existence of Christ in the Eucharistic gifts, the central issue for Catholics will be that of *presence* versus *change*. In this respect also the Windsor Statement represents a striking achievement, though not yet sufficient for the Congregation for the Doctrine of the Faith. Here the Sacred Congregation makes an important point when it refers to the inconsistency between this Anglican–Roman Catholic statement and that between Anglicans and Lutherans of 1972, where the permanence of bread and wine in the Eucharist seems accepted.[30] The Congregation also high-lights the way ARCIC fails to accept the veneration of the reserved sacrament as legitimate. The suggestion is that an agreement on the Eucharist which claims to be 'substantial' would have to include something on this point. In this context the statement of the group of Les Dombes comes closer to the Roman view: 'What is given as the body and blood of Christ remains given as his body and blood and requires to be treated as such.'[31]

The issues of sacrifice and presence, to which we have just referred, are of course the traditional neuralgic points in inter-Church relations on the Eucharist. Before concluding, however, reference should be made to a third area of Eucharistic doctrine, namely that which deals with the effects of the Eucharist. Here agreement is easier to achieve, and here there are some very eloquent formulations of doctrine to be found in these agreed statements. In particular one notes the clear affirmations on the social aspect of the Eucharist, such as that which is made in the Lima Statement. This aspect was the main point which the Second Vatican Council wished to underline in its teaching on this sacrament. In this way one can recognize a certain convergence between the concerns of the Council and those of the theologians of the ecumenical movement.

At this point we have come to the end of the historical section of this book. The story of Eucharistic theology over the centuries, from New Testament times up to our own day, has provided us with a framework for the presentation of evidence and the analysis of the issues. However, as well as the historical way of doing theology, examining the opinions of others, there is also another way. In this the theologian will speak more as an individual, drawing the diverse issues together into a coherent whole and presenting them in a personal synthesis. This will be the approach in the remaining section of this work.[32]

NOTES

1 P. Melanchthon, *Apology for the Confession of Augsburg*, cited by F. Clark, *Eucharistic Sacrifice and the Reformation* (London: Darton, Longman & Todd, 1960), p. 442, n. 21.

2 M. de la Taille, *The Mystery of Faith*, I: *The Sacrifice of Our Lord* (London: Sheed & Ward, 1941); A. Vonier, *A Key to the Doctrine of the Eucharist*

190   *Problems in theology: the Eucharist*

(London: Burns & Oates, 1925). The position of the former will be treated in Chapter 13.

3 Vonier, op. cit., p. 41.
4 Ibid., p. 36.
5 Ibid., p. 38.
6 Ibid., p. 41.
7 The view here expressed is to be contrasted with that of Maurice de la Taille, whose position will be discussed in Chapter 13.
8 Vonier, op. cit., pp. 43 and 18ff.
9 Ibid., p. 31.
10 Ibid., pp. 29–31.
11 Ibid., p. 46, citing Aquinas, ST III, q. 62, a. 5.
12 Ibid., pp. 97ff. See also p. 27.
13 Ibid., p. 111.
14 Ibid., pp. 111–12.
15 DS 3891.
16 L. Ligier, *Il sacramento dell' Eucarestia* (Rome: Gregorian University, 1974), pp. 225–6.
17 J. de Baciocchi, 'Le mystère eucharistique dans les perspectives de la Bible', NRT 77 (1955), pp. 561–80; 'Présence eucharistique et transsubstantiation', *Irénikon* 32 (1959), pp. 139–64.
18 F. Leenhardt, *Ceci est mon corps* (Neuchâtel–Paris: Delachaux & Niestlé, 1955); M. Thurian, *L'Eucharistie: mémorial du Seigneur, sacrifice d'action de grâce et d'intercession* (Paris–Neuchâtel: Delachaux & Niestlé, 1959).
19 B. Lonergan, *Method in Theology* (London: Darton, Longman & Todd, 1972), pp. 81–5.
20 M. Heidegger, *Being and Time* (London: SCM, 1962), p. 100.
21 On 'referential totality' (*Verweisungsganzheit*), see Heidegger, op. cit., p. 99, n. 2.
22 With this we might contrast the attitude of Pius XII in *Humani generis*: DS 3891.
23 Paul VI, AAS 57 (1965), p. 766.
24 For the 1963 statement see P. Rodger and L. Vischer (eds), *The Fourth Conference of Faith and Order* (Faith and Order Paper no. 42; London: SCM, 1964), p. 73. The mode of expression in this 1963 statement for Eucharistic memorial returns in subsequent official texts: for these, see H. McAdoo (ed.), *Modern Eucharistic Agreement* (London: SPCK, 1973), pp. 27, 58, 82, 84.
25 *Baptism Eucharist and Ministry* (Faith and Order Paper no. 111; Geneva: World Council of Churches, 1982), p. 11. We refer to this document below by the letters BEM.
26 BEM, p. 12.
27 McAdoo (ed.), *Modern Eucharistic Agreement*, pp. 28–9.

28 *Churches Respond to BEM: Official Responses to the 'Baptism Eucharist and Ministry' Text*, ed. M. Thurian (several vols; Geneva: World Council of Churches, 1986–).

29 *Churches Respond to BEM*, vol. VI (Faith and Order Paper 144; Geneva: World Council of Churches, 1988), pp. 1–40; SCDF, 'Observations on the Final Report of ARCIC', AAS 74 (1982), pp. 1060–74; 'Rome and Canterbury: the Vatican response to ARCIC', *The Tablet* (7 December 1991), pp. 1521–4.

30 SCDF, AAS 74 (1982), p. 1067, n. 1, citing a passage found in *Anglican–Lutheran International Conversations: The Report of the Conversations 1970–1972 Authorized by the Lambeth Conference and the Lutheran World Federation* (London: SPCK, 1973), pp. 16–17.

31 The 'Les Dombes' Agreed Statement, in McAdoo (ed.), *Modern Eucharistic Agreement*, p. 60.

32 This distinction of methods is inspired by that found in Lonergan, *De Deo trino* (Rome: Gregorian University Press, 1964), vol. II, pp. 33–41, and also by his account of systematics in *Method in Theology*, ch. 13.

Explanatory Section

12

⊠ *Sharing*

For every house there is a key, and, ideally, for every treatise there is an opening chapter which sets the stage for all that is to follow. Here, at the beginning of these personal reflections on the Eucharist, one looks for some concept which will provide a point of entry into the mystery, some commanding idea which, in a sense, will contain within itself all that is to follow.

For such an idea I would like to go back to one of the most ancient terms in our Eucharistic vocabulary. We find it first in St Paul's Greek: *koinōnia*, sharing. Now we break bread in order to share it, so that the notion already contains two aspects within itself, that of giving and that of receiving. In this chapter we will trace this duality through various levels of meaning in the sacrament.

THE BANQUET OF LIFE

When people today begin to ask themselves about the Eucharist, inevitably their minds turn to the night before Our Lord died and to the accounts we have of the institution of the sacrament at the Last Supper. Joachim Jeremias however liked to make the point that we should really begin further back with the meals Our Lord frequently held during his public life with the outcast and sinners.[1] Here I would like to extend the line further still, back into the Old Testament on the one hand, and forward towards the future of the kingdom on the other.

In establishing his worship in a table context, Our Lord was setting it within an ancient biblical tradition, which understood the goal of salvation history under the image of a meal. This thought is suggested already by the gift of manna with which God fed the people in the desert. The prophet Isaiah speaks of the coming of the kingdom under the image of a great banquet. Our Lord himself takes up the image with his many parables about the wedding feast or the festival at the end of time. His own meals with sinners were a way of announcing the same message of the divine offer of universal salvation. He gave the message further emphasis when he fed the multitude at the multiplication of the loaves. Again, after the resurrection, his meals with his disciples have something of the quality of that final banquet.

However we must not think of these meals as referring exclusively to the next life. The plan of salvation which they reveal is saying something about this life also. As an image of God's providence, they remind us of how the Creator wants the whole of creation to participate in the great banquet of life, 'to which all are equally invited by God'[2] – for 'your heavenly Father knows that you have need of all these things' (Matt 6:32).

Seeing this background, it becomes more understandable why Our Lord should turn to the notion of a banquet when he wanted to give shape and form to the central act of worship of Christians. But the reality is not as straightforward as one might at first have supposed. All we have said about the banquet of life is optimistic, positive and consoling, but it leaves something out of account. So far we have been speaking of God's plan for the world and of what it would have been if it depended on him alone. But one of the key points in that plan is that we human beings should play an active part within it. Our co-operation is to be intrinsic to it all, and that is where things begin to fall apart. In the actual course of human history there is the great dislocation of sin. Just as the main cause of famine in today's world is human wars and mismanagement, so the main cause of the imperfections of this world is human selfishness and sin.

Christ's vision of the world, where all human beings are to have their share of the banquet of life, does not come about automatically. There is not only the fact of real hunger and famine, but there is all the injustice and deprivation which manifest the reality of sin. If human beings are to overcome sin and selfishness, a painful process of withdrawal is necessary, withdrawing ourselves from the morass into which human sin has plunged the world. It is precisely because of the pain in such a process that Christ came to lead the way with his sacrifice on the cross. The answer to sin is found on Calvary. Just as Christ's heart was possessed by this vision of the banquet, he realized that it could be purchased only at a price. It is only through self-sacrifice that a new world can be born. It is only in dying to self that we can begin to give reality to the banquet of which Christ dreamed. Not only is there the pain involved in withdrawing ourselves from our personal sinfulness, there is also the necessary struggle against physical and spiritual hunger in the world, so that more and more people can have their share in the banquet of life.

The more we think about it, the clearer it becomes why the celebration of Christian life which Our Lord has left us in the Eucharist comes to us, not in one image, but in two. The Eucharist is not sacrifice alone, nor is it banquet alone. It is both sacrifice and banquet. The Last Supper formed the centre of the great series of salvific meals, in which God's plan for the world was revealed. At that moment, when the events leading to his death were already in train, Our Lord introduced into this line of revelation the element of sacrifice, as the disciples recalled the Passover sacrifice of their ancestors. There is no community without self-denial. There is no resurrection without the cross. There is no banquet without sacrifice. The bread of life is a bread broken for a broken world.

Celebrating a way of life

This duality at the heart of the Eucharist can be approached from another angle. Our Lord had a certain view of how life was to be lived by his followers. One of the most fundamental things he ever said about it was that those who would save their lives must lose them, and that those who lose their lives for Christ's sake will find them (Matt 16:25). This losing of life to find it lies at the heart of what we mean by the Christian way of life. To love is to be unselfish and to give oneself to others. But it is in giving that we receive. The true democracy of Christianity lies here. All that Christianity has to bestow on its followers comes not to those of any particular class or rank in society, nor to those with superior education or large bank accounts, but simply to those who are prepared to be unselfish. For such souls there is a joy and peace in life, a peace which the world cannot give.

There are, therefore, what we might call the two movements of Christian love, a giving and a receiving. They are found in any act of love and unselfishness, and they are the key to the way of life which Our Lord wished his disciples to follow. He himself not only preached this way but practised it, not only throughout his life of love and service, but above all in the events with which his life reached its climax. Christ's death and resurrection are the supreme instance of that losing of life to find life. They are the ultimate model of his way of life.

But these events also constitute 'the paschal mystery'. By this phrase we wish to indicate that they are not simply an heroic paradigm from two thousand years ago. There is a power in these events, which can change our lives here and now, if we let it. These two events together constitute a kind of power-house, a source of energy, flowing into our lives, to enable us to live according to the same pattern. Whenever we Christians love one another, there is present to us something of Our Lord's dying on the cross, helping us to take up the cross of unselfishness. By the same token there is also present something of Our Lord's rising, enabling us to share in the peace and joy which only Christ can give. As a result, the life of a Christian is not only a succession of crosses, which we take up every day; it is also a series of little Easters, as we win through to the graces and benefits of the risen Christ.

It now remains to us to apply this reflection to the Eucharist, since this sacrament is our principal celebration of the Christian way of life. First we might reflect on what it means to celebrate a way of life by considering some examples. Once a year, for instance, during the 70 years of its existence, the Communist state in Russia celebrated a way of life based on force and centralized control, and it did this with a display of military might in Red Square in Moscow. Every so often in Britain the monarch opens Parliament by reading the speech from the throne in the House of Lords. This too is a celebration of a way of life, but in a different key. Here the will of the people and the power of inherited tradition are given expression as central values in that society. In a somewhat similar way the Christian community has been given rituals by Christ and the Church which embody the rather different values on which his community is based. Every week, therefore, our congregations gather together to express and deepen the way of life which we have from Christ. That is one way of explaining what the Eucharist is; but of course it is much more than this, since in our case the founder of the community is part of the celebration, uniting our rituals with those events in his life which are at once the paradigm and the power behind all our living out of his way.

Given the twofold movement of Christian love, it is not surprising that this duality is reflected in the Eucharist itself. First of all it comes out in the very words of the Lord in the Institution Narrative. While these refer predominantly to the death of Christ, they also refer to his resurrection in so far as that death is seen as victorious and issuing in the new covenant and the forgiveness of sins. Then there is the very structure of the rituals Our Lord has left us. Commonly they are broken up into four main parts, reflecting the four original actions of Christ in instituting this sacrament: he took, he blessed, he broke, he gave.[3] This gives us the four parts of the sacrament: the presentation of the gifts, the Eucharistic Prayer, the breaking of the bread, holy communion. Of these the first and the third parts are preparatory to the second and fourth, which thus form the two main sections of the liturgy.

While the death and resurrection of the Lord are present and operative throughout the entire celebration, there is a particular kinship between the offering of Christ's sacrifice and the Eucharistic Prayer on the one hand, and between the resurrection and holy communion on the other. The Eucharist as the actuality of Christ's death and resurrection embodies in this dramatic way not only the two movements of Christian love as they are lived by Christians in their daily lives, but also those two movements as they are found at their zenith in the death and resurrection of the Lord.

The Trinitarian background

It might be thought that, in uncovering the levels of meaning in the Eucharist, one could hardly go deeper than the Lord's paschal mystery. But in fact there is a further level to be explored, without which the picture would not be complete. Our Lord's own life on earth does not contain its full meaning within itself. In coming to understand that life, the early Christians soon found that they had to think in terms of Our Lord's pre-existence and of a life that he led before his Father of which we know next to nothing (John 4:32). From this point of view, Our Lord's earthly existence was but the transposition into time of relationships between Father, Son and Holy Spirit within the Trinity. Schillebeeckx put it well when he wrote: 'The absolute generosity, which the Trinity simply *is*, remains the universally dominant background of the mystery of saving worship in Christ.'[4]

The ancient Eucharistic term 'communion' serves as a useful link between the various levels. The Eucharist is about sharing and communion, not only our communion in the sacrament, but our communion with God and one another in our daily lives. This communion looks back to that communion which Christ shared with his disciples when he was on earth and which he consummated in the events of the paschal mystery; but this in turn has its background and source in the mysterious communion between Father, Son and Holy Spirit, which is part of the very definition of Trinitarian life.

The Father loves the Son and shares his being with him. The Son loves the Father and exists before him in 'perfect active receptivity'.[5] It is in these relationships between the persons of the Trinity that the giving and receiving of created love have their origin. When creation comes out from God and when incarnation and redemption are added to God's gifts, all these are but the overflowing into our world of a Trinitarian love which transcends our understanding and imagination. But in so far as we can discern, all along the line, something of that one pattern of giving and receiving, we can come to regard the Eucharist as the final outreach into our lives of what is the mystery behind the universe. The love, of which the Eucharist is the sacrament, is ultimately the love which God himself is in the mystery of the Trinity.

THE CHURCH

The eternal communion with God, which we have just been considering, is another name for the kingdom of God in its fullness. Oscar Cullmann once remarked that Baptism and Eucharist are for the life of the Church what the miracles were in Our Lord's public life; they are the signs of the presence of that kingdom.[6] For many theologians today the Eucharist is essentially an eschatological sign in the way Cullmann suggested, but to approach it in this way can be done only through another truth, namely that of the Church, since the Church itself is the primary sacrament of the kingdom here below.

Eucharist and Church belong together. There are a number of reasons for this. For one thing, all ritual implies community. A sacrament of love necessarily implies other people. But the basic reason comes out of the way that both mysteries converge on the one goal, that eternal communion with God, which we have just been considering in the previous section. The kingdom of heaven is not only communion with God but communion with one another in God. It is the communion of saints in its fullness, which is another name for the fullness of the Church. Eucharist and Church here below are consequently two different anticipations of the one ultimate reality, and so each in different ways finds its truth in the other. The Eucharist, said de Lubac, is 'the heart of the Church'.[7]

The notion of the coming of God's kingdom is not a straightforward one. Linking kingdom, Church and Eucharist, in the way which has just been indicated, suggests that some of the paradoxes and difficulties associated with the Eucharist have their origin in the tensions and difficulties which attend the Church as the sign of God's kingdom. In one way the kingdom has come about *already* in all the graces of the Christian Church, but in another sense the kingdom has *not yet* come, at least not yet in its fullness. This will happen only at the end of time. In this intermediary period we live in a state of tension between that 'already' and that 'not yet'. On the one hand, therefore, theologians cannot be surprised at the constraints and tensions which seem inseparable from the experience of grace in an imperfect world. On the other hand we must not let this awareness of limitation lead us into underestimating the very real wonders of divine grace which God has put before us in the Church and in the sacraments.

This familiar piece of biblical theology[8] serves as a useful introduction to the section of this chapter in which we broach the ecclesial aspect of the sacrament. The Church really enters into reflection on the Eucharist at two points in particular, as first-fruit of the sacrament and as its presupposition. The Eucharist, as is commonly said today, 'makes the Church', but only if the Church 'makes the Eucharist'.[9] In this section it is the second of these aspects which will be treated, and, as will soon become plain, it is a subject where all that has just been said about tension and constraint will be found to have a special relevance.

Behind what we wish to say in this section lies a particular vision of the Eucharist and of the Church, which I take from one of its earliest exponents, St Ignatius of Antioch. At the heart of this martyr's view of things is the Johannine doctrine that God is *agapē*, love. In the light of this Ignatius sees that the Church is *agapē*.[10] The one reality unites them all. That is the basic insight, and without it much that follows will seem like mere juridicism.

Ignatius is blunt. For him there is no genuine Eucharist apart from the Church, just as there is no genuine Church apart from the hierarchy.[11] It is not so much a matter of law as of the very meaning

of what we do. It is of the very essence of the Eucharist as
sacrament of love, union and community.

Since the implications of what we are saying in this chapter are
practical and often painful, it is good to be clear from the outset
about the spiritual values involved in assigning such a primacy to
the Church in the reality of our celebration. One of the main values
for us here is the sovereignty of grace and our dependence on the
divine initiative in all things. The Eucharist is not the creation of
the human search for the divine. It is a work of God's initiative in
coming to the rescue of a fallen race.

Our dependence on the Church and on its structures, as
manifested in the Eucharist, is a way of saying that we cannot go to
God on our own. Of ourselves we are nothing. This was one of the
issues involved when Luther identified the Mass as a human work.
It is ironic that in rejecting the divine aspect of the Church, Luther
was rejecting the very aspect which would answer his difficulties
about the Mass as a human work. Behind the primacy assigned to
the Church in our celebration lies a profound belief in the Church
as something more than just an organization. It is not just 'the
institutional Church' of so much popular writing, but the Church
as seen by the great saints and mystics, the Church as a mystery of
faith, 'our Catholic Mother', Bride of Christ, Body of Christ. In
the last analysis the Church is Christ for us – the one Christ, the full
Christ, the total Christ, as Augustine put it[12] – and the true
celebrant of the Eucharist is the Church in this plenary and
ultimately mystical sense.[13]

Faith and Baptism

From this primacy of the Church in the Eucharist, certain
practical consequences follow. First of all there is the question of
membership of the Church by faith and Baptism as a condition of
participation. Throughout the history of the sacrament, admission
to the Eucharist has never been indiscriminate. Already John 6
implies that the Eucharist is for believers. St Paul wished to refuse
the sacrament to those who do not examine themselves and discern
the body (1 Cor 11:28–32). The *Didache* withholds it from the
unreconciled.[14] According to St Justin it is only for those who
believe, have been baptized and live according to the gospel.[15]

This juridical fact is suggested by the symbolism of the
sacraments themselves. Baptism is compared to a tomb, or to a

womb.[16] It is that from which new life proceeds. The Eucharist is nourishment for helping us to grow; but before life can grow, it must first be given. One does not feed a corpse; and so Baptism, and its gift of faith, must first cause us to be, before the Eucharist, by its gift of love, can cause us to grow. The Eucharist, therefore, presupposes Baptism and baptismal union in faith, if it is to bestow on us its own specific gift of a deeper union in love.

Of crucial importance here is the way the Eucharist, like all the sacraments, presupposes faith. All the sacraments, said the Second Vatican Council, are sacraments of faith, that is to say, they embody and deepen a human and religious meaning.[17] To separate ritual from meaning is to reduce it to magic. This general truth of our sacramental teaching is the context within which to approach the difficult question of intercommunion. All Church documents on this subject insist on the role of faith in the celebration of the Eucharist. What is at issue is union in faith generally, as well as union in one's belief as to the meaning of the Eucharist in particular.

This sacrament is our highest expression of union in the means of salvation. We have none higher or more solemn, and so this is one reason why it has always been taken as the primary celebration of ecclesial union. The point is significant enough to establish the norm in matters of intercommunion, though it does not exclude some exceptions in particular circumstances, as outlined in the relevant documents. The Eucharist is *the* sign of full ecclesial union. To make it an expression of a union less than this is to falsify the sign. It separates ritual from meaning and upsets the priority of faith over worship.

It is difficult for us in our individualistic age to appreciate the depth of what is involved in the issue we are discussing. To us it can easily seem mere juridicism, whereas to the tradition of the Church there is here a great mystery. It is something of importance not only for theology but also for spirituality. The nuptial aspect of the Eucharist is not something we can easily speak of, but in the tradition of the Church the Eucharist is compared to matrimony in that both are signs of the one profound and mysterious reality, the union between Christ and his Church.[18] The Eucharistic Banquet is the marriage-supper of the Lamb, as the original context of the familiar words before communion imply: 'Happy are those who are called to his supper' (Rev 19:9). In the case of either sacrament one can falsify the sign by anticipating the union in a sinful way.

The sacrament of Orders

There is a further consequence of the primacy of the Church in our Eucharist which it would be helpful to reflect on at this point. The Eucharist presupposes, not only faith and Baptism, but the sacrament of Orders as well. The New Testament, it is true, manifests no great concern to specify who presides over the Eucharist, but one writer summed up the results of the research of recent decades into the approach of the pre-Nicene period as follows:

It falls to those who preside over the building of the Church to preside over the sacraments which, for their part, build the Church. There are exceptions, but they serve only to confirm the general rule, because they are rare and have had no succession.[19]

It is a constant in the practice of the Church, East and West, that the Eucharist must always be presided over by a validly ordained priest. Once again, this requirement of the Church will seem like mere juridicism if it is not seen to be rooted in the very meaning of the sacrament. The Second Vatican Council suggests a helpful approach to this matter when it speaks of the priest as a sign of Christ the Head.[20] This view of the priesthood is sometimes used as a way of making intelligible the entire vocation of the ordained priesthood within the Christian community. One might have reservations about the appropriateness of such a theology, but the usefulness of the idea to throw light on the distinctive *Eucharistic* role of the priest is another matter.[21]

The priest as sign of Christ the Head is the link with the whole Church in time and space. Without him, the congregation remains simply a local assembly, but with him, congregation and celebrant form one organic sign of the whole Christ, Head and members, one priestly people with Christ at its head. It is true that, in one sense, all are priests, for all worship and intercede and 'offer to God the Father the divine Victim',[22] but not all do so in the same way. 'Each in his own place', said Clement of Rome long ago.[23] The priest alone consecrates and only he offers the sacrifice *in the person of Christ*.[24] At the same time, the people present are offering also, not only spiritually in their hearts but also by their active participation in the one organically united liturgy of offering. This Eucharistic assembly is the body of Christ in this place, and it is only the body of Christ, Head and members, which offers the Mass.

Once again we see here at work factors described in a previous point. The requirement of the duly ordained priest will be regarded as a purely juridical detail if it is not seen to express a fundamental spiritual value in our worship. Our dependence on the ordained is an expression of our dependence on Christ himself. Eucharistic worship, though it has roots in human worship generally, is God's gift to human incapacity. The Mass is part of the New Jerusalem descending from on high, as the Roman Canon illustrates so strikingly. It is not something bubbling up 'from below'. It is not natural worship but revealed worship. In this way the priest is a sign to the Eucharistic community of its own divine origin.[25]

NOTES

1 J. Jeremias, *New Testament Theology*, vol. I (London: SCM, 1971), pp. 289–90.

2 John Paul II, ' . . . in the banquet of life, to which all are equally invited by God, we should make "the other" a sharer on a par with ourselves': *Sollicitudo rei socialis* 39: AAS 80 (1988), p. 567.

3 This 'four-action' view of the Eucharist goes back to Gregory Dix, *The Shape of the Liturgy* (Westminster: Dacre Press, 1945), pp. 48–50.

4 E. Schillebeeckx, *Christ the Sacrament of the Encounter with God* (London: Sheed & Ward, 1963), p. 46.

5 Schillebeeckx, ibid., p. 33.

6 O. Cullmann, *Early Christian Worship* (London: SCM, 1953), p. 118.

7 H. de Lubac, *The Splendour of the Church* (London: Sheed & Ward, 1956), p. 87 (title of ch. 6), but in de Lubac the focus is more immediately christological than eschatological: see P. McPartlan, 'Eucharist and Church: the contribution of Henri de Lubac', *The Month* 259 (1988), pp. 847–59.

8 This goes back to Oscar Cullmann, *Christ and Time* (London: SCM, 1965), part I, ch. 5.

9 These expressions are de Lubac's way of summing up his researches into the ancient sources on the point: *The Splendour of the Church*, pp. 92 and 106; also *Corpus mysticum* (Paris: Aubier, 1944), pp. 103, 299. See P. McPartlan, *The Eucharist Makes the Church: Henri de Lubac and John Zizioulas in Dialogue* (Edinburgh: T. & T. Clark, 1993).

10 That God is love is stated in 1 John 4:8, 16; for the Church as *agapē*, see Ignatius, Inscription of his *Letter to the Romans* (RJ 52); for the Eucharist as *agapē*, see his *Letter to the Romans* 7 (PG 5, 693B).

11 Ignatius, *Letter to the Smyrnaeans* 8 (PG 5, 713; RJ 65).

12 Augustine, *On the Merits of Sinners* I, 1, 36, 60 (PL 44, 145). The phrase 'Our Catholic Mother' is also from Augustine: *Sermon* 46, 18 (PL 38, 280).

13 'Every Mass is the celebration of that sacrament by which the Church lives and grows continuously and in which its own nature is especially manifested. For this reason it is, more than any of the other liturgical actions, an action of the entire people of God, hierarchically organized and acting hierarchically': SCR, 'Ecclesiae semper' in A. Flannery (ed.), *Vatican II: Conciliar and Post-Conciliar Documents* (New York: Costello, 1975), p. 58.

14 *Didache* 14, 2 (RJ 8).

15 Justin, I *Apology* 66, 1 (PG 6, 428; RJ 128).

16 Thus the *Mystagogical Catecheses* attributed to St Cyril of Jerusalem: *Cat.* 2, 4–6 (PG 33, 1079–1082).

17 Vatican II, *Sacrosanctum concilium*, art. 59.

18 Aquinas, ST III, q. 65, a. 3.

19 My translation from L. M. Chauvet, *Du symbolique au symbole* (Paris: Cerf, 1979), p. 137.

20 Vatican II, *Presbyterorum ordinis* 2; 6; 12; *Lumen gentium* 28.

21 There is, of course, much more to be said about the place of the Eucharist in the theology of Orders than is attempted here. In this section only the bare minimum required for a generally acceptable theology of the Eucharist is given. For a discussion of some unresolved issues concerning Eucharist and Orders one might turn to P. McPartlan, 'Eucharistic ecclesiology', *One in Christ* 22 (1986), pp. 314–31.

22 Vatican II, *Presbyterorum ordinis* 5.

23 Clement of Rome, *First Letter to the Corinthians* 41 (PG 1, 289A).

24 John Paul II, *Dominicae coenae* 8: AAS 72 (1980), pp. 128–9.

25 This point about our worship being 'from above' and not 'from below' is the same issue as that involved in what at first seems to be the unrelated question of the matter of the Eucharist, namely why it has to be bread and wine and not, for instance, ice-cream and Coca-Cola. It is also involved in the vexed question of whether the ordination of women is at the choice of the Church. The point being made may not decide these vexed questions, but it does put us on our guard that there may be more at stake in them than mere questions of human convention.

13

⊠ *The Eucharistic sacrifice*

At the centre of every Eucharist stands the cross. This truth, reflected as much in art and architecture as in theology, remains one of the key facts about the Mass which keeps coming back to disturb our understanding and even our complacency. It would be so much easier if the Eucharist were simply a kind of party celebrating the resurrection, but at the centre of the celebration there remain the broken body and the blood poured out, and these keep calling us back to the sacrifice of the cross.

CROSS AND EUCHARIST

The Mass is the same sacrifice as that of the cross, though offered in a different manner. We have already seen the formation of that expression of the doctrine at the Council of Trent. Vatican II taught the same mysterious truth in a more congenial fashion:

At the Last Supper, on the night when he was betrayed, our Saviour instituted the Eucharistic Sacrifice of His Body and Blood. He did this in order to perpetuate the sacrifice of the Cross throughout the centuries until He should come again.[1]

To throw more light on that identity between the Eucharist and the cross is the purpose of this section of the chapter.

The issue is one about time, how the walls dividing the centuries seem to fall aside, and the past becomes actual in the present. Of course this is not our ordinary way of thinking about time, but it is not uncommon in human religion generally. There is a distinction to be made, said Eliade, between liturgical time and ordinary time. Ordinary time marks the relentless rhythm of ordinary experience as the future rushes into the past. Liturgical time is not a matter of ordinary experience, since God is explicitly part of it, and something of his transcendence passes into our worship. Liturgical time is 'the time that floweth not', the indestructible time, the eternal present that is indefinitely recoverable.[2] The human being, caught up in the inexorable movement of ordinary experience, has need to plunge periodically into this liturgical time.

Sometimes in this matter our theologians can be as much a hindrance as a help. They come too quickly on the scene with their complicated speculations, necessary as these are in the long run. Is it not simpler to begin with the observation of the anthropologist that a certain transcendence of liturgy over time is only to be expected in the world of human religion? This helps us in approaching Jewish ritual memorial also, where the roots of Eucharistic *anamnesis* lie. Of course, in the Old Testament the notion was overlaid with specifically Jewish ideas of time, history and salvation, and in Late Judaism this moved even further from our ordinary patterns of thought with the contribution of apocalyptic.[3] Consequently, in approaching the Eucharistic memorial, we have to bear in mind that it comes to us from a world very different to that of our own rationalistic prejudices.

However the need to press on into a more searching theological analysis soon becomes apparent once one considers some of the questions which theologians wish to ask.[4] One might start from the notion of *anamnesis*, or memory/memorial, which we have just mentioned. This category has been explained in Chapter 3 above, and it carries us a certain distance in grappling with the issue, but ultimately it remains somewhat imprecise. What kind of an identity between the cross and the Eucharist is being asserted? Does *anamnesis* imply a repetition of the cross in the Mass, even a bloodless repetition? Does it involve a presence across time of Christ in his sufferings, i.e. not only of the *Christus passus*, as Aquinas always phrased it, but of the *Christus patiens*?[5] The category of *anamnesis* undoubtedly gives us a scriptural basis for our reflections, but in itself it does not answer our questions with an adequate theological density.

A common approach in the middle decades of the twentieth century was that stemming from Maurice de la Taille. This view was worked out before the appreciation of the biblical notion of *anamnesis* became widespread. It centres on the idea that to offer the victim of Calvary is to offer Calvary. Calvary was the immolation of the offered victim, and the Mass is the offering of the immolated victim. While this approach can still be useful catechetically, it remains insufficient as a comprehensive theological explanation. It locates the union of Eucharist and cross in the identity of what is offered rather than in the act of offering, and it scarcely does justice to the notion of sacramentality in the way it relates the Last Supper to the cross as but parts of one total event. Rather must we say that, as the Mass is an integral sign of the cross, so too was the Last Supper.

Another contribution of French theology was that of M. Lepin, *L'idée du sacrifice de la Messe* (Paris, 1926). It is one of the clearest instances of a theory of the Mass focused on Christ's mediation in heaven. French spirituality has always stressed the aspect of *abandon*, surrender. Writing in this tradition, Lepin pointed out how Christ's sacrificial will continues in heaven. This then is what is made present in the Mass and constitutes the union between it and the work of Christ. While such an emphasis on the heavenly 'sacrifice' fits in well with Eastern liturgy, it does not account for the constant reference of the Eucharistic tradition to the cross, especially in the West. This emphasis goes right back to the Institution Narrative itself, where the words of Christ give much more weight to the death of Christ than to the resurrection. As Karl Rahner put it in one place: 'In the Eucharist it is the death of the Lord that is to be proclaimed, for it is only through this that life is brought to the world.'[6] In particular, Lepin's approach can scarcely provide a basis for the aspect of merit in the Eucharistic offering, since, as theology has always held, Christ does not merit in heaven.[7]

A parallel difficulty attaches to the approach in Schillebeeckx's book *Christ the Sacrament of the Encounter with God* (London, 1963). Here the emphasis shifts from the risen humanity to the timeless divinity in so far as all of Christ's acts, whether on the cross or in the Mass, are acts of a divine person. While this must be an aspect of the explanation, it is still incomplete, since it does not give enough place to Christ's humanity. In the tradition it is what Christ did in his humanity on the cross which is understood to be present in the Mass.

The theory of Abbot Vonier has been outlined in a previous chapter.[8] The sacramental principle, as put forward by Dom Anscar, seems to the present writer to provide the most satisfactory basis for a theological explanation of the unity of the Eucharist and the cross. One criticism, however, which could be mounted against this view is that it concentrates overmuch on the ritualistic aspect; contemporary concerns would wish to make more of the meaning of ritual in relation to ordinary living and to our responsibility for contemporary history. In what follows I intend to face up to this criticism, while holding to the essence of Vonier's approach.

The sacrifice of Christ is an actuality of daily life before it is an actuality in the Mass. 'The passion of Christ', said St Leo, 'goes on until the end of the world; it is he who suffers in and with all who bear adversity.'[9] The death and resurrection of the Lord are not just crucial events in our past; they are the watershed of a whole current of life and energy flowing through all of our history. In the mystery of the body of Christ, wherever Christians rise above themselves, losing life to find life, there the mystery of Christ's dying and rising is working itself out in the daily dying and rising of his members.

This is the reality which the mystery of the Mass is called to celebrate and deepen. As the manifestation of what Christian life is, the Mass concentrates into a unique ritual moment the reality of our daily living. Such an approach helps to make it more understandable that the presence of Christ's paschal mystery, which so pervades our daily lives, should come to a high point when the Church gathers in Eucharistic worship.

This viewpoint also helps to highlight our love, our dying to self, our 'losing life', as the point of entry of the paschal mystery into our world. To accept this pattern into our lives is to offer ourselves to God, so that in this way the oblationary aspect is clearly the crucial link between the cross, our daily lives and the Eucharist. The Eucharist does not make present all aspects of the sacrifice of the cross equally. The Mass is not the crucifixion of Christ.[10] Its symbolism centres ultimately on what Christ *did* on the cross rather than on what was done to him. What he did was to offer himself out of love for the Father and for us, and by that means, as Aquinas put it, he initiated the rite of the Christian religion.[11] This self-offering in freedom is the kernel of what happened in his sacrifice, and it is this more than anything else which is made present in the Mass. The self-offering of Christ becomes actual in the self-offering which runs through the life of Christians, and the Eucharist expresses, celebrates and deepens the union of the two. 'The Eucharist', said Aquinas, 'is the sacrament of the Passion of Christ, in so far as the human being is perfected by being united with the Christ who suffered.'[12]

The Mass, then, might be described as a three-point mystery. It draws into one the cross of Christ, our daily lives and the Eucharist. But a philosophical mind might still be looking for clarity as to what holds it all together. In one way, it is the divinity of Christ, which draws us all into the unity of his body. But the humanity of Christ is an essential part of it also, beginning with what Christ did and suffered on the cross.

It is a question of presence, and as we will see again in the next chapter, presence is a function of action. Presence is ultimately the presence of a cause in its effect.[13] By his activity in the flesh, and especially by what he did on the cross, Christ established a whole history flowing from his acts, an unbroken series of cause and effect reaching down through the centuries 'until he come' (1 Cor 11:26). In this series the activities of Christ are present, especially when they are highlighted and celebrated by his Church. The indefectibility of the Church is part of it, as is the continuity of the priesthood. It is all part of one divine plan by which the divinity and humanity of Christ are at work theandrically to unite us to him and him to us. The causal series in history is the human substrate through which the divine plan becomes incarnate in our world.

There are therefore three elements which help to throw light on the unity between the Eucharist and the cross. The first is the notion of a Jewish ritual memorial, which emerges from the New Testament as the scriptural basis for theological reflection. The second is the idea of a sacramental sacrifice, such as it has been explained by Anscar Vonier, giving a scholastic underpinning to the scriptural notion. Thirdly there is the metaphysics of presence by which the series of cause and effect down through history is supported, not simply by the present activity of the divinity, but by this as working through the historical influences issuing from the humanity of Christ on the cross. These three aspects, when drawn into the unity of a single viewpoint, provide some understanding of the unity of the Eucharist and the cross.

Finally in this section I would like to draw attention to the order of treatment between this section and the next. In an explanatory approach it is necessary to deal first with the question of the unity between the Eucharist and the cross, before going on to the issue of Eucharistic sacrifice. The latter doctrine is more properly seen as derived from the former, rather than vice versa, as is commonly held.

THE EUCHARIST AS SACRIFICE

Like most of the great religions of humanity, Christianity is a sacrificing religion. Such is the legacy of faith bequeathed to us by the ancient Church, East and West, rejected only in recent centuries by the Protestant tradition; yet it is a truth with which many, not only Protestants, are uncomfortable today. In contemporary sophisticated societies, talk of sacrifice can easily seem primitive and alien. One wonders how many people in our Eucharistic congregations really intend to *sacrifice*. The issue, of course, is how sacrifice is to be understood, and that is the subject of this section.

We can readily grant that in the history of human religion sacrifice has often been a crude and brutish ritual. Sometimes it may even have been associated with magic, orgy and other deviant forms of worship. But this does not mean that the notion is beyond redemption. Sacrifice has also been the vehicle of some of humanity's noblest instincts before God. In the Old Testament we see the notion of sacrifice undergoing a gradual purification. When at last the term is used in the New Testament, it has travelled a long way, through many dubious ideas about God and religion, until finally it comes to the cross, where alone it receives its true significance in Our Lord's enactment of what it means to be a person for others under God.[14]

In this way the primary meaning of sacrifice for Christians points to the cross. That is why we first considered the union between the Eucharist and the cross in the previous section. As was remarked there, the sacrificial nature of the Eucharist is the consequence of that union rather than its premiss. Sacrifice as studied in comparative religion is based primarily on nature, as human beings express in ritual an inward sacrificial attitude. Eucharistic sacrifice, on the other hand, is primarily an expression of history rather than of nature, of an historical event rather than simply of the worshipper's attitude. This already puts the Eucharist in a class of its own, which theologians have tried to express by such terms as 'relative sacrifice' or 'sacramental sacrifice'.

The doctrine of the Eucharist as sacrifice, then, takes its stand on Calvary. It is the sacramental renewal, not of Calvary's brutality and blood-letting, but of the loving surrender with which those realities were borne and offered. Consequently it is not a crude

blood-ritual nor the placating of an angry God, but the embodiment of that plenitude of religious values which Christ achieved on
the cross. Christ's self-surrender on Calvary was in fact the highest
instance known to us of the human sacrificial attitude, so that in
this indirect way the traditional ends of sacrifice associated with
that attitude – thanksgiving, propitiation, petition and praise –
find their way back into our understanding of the sacramental
sacrifice of the Mass.[15]

The sacrificial depths of the Eucharistic liturgy bring home to us
the seriousness of the Mass. Here we are at the very heart of its
meaning. Very easily today we can get so absorbed in questions of
how to celebrate that we fail to do justice to what we celebrate. We
lose sight of the 'what' in the 'how'. Or perhaps we focus on the
resurrection and forget the cross, which is what neglecting the
sacrificial aspect involves; and that, as one writer put it, is to turn
the resurrection into 'an ideogram of the glorification of the
world'.[16] But over against such an approach stands the central
challenge of the gospel way of life, that it is only in 'losing life' that
we 'find life' (Matt 16:25).

Nature and instinct

In this section I wish to pick out and develop three religious values
in particular which are embodied in the sacrificial nature of the
Eucharist. The first of these concerns the natural basis of worship.
Grace builds on nature, say the theologians, but, ever since the rise
of nominalism, the natural underpinnings of our worship have
been under threat in our sophisticated culture.[17] This is particularly the case in our Western world, where in our experience we
have no natural analogue for the Eucharist as sacrifice. In Africa,
for instance, it is somewhat different, and the African experience
helps to point to values in the religious psyche with which our
technological age has long lost touch.[18]

Earlier in this chapter it was pointed out that the Eucharist is
primarily an expression of history rather than of nature, but that
does not mean that all links between nature and our ritual can be
ignored. In accepting sacrificial categories into its understanding
of the Eucharist, the New Testament was asserting a continuity
between the ritual instituted by Christ and those natural instincts
of the human being of which sacrifice is the traditional mode of
expression. The instinct to sacrifice wells up from those depths

within us, so unforgettably described by Karl Rahner, where the human heart is orientated to the mystery of being itself.[19] Sacrifice is part of our response to that mystery and to the experience of 'the holy' which it bestows.[20] It is a way of acknowledging that God is the source of our being and of all being. From him we come, to him we return. Indeed if an authentic response to being includes an acceptance of our own death, in the way that Heidegger and Rahner have described it, then every sacrifice is a celebration of one's own death, the surrender of life to the one Being who has total disposal of one's life. In that way it means laying one's total being on the line before the source of all being, in order to acknowledge one's place in the world and a right relationship to the totality of existence.

Once one tries to put the meaning of sacrifice into words in this way, language falters, because the instincts to which we refer lie so deep. They are a matter of what Rahner would call 'basic consciousness', lying beneath the conceptual and the thematic. At the same time it must be stressed that sacrifice is about the absolute and the objective. The absolute order is clearly something beyond ourselves, but people today so easily get caught up in their own inner world! That helps explain why they have such a problem with sacrifice. For so many of us religion and its symbols have become merely instruments of our own subjectivity, and so they tend to be valued only as embodiments of ideas. Ritual is reduced to verbalism and sacrifice to metaphor.[21]

The sacrifice of the Mass confronts that mentality. By its own assertion it is a matter of flesh and blood, of body given and blood poured out. Indeed it is not too much to say that the Mass is a matter of life and death – Christ's death, our death, death and judgement, for, as St Paul warns us, if we are not discerning of what we are doing in the Eucharist, we may well be eating judgement to ourselves (1 Cor 11:29).

Love and surrender

The second value which sacrifice embodies for us concerns the aspect of love and surrender in our worship as in our daily living. Love is the form of our freedom, and the language of sacrifice is the language of love. It is this way of understanding sacrifice which marks the definitive break with ancient pagan notions of placating angry gods through the shedding of blood. Our notion of sacrifice has to take its inspiration from Our Lord's great act of love and surrender on the cross, and from his revelation of the Father's love, which is the sole source of the whole movement of redemption in the New Testament.[22]

Here I would like to reflect for a moment on the need to try to get behind much of the religious jargon which is often used in this context. A sacrifice, we have said, is the giving of a gift as a sign of self-giving. It is the transfer of ownership over a gift to signify my acknowledgement that I belong to God. Now what do these phrases, 'to belong to God' and 'to give oneself to God', mean? The best analogy lies in the way we belong to anyone who loves us and whom we love in return. We belong to that person by making him or her the centre of reference in our lives. Everything we do is done by reference to that person, so that he or she becomes the centre of one's universe. When two lives flow into each other in this way, it is an experience that lies too deep for words. That is why, in order to express it, lovers commonly have recourse to signs such as the interchange of gifts.

It is something similar in our relationship with God, and here too it is true that the notion of belonging to the other person, God, is really a statement about how we live and how we wish to live. All that we do in life is to be done in reference to God. Liturgy and life go together, and, in order to express, seal and deepen this relationship, we give God a gift as lovers do, though in our case the gift is altogether unique.

To sacrifice, then, in the Christian context, is an act of self-surrender after the pattern of Christ. As he did not defend himself, but handed himself over to what his Father was doing in the world, so we in our self-offering hand ourselves over to something larger than ourselves which God is bringing about. 'Not my will but thine be done' was the kernel of Christ's sacrificial attitude. The sentiment is echoed by us in the Mass when we recite together the Our Father over the body and blood of Christ. 'Thy will be done' may be seen as expressing the inmost heart of our sacrifice and as the epitome of the whole view of life which flows from it.

Freedom and co-operation

A third religious value involved in the Eucharistic sacrifice is that of human freedom and the principle of co-operation with God in the workings of divine grace. At this point we are at the very nub of the differences between Catholics and Protestants on the Mass and, indeed, on the whole economy of grace. As was remarked above in Chapter II in the discussion of the ecumenical statements on the Eucharist, agreement on the Eucharistic sacrifice is intimately connected with agreement on justification by faith.

To offer is an act of human freedom, but can human freedom be reconciled with divine sovereignty and divine initiative? Commonly Protestants have approached this question with an *either–or*, whereas Catholics insist on *both–and*. In other words, Protestants tend to say that the initiative lies either with God or with the human being. Catholics will insist, no less than Protestants, that the initiative is always God's, but they add that this initiative constitutes human freedom rather than restricts it. Human freedom can be reconciled with divine initiative only where God is transcendent. Indeed this is the clearest demonstration of what divine transcendence means, that God can control contingent events, even in their very contingency: 'The heart of the king is in the hands of the Lord.'[23] Our freedom is in the hands of God, so that our free acts proceed on one level from ourselves and on another level from God. The only reality God in no way causes is sin.

Running through Catholic theology and spirituality is this deep conviction that our freedom under grace, far from robbing God of his transcendence, only demonstrates it all the more. We might see a pale reflection of this paradox in the analogy of a good superior. Such superiors demonstrate their qualities, not by surrounding themselves with passive conformists, but with those who display initiative and enterprise. The skill of a good superior lies in inspiring such initiative and in drawing it into the unity of a total plan. St Augustine, as so often, put his finger on it: God who made us without our co-operation will not save us without our co-operation.[24] The very possibility of our co-operating is given us by God, so that he is active in our very activity. Our causality is a 'caused causality', or, as one writer put it, a 'received activity'.[25]

It is clear that this way of thinking is far removed from classical explanations of justification by faith alone. If one grants that this opposition on the nature of grace lies behind the opposition on the nature of the Eucharist, one might well at first despair of any coming together about the sacrament. But in fact the language of co-operation is so deeply imbedded in the common sources of the faith that, even after being excluded on the theological level, one sees again and again that it returns in Protestant writing on concrete and pastoral issues. This should surely encourage those engaged in ecumenical dialogue that a way forward may still be found.[26]

Digression on propitiation

To this discussion of the principle of co-operation I would like to add a digression on one particular aspect of the issue, namely on the nature of propitiation. This subject belongs more directly to soteriology than to Eucharistic theology, so it cannot be treated here in a fully systematic way, but it is one which keeps coming back wherever sacrifice is discussed. When the Council of Trent made propitiation central to its notion of Eucharistic sacrifice, it was giving it a prominence which it did not always have in the tradition. At the same time, propitiation is certainly part of the Church's liturgical heritage, as one can see, for instance, in the Maronite Anaphora of Peter.[27]

Close to the centre of the difficulty with the notion of propitiation lies a confusion between two different issues, neither of them straightforward in itself, but doubly confusing when combined in this way. On the one hand there is the issue of the anthropomorphism involved in speaking of the wrath of God. On the other there is the principle of our activity, our 'caused causality', in the mystery of our redemption. The necessity of setting the first aside easily leads one to set the second aside also, thereby eliminating the role of offering altogether and reducing 'propitiation' to the descending aspect of God's mercy.

Clearly reflection on the second of these issues brings one back to reflection on the first and to deciding what is the authentic affirmation behind the original imagery.[28] Some writers, for instance, seem to take propitiation in the sense of 'changing God's mind'.[29] If this is meant as simply a description, then it is certainly true to the way many people conceive the notion. If it is taken as the only possible account from the explanatory viewpoint proper to the realm of theory, then it is clearly incompatible with the revealed transcendence of God.

This unease is already reflected in the Old Testament where the word most closely corresponding to propitiation, *kipper*, does not have God as an object. At the same time, *kipper* is associated with making oblation to God, oblations that are pleasing to him and are commonly said to remove his anger. It is this association with sacrificial offerings which justifies the acceptance by Irenaeus and subsequent Christian writers of the usage where God is the object of propitiation, while it must be stressed that no one is more emphatic on the divine transcendence than the same Irenaeus.[30]

Once propitiation is carried out through oblation, there has to be an ascending aspect to the notion. The essence of propitiation is vindicated once one grants that our prayers and oblations are pleasing to God. When such acts are carried out by the repentant sinner, they cannot but be set in contrast to one's evil deeds and offered up in the hope of outweighing the offence of one's sins; but any suggestion that this 'changes God's mind' cannot be reconciled with the divine transcendence. Propitiation, like every other instance of our activity under grace, is a 'caused causality'. It begins with the divine mercy and the plan of God who in his goodness so honours us that many of the effects of grace come about only in dependence on the activity which he makes possible in us. As Aquinas put it so succinctly, it is not because of A (our propitiating) that God wills B (our reconciliation) but he wills that B comes about because of A.[31]

This principle of divine providence applies in the first place to Christ's own work of atonement on the cross, a work formally attributed to his humanity. God could have arranged it that our liberation from sin should have come about some other way, 'vertically from above', as Barth would say. In fact he willed that it come about in dependence on the cross. We share in that plan. Just as all our activity under grace is possible only with Christ and in him, so any propitiatory value attaching to our prayers and oblations is possible only through, with and in the propitiating activity of the cross. If this is true of Christian life generally, then it fits in that it should be part of the Eucharistic action also. It is not the case that we change the mind of God. The initiative is entirely and always God's; but God, in his mercy, has wished to honour us in such a way that our reconciliation should flow from our making offerings that are pleasing to him.

With these thoughts it should be possible to bring new life to the notion of sacrificing at the Eucharist. Certainly in today's world we cannot take the idea for granted. Some have even gone so far as to suggest that, however valid the idea may have been in the past, it should be dropped from the language and content of catechesis today. However, when one recalls how deeply the idea is enmeshed in the tradition of the Church on the Eucharist, and when one considers the kind of issues this chapter sees as involved in the notion, it does not seem that there is any alternative to the challenge of making the idea more understandable for the people of today.[32]

NOTES

1 Vatican II, *Sacrosanctum concilium*, art. 47, as translated in W. M. Abbott (ed.), *The Documents of Vatican II* (London: Geoffrey Chapman, 1967), p. 154.
2 M. Eliade, *The Sacred and the Profane* (New York: Harper & Row, 1961), pp. 88–9.
3 Cf. Rev 13:8, especially in the older translations. On these tendencies in Jewish thought see M. Hengel, *The Son of God* (London: SCM, 1976), pp. 66–76; E. Schillebeeckx, *Christ* (London: SCM, 1983), pp. 241–5.
4 The philosophical theology behind the discussion in this chapter and in the next is especially dependent on chs 4 and 5 of B. Lonergan, *Grace and Freedom* (London: Darton, Longman & Todd, 1971).
5 Here I would like to draw attention to an article by my late colleague B. McNamara, 'Christus Patiens in Mass and sacraments: higher perspectives', ITQ 42 (1975), pp. 17–35. The approach in this article is very similar to my own, largely due to the fact that we were both students of the same great, but too little known, Irish theologian, the late John Hyde SJ.
6 K. Rahner, *Theological Investigations*, vol. 10 (London: Darton, Longman & Todd, 1973), p. 96.
7 E.g. Aquinas, ST III, q. 56, a. 1, obj. 3 and 4.
8 See Chapter 11, above.
9 St Leo, *On the Passion*, 19 (PL 54, 383).
10 *Signum passionis . . . non ipsa passio*: Aquinas, *In IV Sent.*, d. 12, q. 1, a. 3, q. III. See also Aquinas, ST III, q. 83, a. 1, ad 2.
11 ST III, q. 62, a. 5, c. The distinction between what Christ did on the cross and what was done to him (*actio* and *passio*) is a frequent one in Aquinas, e.g., ST III, q. 22, a. 2, ad 2; q. 47, a. 4, ad 2; q. 48, a. 3, ad 3. Perhaps this is part of the reason why Aquinas spoke of the presence of the *Christus passus* and not of the *Christus patiens* in the Eucharist. Christ's oblationary activity on the cross is the presage of his resurrection, and it is the risen Christ who is present in the Eucharist.
12 ST III, q. 73, a. 3, ad 3. In the article referred to in note 5 above, the writer does not bring out sufficiently the aspect which is present in the

Eucharistic sacrifice as distinct from the other sacraments. Although it is true that 'all the actions and passions of Christ' are instrumental in our salvation (ST III, q. 48, a. 6), once presence is a function of action in the way outlined by B. McNamara in his article, then the presence of Christ's sacrifice comes to a head in his *action*, which is his oblation.

13 See Lonergan, *Grace and Freedom*, pp. 64–9; also Lonergan, 'On God and secondary causes' in *Collection* (*Collected Works*, vol. 4; Toronto: Toronto University Press, 1988), pp. 53–65.

14 Even if it be true that the notion of sacrifice was originally to be interpreted as a kind of katharsis of violence in the manner proposed by Girard, the development described in this and the next paragraphs sets a distance between such origins and the Mass, so that such ideas can now be surmounted and left behind. See R. Girard, *Violence and the Sacred* (London–Baltimore: Johns Hopkins University Press, 1977).

15 The ends of sacrifice are expressed slightly differently in different Church documents. The formulation used in the text will be found in: SCR, *Eucharisticum mysterium*, art. 3/e, AAS 59 (1967), p. 542; also at somewhat more length in Pius XII, *Mediator Dei*, AAS 39 (1947), pp. 549–50.

16 E. Käsemann, cited by W. Thompson, *Jesus Lord and Saviour* (New York: Paulist Press, 1980), p. 116.

17 Nominalism, already described in Chapter 9, note 25 above, tended to treat things as absolutely singular and so to consider universal concepts as devoid of any essential meaning: they are only names, *nomina*. It would thus be sceptical of the notion of nature. This scepticism was intensified by the Reformers' notion of human nature as totally corrupted by sin. Hence manifestations of natural religion can only be from the devil! The effects of nominalism on liturgy, shifting the emphasis from the symbolic to the verbal and the conceptual, are well discussed by L. Bouyer, *Rite and Man* (London: Burns & Oates, 1963), pp. 14–77.

18 As examples of learning from Africa in this matter see M. F. C. Bourdillon and M. Fortes (eds), *Sacrifice* (London: Academic Press, 1980); G. Ashby, *Sacrifice: Its Nature and Purpose* (London: SCM, 1988).

19 K. Rahner, *Theological Investigations*, vol. 4 (London: Darton, Longman & Todd, 1966), pp. 48–60; *On the Theology of Death* (Quaestiones Disputatae no. 2; London: Burns & Oates, 1964), especially pp. 21–39.

20 Parallel to Rahner, even the agnostic Heidegger realized that the mystery of being lays a claim on us, to which we can respond only by 'sacrifice', that is by self-surrender, and by thanksgiving. 'In sacrifice there is expressed that hidden *thanking* which alone does homage to the grace wherewith Being has endowed the nature of man . . . Original thanking is the echo of Being's favour . . . This echo is man's answer to the Word of the soundless voice of Being': M. Heidegger, 'What is metaphysics?' in *Existence and Being*, ed. W. Brock (London: Vision Press, 1949), p. 389.

21 R. Williams, *Eucharistic Sacrifice – The Roots of a Metaphor* (Bramcote: Grove Books, 1982); D. Power, *The Eucharistic Mystery* (Dublin: Gill & Macmillan, 1992), pp. 142–3, 320–4. These writers have reduced sacrifice to metaphor, seemingly as a way of bypassing the ecumenical problem about sacrifice. Not only does this not fit in with the hypothesis I have proposed in Chapter 3, but I do not see it as doing justice to the fundamental ecumenical problem about justification and co-operation.

22 Rom 5:8; Eph 2:4; John 3:16; 1 John 4:10.

23 On divine transcendence and human liberty see B. Lonergan, *Grace and Freedom*, ch. 5. The quotation in the text is from Prov 21:1, a favourite one of Aquinas in this context, as frequently noted by Lonergan, op. cit., pp. 54, 99, 101, 103, 136 note 94.

24 Augustine, *Sermon* 169, 11, 13 (PL 38, 923; RJ 1515).

25 E. Schillebeeckx in *Gott in Welt*, ed. J. B. Metz and others (Freiburg–Basel–Vienna: Herder, 1964), vol. 2, pp. 46–7. See also Lonergan, *Grace and Freedom*, pp. 84–8.

26 I think that there is an example of just such an approach at work in the recent Catholic–Lutheran dialogue in Germany as presented in K. Lehmann and W. Pannenberg (eds), *The Condemnations of the Reformation Era: Do They Still Divide?* (Minneapolis: Fortress, 1990). On justification as not purely passive, see pp. 46–7, and on the Eucharistic sacrifice considered acceptable as a *response* to God, see p. 87. The notion of sacrifice as response rather than as metaphor seems to me a better way forward than that proposed by the writers referred to in note 21 of this chapter.

27 A. Hänggi and I. Pahl (eds), *Prex eucharistica* (Fribourg: Editions Universitaires, 1968), pp. 410–15.

28 To face this problem a distinction may be made between the language of 'common sense' and that proper to 'the realm of theory' as is done by B. Lonergan, *Method in Theology* (London: Darton, Longman & Todd, 1972), pp. 81–5.

29 For example, this seems to be the implication, though not the expression, of Robert Daly. In his own words, actions of propitiation 'have the specific purpose of soothing the anger or ill-will of the deity and/or of securing his favour': *Christian Sacrifice* (Washington: Catholic University of America Press, 1978), p. 44.

30 Irenaeus speaks of 'the true sacrifice, by offering which they shall propitiate God, that they may receive life': *Against the Heresies* IV, 17, 2 (Har 2, 195; SC 100, 580). See the discussion of Irenaeus and Origen in Chapter 6 above.

31 Aquinas, ST I, q. 19, a. 5. In the background here is the problem of God's transcendence over time, well treated in B. Lonergan, *Grace and Freedom*, chs 4 and 5, especially pp. 103–9; the same is presented in a summary form in the article referred to in note 5 of this chapter.

32 A good example of a writer attempting to do just that, and that from a
Protestant background, is Frances Young, *Sacrifice and the Death of Christ*
(London: SCM, 1983); *Can These Dry Bones Live?* (London: SCM, 1982),
pp. 65–83; 'Sacrifice' in *A New Dictionary of Christian Theology* (London:
SCM, 1983), pp. 516–18.

14

When confronted with the doctrine of the Eucharistic presence, the task of systematic theology is not an obvious one. Theologians will sometimes limit themselves to asserting the fact of that presence, disclaiming any attempt to treat of the 'how'. This is more than simply intellectual modesty. At the end of the day, the 'how' of the Eucharistic Change will always remain mysterious, and there are good historical precedents for disavowing the very question.[1] At the same time, the probing of the human mind knows no rest, and the fact of the matter is that over the centuries scholars have delved into the issue, not on the assumption that they can remove the mystery, but simply in order to throw a little light, in so far as that is possible at all, and to avoid taking refuge too soon in the appeal to mystery. The approach adopted in this chapter will be, first of all, to elucidate a fundamental philosophical division which, even when recognized, bedevils all discussion of this topic. Secondly, the reader will be presented with three considerations of a more existential theology which attempt to throw some light on this perennial mystery.

A PHILOSOPHICAL DIVISION

Edward Schillebeeckx surely put his finger on the nerve-centre of this whole problem when he wrote that the central question in this discussion is 'What is reality?'[2] Even among Catholic thinkers there can be different answers to this question. Bernard Lonergan sees a divergence on the nature of reality as establishing a fundamental line of division between Thomists and Scotists, who in fact are traditional adversaries in Eucharistic theology. According to Lonergan, Scotism operates on an empirical notion of objectivity, where knowing is understood on the analogy of seeing. The 'real' in this approach is the 'already-out-there-now-real'. In other words, intelligible reality is confused with the kind of reality reached by sensation.[3]

According to the position of Lonergan, which may be described as one of critical realism, 'the real' is not adequately established by simply pointing it out. It should rather be defined in terms of an act of meaning. The real is that which is reached by the intellect's completion of the process of understanding and judging. It can be defined as the content of a true affirmation. Such an approach rests on a firm conviction that the intellect, not sensation, is the faculty of the real, and that the validated judgement is the index of reality.

This distinction between a naïve realism on the one hand and a critical realism on the other helps to make sense of a number of Eucharistic controversies of the past. Once one is thinking, consciously or unconsciously, along the lines of naïve realism, there is an inescapable tendency, either to interpret Eucharistic presence in a physicalist way, or else to react in the opposite direction towards a purely figurative sense. An example of the first would be Paschase Radbert and the authors of the first Oath of Berengar in 1059. An example of the second would be Zwingli or the pure symbolists of the Berengarian controversy. If, with Lonergan, one grounds naïve realism in a particular interpretation of the human mind, then it is understandable that the tendency should surface from time to time, without necessarily reaching the point of heresy. Thus one can see it at work in the Scotist hesitations over transubstantiation, in the surprising physicalism of Luther, and in the tendency among many today to favour 'presence' rather than 'change' as the key category for the Blessed Sacrament.

Critical realism will focus the sense of Christ's presence on the truth of the affirmation 'This is my body . . . this is my blood'. That which all along in this book has been called 'the Eucharistic Change' can then be understood as a change of meaning, from 'This is bread – the sign of our offering' to 'This is Christ's body – the sign of his offering'. The change of meaning in these judgements is, for ordinary purposes, a sufficient signal of the change of reality. If you are not a critical realist, however, you are going to have a gnawing dissatisfaction with such an approach, feeling that it is not 'real' enough.

The division between critical and naïve realists is even more significant in the understanding of presence. Most people think of presence in an imaginative way. In the mind's eye they see two bodies coming close to each other and then touching. For them presence is a precondition of action. However, Aristotle's famous saying 'Action is in the recipient' sets us on the way to a different view of presence. The reality of action, he insisted, is a perfection within the recipient. Action cannot be some kind of intermediary entity between agent and recipient, since the whole question would keep returning with regard to the relationship between this intermediary and the agent, and so on to infinity. Consequently there is no intrinsic relationship between the two bodies until one acts on the other. Action, therefore, is the precondition of presence, rather than vice versa.[4]

Clearly this piece of systematic thought has fundamental consequences for the theology of the Eucharist, where not only the presence of Christ's body but also that of his sacrifice are central issues. The fact that it flies in the face of the image-bound categories of ordinary thinking throws considerable light on the ever-recurring difficulties which people have as regards this sacrament. In the case of the presence of Christ's body in the host, Aristotle's principle about action forces us to think of the 'action' which substance exercises on its accidents, holding them in being and through them acting on the things around. This raises a previously unsuspected question as to what happens to this action in the case of host and cup. It also requires us to ask 'What is the action by which Christ's sacrifice becomes present in the Mass?'

The answer to that second question can only point to the action of Christ in offering himself, and us in him, to the Father. In this way this action becomes fundamental to all our considerations of presence. Leaving aside the more metaphysical issue of the action of substance on accidents, I would like to draw together the concerns raised by our reflections both on 'the real' and on 'presence'. Taking as a fundamental premiss that action is the precondition of presence, one can focus the question we have just been asking in the following way: 'What is the basic action which grounds the notion of Eucharistic Presence?' Ultimately it has to be that same action which grounds the presence of Christ's sacrifice in the Mass, namely that by which he offers himself, and us in him, to the Father. This action, then, is the context which helps to make the mystery of the Eucharistic Change a little more understandable.

There has been a strong tendency in Eucharistic theology to isolate the elements from their context. This is all the more likely to happen when one thinks of presence along the spatial lines of naïve realism. Commonly the question of presence is seen as one of Christ's presence to us, and the more fundamental question of Christ's presence to the Father is neglected. What is being argued in this book is that we should put the elements back into their context. It is only within the movement of Christ's sacrificial action, Christ giving himself to the Father, that the intelligibility of the Eucharistic Change can be adequately grounded.

The relevance of this approach can be brought out by considering a challenging question which Luther once posed to Catholics. One could phrase his question this way: 'What difference does it make whether Christ is present under the substance of bread, as the Lutherans say, or under the accidents of bread, as the Catholics say, as long as Christ is present?'[5] One response, of course, in the best Thomist tradition, can be philosophical, insisting that the distinction of presence from change in this case makes no sense; unfortunately, this response will not satisfy everybody, not even Catholic theologians.

A more theological response, and one that illustrates the approach we are discussing, is to point to the interdependence of the two basic truths about the Eucharist, that of sacrifice and that of Eucharistic Change. We can now see that the separation of sacrament from sacrifice, which had occurred in theology before Luther's time, was fraught with fateful consequences for the sacrament ever since. Having neglected the aspect of sacrifice, Luther had set aside the fundamental perspective which makes the Eucharistic Change meaningful. As we saw in Chapter 4 above, what is 'given' in the Eucharist is that which Christ gives in sacrifice to the Father, namely himself, his body and his blood. One does not offer accidents. When one offers something, one offers *what it is*, and in the New Law that can only be Christ's body and blood. Once one admits that the Eucharist is in some sense sacrificial, one has taken the fundamental step towards the doctrine of Eucharistic Change. The key issue is not Christ's presence to us spatially but Christ's self-gift to the Father in a ritual that is also ours.

THE CHANGE AS SIGNIFICANT

Change of meaning

On the basis of the orientation that has just been established we can now develop our approach according to three different aspects, each of them lighting up the basic truth from a different point of view. The first of them represents the final attempt of this book to say something about the problems raised under the heading of transignification, but, for the reasons indicated in Chapter 11 above, it will be simply one theologian's approach along the lines indicated by that term. In that earlier discussion it was pointed out that we must resist having our categories narrowed down to those of the exact sciences. The reality of our world is so much more than that which scientists dissect in their laboratories and examine by their microscopes. Our world is a human world, and the meaning things have in our world are as much a part of their reality as their physical constitution.

Thus when a housewife sets a cake before her guests, the reality of what is before them is to be measured, not just by considering her cake as a concoction of various physical ingredients, but as the bearer of a human meaning, born of the effort to prepare it. The cake is essentially a symbol, and symbols are not just cyphers on the fringe of consciousness; they are an intrinsic part of a human world and of its reality. Gifts, for instance, should never be seen apart from the meaning they embody, for that meaning is part of their reality. At the same time, the physical constitution of such gifts is not irrelevant. Commonly it is determined by the intended meaning. In the example just given, any old soggy loaf just would not do.

Now when we apply this idea to the Eucharist, the first thing we discover is that this is in fact the way the new liturgy regards the bread and wine in the Mass. Here the elements are not just objects but gifts: ' . . . what earth has given and human hands have made'. In the context this significance is not just human but religious. The bread and wine are part of a whole ritual of self-giving to God, one of the abiding patterns of human worship. In our liturgy they are brought to the altar as signs of our existence, for through them we wish to place in the hands of our Maker our entire existence, the bread of our labour and the wine of our joy.

Commonly, in the language of signs, there is a certain identity between a giver and a gift. This is true when a young person gives a gift to the one he or she intends to marry, but it is especially true in religious signs: our gifts are ourselves which we wish to give to God. Both levels of meaning, the human and the religious, are exemplified in the Jewish table-ritual from which the Eucharist takes its origin. In breaking bread for his household, the father of the family is giving something of himself to them and to God.

In our case, however, such giving is always imperfect and incomplete. Through our human limitations, and even more through our sinfulness, we always hold something back. 'Your guilty deeds have made a gulf between you and your God', said the prophet (Isa 59:2). In this predicament we are left with the problem of bridging that divide and reaching the divine presence. Left to ourselves, we could not have bridged it, but part of the meaning of Christ's redemptive incarnation is that he has come to lift our worship on to a new level by changing it into his own. In our liturgy he takes over, and when he says 'This is my body . . . this is my blood', he is equivalently saying 'This is my worship'. It is not just bread and wine which he is changing, but the whole action of worship, from being simply ours to being his, and ours in his. Part of what that means is that he changes our offerings into his offerings. From being signs of our existence and of the way we give, they become signs of his existence and of the way he gives.

Christ is the perfect giver. When he gives, he holds nothing back. He gives himself completely, and in his case the identity between giver and gift is complete. Total self-giving is the key. On the stage of human history it meant Christ's death on the cross, when he gave the last breath of his body and the last drop of his blood. Here these gifts are not regarded as simply physical objects. They are the embodiment, the incarnation of the love behind the giving, for on Calvary what saved us ultimately was not the physical pain in itself but the love with which it was offered for the salvation of the world. In this spirit Christ laid down on the altar of the cross his very body and his very blood. Nothing less would do.

Having once occurred on the stage of human history, Christ's great act of sacrifice can now enter the world of signs. Total self-giving on the stage of the sacraments means that here too Christ lays down his very body and his very blood, with a perfect identity between giver and gift. In this sacrament he gives us, not just a sign of himself, nor a part of himself, nor an influence flowing from himself, but his very self and his whole self, body, blood, soul and divinity, for that is the way that Christ gives, and nothing less would do.

When in his encyclical *Mysterium fidei* Paul VI used some of the language of transignification to express the Eucharistic mystery, he was arguing from the change of reality to the change of meaning. In this consideration I am suggesting that one can also move in the opposite direction, arguing from the change of meaning to a change of reality. The Eucharistic gifts, which started off in the liturgy as simply our gifts, have now become primarily Christ's gifts. That is their new meaning, and this new meaning requires in them the new reality, so that they may truly express the perfect sacrifice of the perfect lover under the eye of the perfect Father.

Change of purpose

Our second consideration will be a more traditional one, building on ideas already present in the patristic writers. Where the previous consideration was directed to the human subject who contemplates the Eucharist, this one looks outward on the ultimate reality conveyed by the sacrament, underlining what the sacrament must be in order to produce such an effect.

What is the purpose of the Eucharist? The answer to that question in the tradition is a torrent of images, bewildering in their richness. The final chapter of this book will be devoted to sorting them out. In the meantime we might focus on the clue given us by the kind of sign Our Lord has chosen, that of *nourishment*. The purpose of nourishment is to maintain life, and one of the purposes of the Eucharist is precisely to sustain life in us (John 6:53ff.).

But what kind of life is the Eucharist to sustain? At first our gifts are simply bread and wine, and these, as we all know, are nourishment for our ordinary natural existence. But that is not the kind of life Our Lord is speaking of when he says 'I have come that they may have life, and have it more abundantly' (John 10:10). Christ has not come simply to repair the original creation but to inaugurate a new one, a 'new creation' (2 Cor 5:17), a new life, a 'born-again' life.

One of the central wonders of the New Testament is the fact that the life which Christ is bringing us is the life of God himself, the life of Father, Son and Holy Spirit shared with us. The life of the Eucharist is the life of God, which we are to share with him

through all eternity: 'He who eats my flesh and drinks my blood
has eternal life' (John 6:54). Now nourishment acts in virtue of
that which it is. Bread and wine are appropriate nourishment of
natural physical life within us, but to nourish the divine life our
gifts need to be changed into something of a higher order, the very
flesh and blood of God. That is what tradition has always declared
the Eucharist to be, and that alone seems adequate to explaining
the objective change which the Eucharist works in those who
receive it with faith.

At this point we stand at the very limits of what human language
can express. Though words have their role in this interchange
between God and his people, the basic message is really in the
whole ritual event in a way that is ultimately deeper than words.
The nature of the gifts he gives is Our Lord's way of conveying the
depth of the intimacy he wishes to establish with us. Conversely
the only measure of the wonder of the Eucharist is the depth of the
mystery of divine grace. There is really no natural analogy for the
way God wishes to live in his friends. We might think, for
instance, of the child in the womb or the lover in the beloved, but
the divine reality transcends such examples. The divine way of
entering into our lives and remaining with us is best conveyed
when his body and blood passes into ours, and that is it. Ultimately
there is no analogy for such a means, just as there is no analogy for
such an end. The mystery stands before us in its wordless wonder.

Transfiguration

A third consideration draws its inspiration from some statements
of the early writers, but even more from Teilhard de Chardin.[6]
'Transfiguration' was a term applied to the Eucharistic Change by
St Ambrose,[7] but it has acquired a new relevance through the
writings of the French theologian-scientist. Already the New
Testament itself seems to look forward to an ultimate cosmic
change, when a great conflagration will be the prelude to a new
heaven and a new earth.[8] The agent of this new dawn will be the
Holy Spirit, whose role in it is already suggested by his New
Testament title as 'the Spirit of Glory' (1 Pet 4:14). The new earth
will be one glorified by the presence of the Holy Spirit. He will take
over all things, and God will be 'all in all' (1 Cor 15:28).

Such is our future, but the future has a way of being at work in
the present, and one of the ways in which this happens is found in

the Blessed Sacrament. Here we have a fragment of that 'new age' where the change of this material world into a new earth has already come about. Just as at the transfiguration on the mountain-side Christ's body seems to have been endowed with the characteristics of the glorified state, so in the Eucharist something of that process has been carried a stage further.

It is all a question of change. Just as Christ was changed on the mountain-side, just as the world will be changed at the end of time, so in the Eucharist the Holy Spirit has changed our bread and wine, fragments of this material universe, into the body and blood of Christ, anticipations of the world to come. God changing our gifts, God changing us, God changing the world – clearly it fits in that we should go out from this encounter and this banquet to help change the world, making Christ more present within it, so that the community of men and women may become more fully the ultimate body of Christ.

THE RESERVED SACRAMENT

At various times in the course of the preceding pages the subject of the reserved sacrament has come to the fore. Clearly one cannot deal with the issues of this chapter without raising the subject once again, and so this is where, in the light of all that has gone before, a final word will be attempted concerning the place of this devotion in the contemporary Church.

One of the most fundamental things we discovered about patristic theology was that at that time the Eucharistic celebration was the centre of the Church and the Church was the centre of the Eucharist.[9] This was part of that ancient synthesis which, with the onset of the medieval period, began to fall apart. A shift in the centre of gravity took place, with the result that, from that time on, the theology of the Church came to centre more and more on the aspect of authority, especially that of the Papacy, and the Eucharist, at least in the popular mind, tended to centre more and more on the Real Presence.

The liturgical reforms of Vatican II have marked one of the most profound changes of consciousness with regard to our worship in the whole history of the Church, and much of this has been marked by an explicit desire to rediscover the values of the patristic age.[10] As theologians and liturgists turn to that ancient synthesis for their inspiration, inevitably a question-mark begins to form around the status of tabernacle devotion in a way that would have been inconceivable fifty years ago. People have begun to ask whether it has a future at all, and if so, how can it be fitted into the new situation of theology and liturgy. If a knowledge of history creates the problem for us, perhaps an even wider knowledge of history will help towards a solution. In formulating a reply, it will be useful to go back beyond the twelfth century and to appreciate how, despite its largely medieval and Western associations, tabernacle devotion has its roots in the common heritage of the faith.

The principle behind the reservation of the sacrament is the permanence of Christ's presence in the Eucharistic species until they are consumed. In the New Testament this permanence is implicit in the way the words 'This is my body' are understood as a statement of objective fact. One striking illustration of this objective understanding is the notion of *manducatio impiorum* found in I Corinthians 11:27–30. There the Apostle assumes that evil people can still objectively receive the body of the Lord, albeit to their own condemnation.

Explicit testimony to this permanence comes in the patristic writings. The first instance known to us can be found in Justin's witness to the custom of bringing communion to the sick.[11] This dates from the middle of the second century. From the third century we hear of Christians keeping the Blessed Sacrament in their homes to enable them to have communion on days when there was no Mass.[12] Later we hear of their carrying the sacrament with them on their persons, a custom destined to become widespread among the Irish monks.[13]

There is evidence of the reservation of the sacrament in churches from the seventh century, but it is only from the ninth century that it became a common practice. It was reserved in a wall-cupboard, or sometimes at an altar, suspended over it in a pyx. Reservation on the main altar became general only from the sixteenth century.

The primary purpose of reservation has always been, and remains to this day, the communion of the faithful. This sacrament, says the Council of Trent, was 'instituted in order to be received'.[14] However, particularly from the eleventh century on, a secondary purpose has emerged, namely the veneration of the sacrament itself. In previous chapters some indications have been given of the background to this development. To some extent it was a reaction against the denials of Berengar and the Cathars, but more fundamentally it embodied medieval devotion to the human and historical Christ. Where the people of earlier times had seen the body and blood of Christ as a means through which the divine life comes to change us, the medievals began to see in them simply the person of Christ, present before us on earth once again. Ever since that time the language and theology of presence have come to play a key role in the spirituality of the Western Church.

Among the difficulties raised against this practice, from within the Church itself, the principal one lies in the way it seems to diminish the place of Mass and holy communion as the primary instance of the Eucharist. It is pointed out that, as food, the sacrament is essentially something to be eaten in a banquet, not something to be looked at and locked up. It is sometimes suggested that this devotion stresses one mode of Christ's presence at the expense of the other modes, but especially that of his real presence in the community. With a tabernacle in a dominant position in a church, it is difficult to develop among the faithful a sense of Christ's presence in the liturgical assembly.

Despite such criticisms, the Vatican Council itself, and the Magisterium since then, have continued to endorse this devotion as a source of spiritual benefit. A sample of this teaching may be quoted:

Since the Eucharistic mystery was instituted out of love, and makes Christ sacramentally present, it is worthy of thanksgiving and worship, and this worship must be present in all our encounters with the Blessed Sacrament . . . Jesus waits for us in this sacrament of love. Let us be generous with our time in going to meet him in adoration and in contemplation that is full of faith and ready to make reparation for the great faults and crimes of the world. May our adoration never cease.[15]

The confusion in this matter, which was a feature of the years immediately after Vatican II, has now given way to a new confidence in the devotion. Karl Rahner spoke for many when he wrote towards the end of his life that the adoration of the Blessed Sacrament should certainly be part of the spirituality of the future.[16] One cannot turn one's back on the values which centuries of spirituality have found in this tradition; yet, at the same time, there are some qualifications to be introduced in the light of the experience of the new liturgy.

First of all, it must be insisted on that the primary instance of the
Eucharist will always be Mass with holy communion. The
reserved sacrament, and the various forms of devotion to it, such
as exposition, processions, visits, must remain in a subordinate
position. This has not always been the case in the past, leading to
an imbalance in the perception of the Eucharist, but today the
Church is endeavouring to remedy that emphasis.[17] Tabernacle
devotion must be seen as intrinsically related to Mass and holy
communion. This devotion can only gain if one keeps in view that
it comes from the Mass and leads back to the Mass. The tabernacle
may be seen as a memorial of the Mass, helping us to extend our
Mass and holy communion throughout the day or week and so to
prepare for our next celebration of the sacrament. So full is the
Eucharist of the wonders of God's mercy that we cannot take them
all in during the course of the Mass. Consequently there is room
for returning every so often during the day to the Eucharistic
presence, so that this powerful sign of God's love may speak to our
worship and adoration.

As regards the other ways of Christ's presence to his Church, it
is important that the reality of these ways be made clear, but it
would be wrong to imply a kind of rivalry between them, as though
one were to say 'I do not need the tabernacle, since God is present
all around me'. The truth of the matter is that each mode of
presence helps the other. Between the various modes of presence
there is, not rivalry, but complementarity.

Central to all the modes of Christ's presence, and source of
inspiration for appreciating them, is Christ's presence in the
Eucharist. This is properly called *the* sacrament of presence. In the
New Testament the primary tabernacle of God among the people is
that flesh in which the Divine Word 'pitched his tent among us'.[18]
But this is the very flesh which exists for us in the Blessed
Sacrament. The sacramental species lend to the Eternal Word the
'here-and-now' of their material reality, so that he continues to
meet us in that immediacy of space and time which is so important
for human meeting and a sense of mutual presence. As Paul VI put
it, in the sacrament he continues to be our Emmanuel,
God-with-us.[19]

However we must not think of presence in purely spatial terms.
A modern philosophy of presence, as was indicated in Chapter 11
above, stresses that the higher forms of presence are personal.

Personal presence admits of degrees as we advance in understanding and love, so that in its highest manifestations presence is mutual. In this way the extent to which we respond to presence becomes part of the reality of the presence itself. Now different modes of presence have different modes of appropriate response. To Christ present in one's neighbour, the appropriate response is service. To Christ present in the Mass the appropriate response is active participation in the liturgy. To Christ present in the tabernacle the appropriate response is adoration and prayer.

Such a differentiation of the modes of our response also has implications for the liturgy. Sometimes liturgists have not distinguished sufficiently the norms appropriate in the Mass from those appropriate for the worship of the sacrament outside Mass. While the Mass is clearly a matter of liturgical action, where active participation is primary, benediction and other forms of devotion to the reserved sacrament have about them more of contemplation. Furthermore, where the Mass is primarily theocentric, in the sense that it moves through Christ to the Father, devotion to the Blessed Sacrament can afford to be more Christocentric. All this is in line with the way this devotion was originally shaped by the contemplative and mystical movements of the Middle Ages and by their devotion to the historical Christ.

As people of our own time, we inevitably give our own accent to this devotion, but that does not preclude our benefiting from the rich patrimony of the past, which continues to nourish and inspire, even today. A chapel of reservation is an especially appropriate place for letting the many riches of this mystery, past and present, which we have been considering throughout this chapter, come home to us and enter into our hearts.

NOTES

1 Cyril of Alexandria, *Commentary on John* IV, 2 (PG 73, 573B, 578B), text in English in A. Hamman (ed.), *The Mass: Ancient Liturgies and Patristic Texts* (Staten Island: Alba House, 1967), pp. 133–6.

2 E. Schillebeeckx, *The Eucharist* (London: Sheed & Ward, 1968), p. 76. The context there is a criticism of the 'ontological voluntarism' of Leenhardt from the point of view of 'the specifically Catholic view of reality' (ibid., p. 79).

3 B. Lonergan, *Insight* (London: Longmans, 1967), pp. 250–3, 372 and 387–8.

4 See B. Lonergan, *Grace and Freedom* (London: Darton, Longman & Todd, 1971), chs 4 and 5. Also still helpful is F. de Lanversin, 'Le concept de présence et quelques-unes de ses applications théologiques', *Recherches de science religieuse* 23 (1933), pp. 58–80, 176–96.

5 Luther's own words were 'And why could not Christ include his body in the substance of the bread just as well as in the accidents?': *Luther's Works*, vol. 36 (Philadelphia: Fortress, 1959), p. 32.

6 P. Teilhard de Chardin, *Hymn of the Universe* (London: Collins, 1973), especially pp. 44–51, 28–31.

7 Ambrose, *On the Faith* IV, 124 (PL 16, 641). In the Middle Ages some found this term insufficient: *Non enim transfiguratur panis, sed transubstantiatur*: Baldwin of Ford, *De sacramento altaris* (PL 204, 678A; SC 93, 204).

8 2 Pet 3:10–13, citing Isa 65:17.

9 P. McPartlan, *The Eucharist Makes the Church* (Edinburgh: T. & T. Clark, 1993), chapter 4.

10 Vatican II, *Sacrosanctum concilium* 50.

11 Justin, I *Apology* 65 (PG 6, 428B).

12 Tertullian, *De oratione* 19 (PL 1, 1181); *Ad uxorem* 2, 5 (PL 1, 1296); Novatian, *De spectaculis*: CSEL III, p. 8.

13 Ambrose, *On the Death of His Brother Satyrus* I, 43 (PL 16, 1304B); Rule of St Columbanus, in G. S. M. Walker (ed.), *Sancti Columbani Opera* (Dublin: The Dublin Institute for Advanced Studies, 1957), pp. 143 and 149.

14 Council of Trent, Decree on the Eucharist, chapter 5 (DS 1643).

15 John Paul II, *Dominicae coenae* 3 (London: CTS, 1979), pp. 9–11. Other relevant passages from recent Church teaching are: Vatican II, *Presbyterorum ordinis*, arts 5 and 18; SCR, *Eucharisticum mysterium* (1967), arts 49–51; Paul VI, *Mysterium fidei*, ss. 63–69: AAS 57 (1965), pp. 770–2; SCDW, *On Holy Communion and the Worship of the Eucharist Outside Mass* (1973): *Notitiae* 9 (1973), pp. 306–24.

16 K. Rahner, *Theological Investigations*, vol. 20 (London: Darton, Longman & Todd, 1981), p. 147. The same point more fully in 'Eucharistic worship', ibid., vol. 23 (London: Darton, Longman & Todd, 1992), pp. 113–16.

17 SCDW, *Holy Communion and the Worship of the Eucharist Outside Mass*, n. 81: *Notitiae* 9 (1973), p. 318.

18 John 1:14. This is the force of the Greek verb here (*skēnoun*), with its echoes of the Hebrew *shekinah*, an Old Testament term for the divine presence. The theme of the Fourth Gospel that Christ replaces the Temple (John 2:19-22) and that he is now the locus of intercourse between heaven and earth (John 1:51) is a variation of the same idea: R. Brown, *The Gospel According to John, I–XII* (New York: Doubleday/London: Geoffrey Chapman, 1966), pp. 32–3, 89–91, 124–5.

19 Paul VI, *Mysterium fidei*: AAS 57 (1965), p. 771.

15

⊠ *The fruits of the Eucharist*

In Our Lord's great parable of the vine and the branches, where
the Eucharistic overtones are unmistakable, he tells us that we
should go out and bear fruit, fruit that will last (John 15:2, 16).
This command of the gospel helps to underline the question of the
effects, or fruits, of the Eucharist, which has arisen from time to
time throughout this book, but will now be taken up in a more
systematic way. In this treatment use will be made of the scriptural
term 'fruits' in preference to the more usual 'effects' of which the
manuals commonly speak.

We have already observed in the preceding chapter that, in
Church tradition, this aspect of the sacrament is frequently spoken
of with such an abundance of images that they confuse by their
very richness. Faced by this confusion it will be good to stress at
the outset that the fruits of the Eucharist, whether in Mass or in
holy communion, are basically one. We can use different words to
describe it, like love, union, life, grace, but always they come back
to this: the Eucharist imparts that which it signifies, our ever
deeper identity with that mystery of love which poured itself out
on the cross and, at the resurrection, released into human history
the very life of God.[1] Within that unity, however, theology likes to
pick out different aspects. To examine these in more detail is the
task of this final chapter.

THE FRUITS WE GIVE

The glory of God

We begin with an aspect which is often neglected when people take
up this topic. In the account of the Last Supper in the Fourth
Gospel, where something of Our Lord's attitude before death is

spoken of, we find that his mind is presented as dominated by concern for the glory of the Father. This suggests that one of the first fruits of the sacrament is the greater glory of God, to which every sacrificial offering, by its very nature, wishes to contribute. Too often when people speak of the fruits of the sacrament, their minds are focused on the fruits we receive. But in the Eucharist, as in Christian life generally, it is in giving that we receive, and the first thing we give to God by our sacrifice is the glory and honour of our praise and worship.

By his sacrifice on the cross, Christ gave to the Father a glory that, in virtue of the hypostatic union, is reckoned without limit. In the Mass it is somewhat different and not without controversy. On one level, since the Mass is truly the actuality of that sacrifice of Christ, the glory it gives to God has to be in principle unlimited. However, in the concrete, in so far as the offering is now ours as well as that of Christ, it is always limited by the varying degree of generosity and dedication with which it is offered, whether one thinks of the Church at large at any one time, or of the individuals, priest and laity, who are directly involved in its celebration. This is a particular instance of the general principle of sacramental theology that the intrinsic worth of the rite (the *opus operatum*) is always limited in its effect by the degree of faith and love in those taking part and in those benefiting from the rite (the *opus operantis*). The point has practical implications for the system of Mass offerings, formerly called 'stipends', and for the notion of having more than one Mass said for a particular intention, but it is one which can become extraordinarily complex. For this reason only a general orientation will be attempted here, not a comprehensive treatment of the entire subject.

From the time of Scotus in particular it has been common in the schools to distinguish three kinds of fruit of the Mass: the 'general fruit', the 'special fruit' and the 'most special fruit'.[2] The 'general fruit' refers to the benefit coming to the Church as a whole each time the Mass is offered. The 'special fruit' refers to that which follows on the intention of the officiating priest, commonly on the occasion of a Mass offering, whether the recipient be present at the Mass or not. The 'most special fruit' refers to the benefits which come to those directly involved in carrying out the celebration, and in particular those which come to the celebrant himself.

As regards the first of these, it is important to note that all believers can benefit from every Mass, whether they are aware of that Mass or not. This 'democracy' of the fruits of the Mass is an essential presupposition of any discussion of the distinction of fruits, such as is about to be undertaken here.

The system of monetary Mass offerings, which rests on the principle of the 'special fruit', is one from which controversy is never far distant. Certainly the notion can be abused if the impression is given that the Mass has a price. At the same time, it is a system which opens up to people a way of affirming their identity with the Mass in a very real and expressive manner. It is a contemporary equivalent of the ancient custom of the people bringing the gifts of bread and wine to the church, from which the offerings used in the Mass were taken. Indeed it is a common view today that the present custom of monetary offerings grew out of the ancient offertory system. In the material order this offering of money can help to make the sacrifice humanly possible, and so can express the reality of a person's commitment to the worship of God. It is important to explain to people that its value cannot be reckoned in material terms but only in proportion to the love and generosity which inspire it.

In this whole discussion we are faced with the intractable problem of holding a balance between the external and internal factors which go to make up the worth of any human activity. Only the external is open to human measurement, but we know that the real value of what we do lies ultimately in the degree of faith and love behind it, known only to God. Yet in assigning the primacy to the human heart in this way, one must not rule out all proportion between the external and the internal, if one is to avoid the ancient trap of a dualism between body and spirit.

That there is particular benefit for those taking part in a particular Mass, and one in some way normally proportionate to their faith and love, is a point over which we need not delay except in relation to the celebrant. The question is this: is there a fruit of the Mass *ex opere operato* offered to the celebrant in virtue of his special responsibility for the celebration? Many theologians today, following the lead of Karl Rahner, deny the existence of any such particular fruit. The question can be practical for priests in deciding whether it is better to celebrate or simply to attend Mass, or indeed whether to participate at all on a given day.

Rahner's position is that there is no 'most special fruit' for the celebrant distinct in kind from that involved in any active participation in the Mass by a baptized person.[3] However even this position does not exclude the notion of a priest on his own celebrating Mass out of devotion. Rahner acknowledges the fact of common experience that the actual celebration is normally an occasion of greater faith and devotion for the priest than is mere assistance at Mass.[4] It follows from this that for the priest to celebrate rather than to assist can be reckoned normally to give greater glory to God and greater benefit to those for whom he offers than otherwise would be the case, but one should add that, in an ecclesial context, personal inclination cannot be the only norm. One must also take account of what the Church generally regards as appropriate at a particular time.[5]

Propitiation

Before leaving the question of what we give to God, it seems fitting to make one final reference to the difficult issue of propitiation, which was explained at the end of Chapter 13 above. The glory we give to God takes on a special colouring from the context of our sinfulness, and that is what we really mean by this troublesome word 'propitiation'. If this word can be used at all today, one must insist that in a Christian context it does not mean the placating of an angry God. As we saw already, that is simply not the kind of God revealed to us in the New Testament. Propitiation can be described in the ordinary language of preaching as an honouring of God motivated by repentance and leading to a deeper appropriation of forgiveness. The concept includes the notion of reparation and atonement, though the degree to which these aspects are made explicit varies considerably. However when we speak of the fruits of the Eucharist, the list would hardly be complete if mention was not made of the propitiation of sins.

THE FRUITS WE RECEIVE

As well as the fruits we give in the Eucharist, there are the fruits which we receive. This is the topic which people usually think of when they speak of the effects of the sacrament. The question could well be posed in the following form: 'In what way does the Eucharist make a difference in the lives of those who participate in it?' Our answer will lead us to break up the sacrament's one effect into different aspects, but before doing so it will be helpful to establish first a broader view and to try to have some implied vision of the place of the Eucharist in our world. Does this sacrament really make a difference in human affairs? What is it meant to achieve?

Community

The goal of the Eucharist is the goal of Christianity itself, for this sacrament is our highest manifestation in liturgy of what Christianity is. Now the goal of Christianity could be described as the coming about of the kingdom of God, when God will finally intervene in our world to fulfil the longing in human hearts. But what do people long for? Perhaps they hardly know themselves. Poets and philosophers will speak of some kind of a coming together of human beings in love and peace. A favourite word for it is 'community', but this remains elusive both in reality and in concept.

Then Our Lord comes on the scene. He too speaks of love, union and community. Indeed no one has dreamt this human dream as passionately as Christ has. Day in, day out, he talks of nothing else: 'By this will all know that you are my disciples' (John 13:35); 'This is my commandment, that you love one another' (John 15:12). Christ has a vision for the world. He is looking forward to a whole new set of relationships among human beings based on a whole new relationship of people with God. That is his kingdom, the new covenant, the new Jerusalem, based on what he calls his 'new commandment' (John 13:34).

At this point people might raise the question as to what is new about the commandment to love on the lips of Christ. After all, people had been talking about love and community for many a long day before his time. To this it might be replied that in Christ this commandment has a new basis, for it is now grounded on the universal presence of Christ himself, especially in his suffering members.

One of the best places in Scripture for a blueprint of this community of Christ is the parable in Matthew 25:31–46. There we are given an image of the kingdom, where Christ himself is the king. In this parable all human beings are brothers and sisters of a king, and the passport into that kingdom is the love we have one for another. In his turn St Paul speaks of our all being one single person in Christ (Eph 2:13–18), one body (1 Cor 12:12–30); and in Galatians 2:23 we are told that all the distinctions which divide people from each other, Jew and Greek, slave and free, male and female, are all rendered irrelevant once we find our new being in Christ.

Such a vision of the world can fairly take one's breath away. For such a view of Christianity no apology is needed. Our message began as something human, but the force of Our Lord's teaching and personality have lifted it up to a higher plane altogether. Indeed one might wonder whether it is possible at all. Is it not too idealistic and other-worldly? In a sense, that doubt is justified, and this vision will come about in its fullness only in another world. But if Christ died in order to make it possible, he came back from the grave in order to begin to make it actual. That is part of what was happening in the Resurrection Appearances. Our Lord came back to his disciples in order to gather his community together again, and this he did most notably by eating and drinking and praying with them at a common table. This task goes on even after his Ascension, and every Mass is Jesus of Nazareth coming to his followers in our contemporary world, continuing his work of forming them into the community of his kingdom around the one table.

Eucharist and community go together, just as liturgy and life are inseparable. You cannot have the one without the other. Eucharist without community easily becomes a flight from reality. Community without Eucharist deprives the community of one of its most far-reaching sources of power. Consequently systematic theology sums up this teaching by saying that the primary effect of this sacrament is the greater unity of the people in love.

In one way nothing could be more contemporary than this insistence on the communitarian aspect of the Eucharist. The Second Vatican Council set a headline for us, returning to the point more than once.[6] It is an important application of this Council's general principle that the life of grace has to make a discernible difference in this world.[7] Liberation Theology has made the point its own, giving its own accent to this stress on love in practice.[8]

In another way nothing could be more traditional. Community is part of the meaning of the Greek word *koinōnia*, communion, which, as was pointed out in Chapter 12 above, has been a Eucharistic word ever since the New Testament.[9] St Augustine spoke for the whole tradition when he described the Eucharist as 'the sign of unity, the bond of charity'.[10] De Lubac summed up the teaching of the ancient writers in that phrase of his which has become a slogan for a renewed theology: 'The Eucharist makes the Church.'[11]

Behind this last phrase lies a deep patristic sense of how the body of Christ makes the body of Christ, the sacramental body making the ecclesial body. Indeed it does not seem too much to say that for these early writers Christ's presence in his body, the Church, was *the* real presence and the relevant context for all celebration and for all other modes of presence. Since the Middle Ages we have tended to locate our celebration rather in a context of absence, to be relieved only at the consecration bell. When in the ancient world the context was one of the real presence and life of Christ in his Church, the Eucharist was understood to give to Christians the life of that body, the Church, and so to enable them to go out and deepen that presence and that life in the world.

The Eucharist helps form community, as Vatican II insisted. There is, however, an ambiguity about the word 'community' which one needs to guard against. In one sense the community is the whole Church, of which the local assembly is the sign. The celebration of the Eucharist certainly has its effect on this universal level, and that is an important part of the justification of Masses celebrated without a congregation. But there is a danger that this approach may become an abstraction and so open the door to individualistic celebration under another guise.

Contemporary writers, therefore, are anxious to stress the significance of the Eucharist for Church life in the concrete. This applies both to its impact on the local community and on society at large. The Eucharist, said one author, is the most political thing the Church does.[12] More significantly, the Synod of 1971 put it this way: 'The Eucharist constitutes the community and puts it at the service of the people.'[13]

In the wake of the introduction of the post-conciliar liturgy, many have regretted the scaling down of the sense of mystery in our worship, but it would be wrong to set this development on its own. It must always be seen as simply the other side of the coin as the Church tries to ensure that our liturgy reflects the basic social dimension of any authentic Christianity (cf. Jas 1:27). The promotion of this second value more than compensates for the lessening of emphasis on the first.

As was indicated at the outset of this section, we need a certain vision for the Eucharist, just as we need it for Christianity itself. We cannot lapse into being simply people of ritual at one extreme, or simply people of secular commitment at the other. We need both vertical and horizontal in liturgy as in life.

The most potent force for promoting this view of things is the universal presence of Christ, which it is the work of the Eucharist to celebrate, to nourish and to deepen. As well as making Christ present in the host, the Eucharist is to make him present in the world. Indeed the path to the fulfilment of this plan lies through the one mode of presence to the other. The achievement of Christ's love in this world must be seen as one of the fundamental goals of the Eucharist. Wherever that presence is found, it is due in some way to the celebration of the Eucharist in the Church. The more these values are expressed within the celebration itself, the more they are likely to inspire the participants to carry the presence of Christ with them out into their daily lives, so that the sacramental body may fulfil its destiny in transforming the people into the body of Christ in the world.

A remedy for our sins

The very splendour of the Eucharist, which the teaching of the preceding section illustrates so clearly, poses a problem by its very richness. It is a matter of the contrast between the ideal and the reality. How can we speak of the Eucharist as the celebration of community when our daily experience is so often the denial of that very quality? At times people have felt so overwhelmed by the absence of community in their daily living that an authentic celebration of the Eucharist has seemed impossible. On the other hand, to make this a reason for not celebrating Mass would normally be an exaggeration, a failure to take account of that well-known tension between 'already' and 'not yet' in the coming of the kingdom, to which reference was made in Chapter 12.

Ever since the New Testament, Christians have believed that, in one sense, the kingdom has come *already*, and that gives substance to our celebration and our thanksgiving. But that belief includes the perception that the kingdom has *not yet* come about in its fullness. There remains the reality of our struggle here below with our short-comings and our sins. This is why the Eucharist of the Church cannot be seen as the celebration of the elect. The relationship of the Eucharist to the propitiatory offering of the cross is one consequence of this situation. The fact that the fruitfulness of the Eucharist is more complex than simply the gifts of love and unity is another.

It has already been remarked more than once that the question of the purpose or fruits of the Eucharist has traditionally been answered by a torrent of images. To deal with this wealth of ideas, the intention in this final chapter is to present, not exactly a definitive list of fruits, but rather a structure within which traditional language can be treated in an ordered way. Karl Rahner gave us an important clue when he wrote: 'The first effect and instrumental cause of the other effects of the sacrament of the Eucharist is a profounder incorporation into the unity of the mystical body of Christ, the Church.'[14] This quotation not only endorses the preceding section in its account of the primary fruit which we receive in the Eucharist, but it also suggests how this aspect provides a basis for the other fruits of the sacrament, in a manner to be explained as follows.

The people of God are a reality of history. They take their origin in an event in the past, and are ever on their way through time towards a definitive goal in the future. Consequently, at any moment in that history, this people can be seen to be defined and constituted by this twofold relationship, that to the past and that to the future. As the Eucharist incorporates us ever more fully into the life of this people in the present, it inevitably gives us a deeper share in all that this people has from its origin in the side of Christ on the cross, and in all that they have from their orientation to their destiny, when Christ will come in his fullness at the end of time.

In this way one can come to consider the fruits we receive in the Eucharist within a temporal framework. Incorporated into the Church of the present, we have through this sacrament a deeper share both in the fruits flowing from the cross and in the fruits which are anticipations of the future banquet of the kingdom. In this section of the chapter it is the former category of fruits which is to be considered, and they can be seen to be summed up in a word going back to the Eucharist of Ignatius of Antioch, 'remedy'.[15]

The problem which this section wishes to address may be found in the man at the back of the church who is reluctant to go to holy communion out of a sense of his own unworthiness. He reminds us of the sinner in Our Lord's parable, who would not dare to raise his eyes to heaven (Luke 18:13). The problem stems from the New Testament itself and from the stern warning of St Paul against eating or drinking this sacrament unworthily (I Cor 11:27). In our own day the doctrine is familiar in the requirement of the Council of Trent that a person in mortal sin must first have recourse to the sacrament of Penance before receiving holy communion. The reverence this precaution implies reached its ultimate manifestation under the influence of Jansenism, where whole congregations would fill a church at the later Masses on a Sunday morning and no one would go to communion.

The one who challenged this situation and pointed the Church in a new direction was St Pius X, with his promotion of frequent communion. The decree on this subject, *Quam singulari*, put its finger on the nub of the matter when it criticized those who regarded holy communion as 'a reward for virtue' rather than as 'a remedy for human frailty'.[16] In this the Holy See was going back to an earlier and deeper tradition about the Eucharist, where the aspect of the sacrament as nourishment and remedy was more fully appreciated. Food is for the weak as well as for the strong, but especially for the weak. No less a person than St Ambrose wrote of the Eucharist 'I who am always sinning always have need of a remedy'.[17] One could paraphrase another passage in the same work by saying that the Eucharist is our daily bread for our daily sins.[18]

This aspect of the sacrament became a point of contention at the time of the Reformation. Luther's notion of faith and justification was so centred on the forgiveness of sins that it was inconceivable to him that a sacrament should have been instituted by Christ for any other purpose. This is the background to the teaching of Trent that the forgiveness of sins is not the principal effect of the Eucharist.[19]

In the event, the doctrine of the Council on this point did not have an easy passage through the assembly. That the forgiveness of sins should be attributed to the Eucharist at all seemed to call into question the sacrament of Penance. Something of this tension has a certain basis in the scriptures themselves where, on the one hand, we are told that the Eucharistic cup is Christ's blood 'for the forgiveness of sins' (Matt 26:28), and, on the other, we are warned against unworthy communion (1 Cor 11:28–32). The obligation to self-purification *prior* to the Eucharist has thus got a long tradition behind it, eventually expressed in the Church's norms concerning confession before communion for those who have been in mortal sin.[20] But the idea of purification *through* the Eucharist has an equally significant tradition to support it, not only in the patristic writings, but also in the post-communion prayers of the liturgy.

On the Council floor the remission of sins through the Eucharist was contested by the Pope's theologian, the Jesuit Lainez, but the arguments on the other side were overwhelming.[21] Not only was there the patristic and liturgical tradition, but in the Middle Ages Aquinas had devoted no less than four articles of his *Summa* to the issue.[22] In the end the acceptance of the point by the Council was clear and comprehensive.[23]

The notion that there is a forgiveness of sins available to us from the Church in ways other than the sacrament of Penance is one that has been growing in the consciousness of the faithful since the introduction of the vernacular in the liturgy. As already mentioned, this creates a problem as regards the confessional, but it certainly does not mean that this latter sacrament becomes superfluous, or that it is to be confined to dealing with mortal sin. Rahner indirectly pointed to the distinctive role of Penance when he wrote of the Eucharist: 'The primary and proper purpose of the Eucharist cannot be sinful man's appearance before the tribunal of divine grace, and therefore a man cannot, when receiving the Eucharist, really elicit the acts of a sinner before that tribunal of God.'[24]

Christianity has its positive and negative sides. Positively it means union with God and his love through our union with Christ's paschal mystery. This is the central reality of redemption, which we celebrate in the Eucharist in joy and thanksgiving. It follows that in the Eucharist the forgiveness of sins cannot be the main point. There it is always incidental and mostly related to venial sins.[25]

The negative side of Christianity concerns the darkness from which we have been redeemed in principle but which continues to dog even the just (Prov 24:16). As we have just seen, this aspect cannot be absent from the sacrifice of our redemption, yet if Mass were the only way of facing the truth about ourselves, it would hardly do justice to the existential depth of sin and sinfulness in our lives. This is why so often we need a special sacramental occasion, centred on this darkness within us, when we will seek, not only forgiveness and guidance, but a deepening of the whole penitential process in our lives. The presence of forgiveness in the Eucharist is not an argument for the abolition of the sacrament of

Penance, but rather one for celebrating it in a deeper and more personal way.

Once these qualms about the role of the sacrament of Penance have been set aside, the way is clear for renewing and deepening this consoling truth of our tradition, that the Eucharist is for all of us the healing remedy which our daily sins require. In the ancient world wine was used not only for nourishment but also for healing. Consequently it is appropriate that this healing function of the sacrament should be associated with the cup in a special way. One of the Prefaces of the Blessed Sacrament in the Roman Missal puts it this way:

> As we eat his body which he gave for us, we grow in strength.
> As we drink his blood which he poured out for us, we are
>   washed clean.

The banquet

From the beginning of this book the question of the Eucharist as meal has never been far away. In the opening chapters it was implied that, strictly speaking, the external form of the Eucharist cannot be said to be a meal, though the rite clearly has its origin in a table context. At the same time, the language of meal or banquet has always been part of the Eucharistic tradition. In this, the final chapter of the book, it is time to deal with this anomaly and to explore further the depths of meaning contained in this classic image of the sacrament.

In Chapter 12 we have already seen how the institution of this sacrament fitted into a long line of salvific meals through which the Lord revealed one of the basic images for his plan of life for the world. We also saw how at the Last Supper Jesus incorporated into that tradition a second image, that of a sacrifice, which many theologians, from time to time, have set in opposition to that of a banquet. This way of presenting the matter should be in itself a sufficient refutation of such an opposition, but it must be admitted that, for dogmatic reasons, one or other of these basic images has often been neglected by different groups of Christians. On the Catholic side, when relations with Protestantism were more confrontational than they are today, the image of the banquet was certainly overshadowed by that of the sacrifice, but it should be recorded that the meal aspect was never completely forgotten. It was constantly kept alive, for instance, by the frequent chanting of the antiphon of the Divine Office, *O sacrum convivium*, 'O sacred banquet', which was a common Eucharistic hymn in Catholic churches generally.

The Eucharist as banquet is fundamentally an image of the great feast of the blessed in the kingdom of God with which salvation history will reach its consummation. This feast is really the life of the redeemed in heaven, the future joy of the blessed, absorbed in eternal contemplation and communion. That the Eucharist is the image of this future life is a way of saying that this is the destiny to which the sacrament gives us access. This is suggested to us by the Eucharistic teaching of John's gospel in particular. In Chapter 5 above, devoted to this gospel, attention was drawn to the paradox in John 6:54:

The one who eats my flesh and drinks my blood has eternal life.

'Eternal life' is the life of heaven, to which reference has just been made in the preceding verses. The paradox comes in the contrast between the adjective going with 'life' and the tense of the verb. Eternal life is the life of the future; but, according to this verse, the participant in the Eucharist *has* this life. This future life, therefore, is a present reality in those who are nourished by this sacrament. The Eucharist, in a sense, is heaven on earth.

That is our basic description of the fruit of the Eucharist which we are now trying to understand. Tradition has a number of other terms to describe it: the Eucharist gives grace; the Eucharist is a pledge of future glory; the Eucharist is 'the medicine of immortality' (Ignatius of Antioch)[26]; but all of these come down to the same idea, namely that through this sacrament we anticipate in some degree the life of eternal communion with God.

What is this life to which the Eucharist gives access? Clearly, it is the life of God himself, the new creation inaugurated by the advent of the Word in history. It is not just the life of the old creation refurbished and renewed. That is the mistake of those who understand the Eucharistic banquet as little more than a celebration of 'togetherness' around a common table.

However, can we say more about the nature of this divine life? In its sixth chapter the Fourth Gospel confines itself to the use of the word 'life', but, as was pointed out in a previous discussion of this gospel,[27] it is not unreasonable to expand this notion by invoking the unique revelation of the life of God recorded for us by this same evangelist in the significant context of the Last Supper. There St

John opens up for us, in words of unforgettable mystery and awe, the wonder of the divinity as a drama of personal love, extended from the eternal Three to embrace all those who turn to Christ. One of the great advances in contemporary theology has been the recovery of the sense of grace as not just an accumulation of created graces but as ultimately the Uncreated Grace of Father, Son and Holy Spirit giving themselves to us and making their home in us (John 14:17, 23). This is the sense in which divine grace is to be seen as the fruit of the Eucharist. It is the communion of Father, Son and Holy Spirit, shared with us in the mystery of sacramental communion. In a word, the Eucharist gives us the Trinity.[28]

Another way of stating the same thing is to say that the Eucharist gives the Holy Spirit. The Holy Spirit, particularly in the Eastern tradition, has always had a special role in the doctrine of the Eucharist. By the witness of the New Testament, the Third Person was present to Christ on the cross, transforming his Passion into a sacrifice (Heb 9:14). The same Spirit has commonly been invoked as the agent of transformation in the Eucharistic Change, just as he was the agent of the Incarnation in the womb of Mary. In Eucharistic Prayers this role of the Spirit is frequently joined to his activity in bringing about the fruitfulness of the Eucharist in those who go to holy communion.

It is an understandable extension of this activity to see a deeper possession of the Holy Spirit himself as one of the effects of the sacrament that remain with us after the specifically sacramental presence has passed. We can find this idea in the patristic writers, for instance in St Ephraem the Syrian (*c.* 306–373):

> Spirit that cannot be eaten is hidden in your bread,
> Fire that cannot be drunk dwells in your wine.[29]

Again:

He called the bread his living body, and filled it with himself and the Spirit

   . . .

He who eats it with faith eats fire and Spirit.[30]

Yet another expression of this truth would be to say that the Eucharist gives us the presence of God in our lives. The divine presence has been one of the great themes of the Bible from the Old Testament onwards. The closeness of that presence, eventually centred in the Temple, was one of the privileges which marked Israel out as the favoured people of God. While this presence reaches a new climax within the Eucharistic celebration, it is helpful to underline that afterwards it continues within us as one of the fruits of the sacrament. God's presence within us through Christ's body and blood probably lasts only a few moments, but his presence through the Holy Spirit continues and grows within us as long as we remain in the state of grace. It is like the fire that engulfed the burning bush. The gift of Christ's body and blood in the Eucharist is the fuel that feeds that fire.

These thoughts are the basis of a custom which once was strong amongst the faithful but has sometimes been swept aside in the new liturgy. It is that of thanksgiving after communion. This custom is explicitly encouraged by the suggested moments of silent prayer within the liturgy itself. The principle is an important one. On the one hand there is this sublime doctrine on the presence of the Trinity in those who go to communion; but if, on the other hand, one does not respond to that presence in an appropriate way, then, though the doctrine be true in itself, it will scarcely be a significant reality in one's own life. Indeed the more one thinks about it, the more it may seem that an appropriate response can scarcely be contained within a few moments of communal silence within the Mass.[31]

Here we might recall the experience of an older generation who found the time after communion a moment of special closeness to God. Aquinas surely gave us an insight into his own spiritual life when he wrote:

By the power of this sacrament the soul is spiritually nourished in that it is filled with delight in a spiritual way and, in a sense, intoxicated with the sweetness of the divine goodness, according to that verse of the Song of Songs 5:1, 'Eat my friends, and drink, and be inebriated, my dear ones'.[32]

The point is that, for such an experience to occur, one must give it the time it requires. On the other hand, lest one's expectations be premature, it is good to bear in mind that dryness after holy communion was a frequent experience of even such a saint as Thérèse of Lisieux.[33]

The great saints and mystics sometimes leave us breathless with their accounts of what the Eucharist has come to mean for them. Indeed if our doctrine on the Eucharist were not sufficient to ground such mystical teaching, it would clearly be defective in a major way. St Cyril of Alexandria wrote more than once of how the power of Christ's sacred flesh makes us 'co-corporeal' with him. In one place he says that we are united with him 'like wax with wax'.[34]

One of the most emphatic on the depths of our union with the divinity in the Eucharist was Hilary of Poitiers. It is, he says, no mere moral union or union of wills but a physical union or union of nature. The final statement in the following passage is particularly remarkable:

If truly 'the Word was made flesh', and if we truly receive that Word made flesh in holy communion, is it not understandable that Christ should dwell in us on the level of nature? By his birth as a human being he has taken our fleshly nature into an inseparable union with himself. In the sacrament by which his flesh is shared with us he has joined his fleshly nature with his eternal nature. In this way we are all one, because the Father is in Christ, and Christ is in us . . . Consequently he is in us through his flesh and we are in him, while that which we are with him is in God . . . For no one will be in Christ unless Christ has been in that person; and Christ has assumed into himself the flesh only of that person who has received his (in holy communion).[35]

Inevitably the Eucharist has had a special significance in the mystical tradition of the Church. As the sacrament of union with the divinity it is one of the main symbols of that unitive way which mystical theology places at the summit of spirituality. Henri de Lubac always assumed that this was part of the meaning of that famous passage in Augustine:

I found that I was far from you in the region of unlikeness, as though I heard your voice crying out from on high 'I am the food of the full-grown; grow, and you will eat me; and you will not change me into yourself like the food of your flesh, but you will be changed into me'.[36]

The Eucharist not only supports the mystics along their way but it gives them an image of the experience itself. An example would be the following passage from Blessed Henry Suso (*c.* 1295–1366):

When the good and faithful servant enters into the joy of his Lord, he is inebriated by the riches of the house of God; for he feels, in an ineffable degree, that which is felt by an inebriated man. He forgets himself, he is no longer conscious of his selfhood; he disappears and loses himself in God, and becomes one spirit with Him, as a drop of water which is drowned in a great quantity of wine. For even as such a drop disappears, taking the colour of wine, so it is with those who are in full possession of blessedness. All human desires are taken from them in an indescribable manner, they are rapt from themselves, and are immersed in the Divine Will.[37]

Even more striking is the statement of Blessed Jan van Ruysbroeck (1293–1381), recalling the passage from Augustine above:

To eat and be eaten! This is union! . . . Since his desire is immensity itself, to be wholly devoured of him does not greatly amaze me.[38]

One of the great Eucharistic mystics was Ignatius Loyola, whose experiences of the Trinity during Mass and holy communion are recounted for us in some pages of his personal notes which, contrary to his intention, have survived. A few quotations from this source will serve as a fitting conclusion to these reflections on Eucharistic mysticism:

4.3.1544   When I wanted to begin Mass, I felt very great touches and intense devotion to the Most Holy Trinity . . . Later on, almost at the end, turning to Jesus, and recovering something of what was lost, at the prayer, 'Placeat tibi Sancta Trinitas', etc., ending in His Divine Majesty, a great and excessive love covered me with intense tears, so that every time throughout the Mass and before I had special spiritual consolations, they all terminated in the Most Holy Trinity, bearing me on and drawing me to its Love.

5.3.1544   . . . From here on I continued the Mass with many tears, courage and spiritual vigour, the greater consolations terminating in the Most Holy Trinity, and less in Jesus, and much less in the Father; always, on the one hand, increasing in confidence regarding reconciliation with the Most Holy Trinity, so that when Mass was ended, I felt in the oration a tranquility and repose.

6.3.1544   Beginning the Mass with an interior and humble satisfaction, and continuing as far as the *Te igitur* with great interior and sweet devotion which came several times with a slight interior sweetness as though to weep. At the *Te igitur*, I felt and saw, not obscurely, but clearly and very clearly the very Being or Essence of God, under the figure of a sphere, slightly larger than the appearance of the sun, and from this Essence the Father seemed to go forth or derive, in such a way that on saying 'Te', that is, 'Pater', the Divine Essence was represented to me before the Father, and in this vision, I saw represented the Being of the Most Holy Trinity without distinction or sight of the other Persons, and with intense devotion to what was represented to me, with many movements and shedding of tears. Thus I went through the Mass, considering, remembering and again seeing the same, with a great flood of tears and increase of love for the Being of the Most Holy Trinity, without seeing or distinguishing the Persons, except that they proceed from the Father, as I said.[39]

Appropriately the subject of Eucharistic mysticism brings this book to an end. Looking back over the journey we have travelled, with all its twistings and turnings, the reader might legitimately ask for some overview which draws it all together. We began with a consideration of the external form of the Eucharist, owing its origin to the table rites of the Jews. This consideration, illuminating as it is, only brings one a certain distance. The real significance of the Eucharist comes from its inner content, a new and profound reality with which Our Lord has filled the simple table rituals of his people.

The inner content of this symbolic ritual is twofold. It is a sacrifice and a banquet. On the level of external form, the Eucharist is not a sacrifice; it is a stylized ritual in bread and wine and prayer. But the Eucharist looks back to Christ's paschal mystery. As a sacramental sign of those events, it contains them, and so it is a real sacrifice.

Similarly the Eucharist looks forward to the great banquet of the kingdom at the end of time. Again, on the level of external form, it can scarcely be considered a banquet. Where do a piece of wafer and a sip of a cup constitute a banquet? But because it is the sacramental sign of that future banquet, it really is a banquet and really contains an anticipation of those exalted events of the end of time. The Eucharist, then, is the supreme gesture of Our Lord's love in the life of the Church, summoning us to immerse ourselves every so often in the reality and in the graces of our origin and our goal.

NOTES

1 Rahner put it this way: 'Union by grace in faith and love with Christ's sacrifice is the *one* effect of the sacrifice itself': in K. Rahner and A. Häussling, *The Celebration of the Eucharist* (London: Burns & Oates, 1968), p. 78.

2 In Latin: *fructus generalis, fructus specialis, fructus specialissimus*. See Rahner, op. cit., pp. 54 and 46.

3 Ibid., p. 84. Rahner has been criticized for not distinguishing sufficiently between the act performed and the fruit received: J. T. O'Connor, *The Hidden Manna: A Theology of the Eucharist* (San Francisco: Ignatius Press, 1988), pp. 254-9, with quotations there from Pius XII and Paul VI. It seems to me that a more fundamental limitation lies in his treating the matter simply from the point of view of the graces of the Eucharist and not from those of the sacrament of Orders. For Pius XII see allocutions in AAS 46 (1954), pp. 668ff.; 48 (1956), pp. 716-18. For Paul VI, see *Mysterium fidei*: AAS 57 (1965), p. 762.

4 K. Rahner and A. Häussling, *The Celebration of the Eucharist*, p. 103.

5 That the value of a celebration is in some sense relative is illustrated by the associated question of the frequency of the Mass. See R. Taft, 'The

frequency of the Eucharist throughout history', *Concilium*, no. 152 (1982/2), pp. 13–24; P. de Clerck, 'La fréquence des messes. Realités économiques et théologiques', *La Maison-Dieu* no. 121 (1975), pp. 151–8.

6 Vatican II, *Presbyterorum ordinis*, arts 5 and 6; *Lumen gentium*, arts 3, 7, 11, 26; *Unitatis redintegratio*, art. 15.

7 Vatican II, *Gaudium et spes*, arts 39, 43, 44, 93.

8 G. Gutiérrez, *A Theology of Liberation* (London: SCM, 1974), pp. 258–65; T. Balasuriya, *The Eucharist and Human Liberation* (Maryknoll, NY: Orbis, 1979).

9 Acts 2:42; 1 Cor 10:16–17.

10 Augustine, *Treatises on John* 26, 13 (PL 35, 1612).

11 H. de Lubac, *Corpus mysticum: l'eucharistie et l'église au moyen-âge* (Paris, Aubier, 1944), p. 103; *Catholicism* (London, 1950), pp. 38–50; *The Splendour of the Church* (London: Sheed & Ward, 1956), pp. 106–13. See also above at Chapter 12, note 9.

12 J. A. T. Robinson, *Liturgy Coming to Life* (London: Mowbray, 1964), p. 31.

13 Synod of 1971, *Justice in the World*, part III.

14 Rahner and Häussling, *The Celebration of the Eucharist*, p. 94.

15 Ignatius refers to the Eucharist as 'a medicine of immortality and an antidote against death': *Letter to the Ephesians* 20, 2 (PG 5, 661).

16 SCS, Decree *Quam singulari* (8 August 1910): AAS 2 (1910), pp. 577–83, reference at p. 582.

17 Ambrose, *On the Sacraments* IV, 28 (PL 16, 446–447).

18 Ibid., V, 25.

19 Council of Trent, Decree on the Eucharist, canon 5 (DS 1655).

20 Council of Trent, Decree on the Eucharist, canon 11 (DS 1661).

21 *Sacramentum refectionis, non remissionis*: Lainez, February 1547: CT, V, p. 934.

22 Aquinas, ST III, q. 79, aa. 3–6.

23 Council of Trent, Decree on the Eucharist, chapter 2 (DS 1638). For the discussion of the point in September 1551, see CT, tome VII, vol. 1, pp. 132, 136–8.

24 K. Rahner, *Servants of the Lord* (London: Burns & Oates, 1968), p. 179.

25 As regards mortal sin, the role of the Eucharist is basically that of preserving us against future sin, as the Council of Trent teaches (DS 1638). Where such sins have already been committed, the obligation of confession, referred to in note 20 above, will normally deal with the situation (DS 1661).

26 Ignatius, *Letter to the Ephesians*, 20, 2 (PG 5, 661; RJ 43).

27 Chapter 5 above.

28 See Vatican II, *Unitatis redintegratio*, art. 15, for a fine statement of this teaching.

29 St Ephraem the Syrian, *Hymnen 'De Fide'* 10, 8, ed. E. Beck (Louvain: Secretariat of Corpus Scriptorum Christianorum Orientalium, 1967), vol. 2, p. 34.

30 St Ephraem the Syrian, *Sermons for Holy Week* 4, 4 (Lamy I, 416; RJ 707).

31 This is suggested by SCDW, *Inaestimabile donum*, art. 17: AAS 72 (1980), p. 338. Especially appropriate material for such thanksgiving will be found in the Fourth Gospel, chapters 13–17.

32 Aquinas, ST III, q. 79, a. 1, ad 2; cf. III, q. 81, a. 1, ad 3. In this context P. Gy also cites Readings I and II of the *legenda* of the Office of Corpus Christi: in J. Doré (ed.), *Sacrements de Jésus-Christ* (Paris: Desclée, 1983), p. 95.

33 Thérèse of Lisieux, *Autobiography of a Saint*, translated by R. Knox (London: Collins, 1960), p. 168.

34 'Co-corporeal' (Greek: *sussōmos*) is found already in the *Mystagogical Catecheses* attributed to Cyril of Jerusalem, IV, 3 (PG 33, 1100), then in Cyril of Alexandria, *Commentary on John* XI, 11 (PG 74, 560); 'wax with wax' is from the same commentary, IV, 2 (PG 73, 584B).

35 Hilary, *On the Trinity* VIII, 13–16 (PL 10, 245–249); text in English in A. Hamman (ed.), *The Mass: Ancient Liturgy and Patristic Texts* (Staten Island: Alba House, 1967), pp. 198–201.

36 Augustine, *Confessions*, 7, 10 (CSEL 33, 157; RJ 1593). On de Lubac, see P. McPartlan, 'Tu seras transformé en moi', *Communio* (edition in French) 17, no. 103 (1992/5), pp. 38–52.

37 Cited by E. Underhill, *Mysticism* (London: Methuen, 1911), p. 507.

38 Cited by Underhill, op. cit., p. 509.

39 *The Spiritual Journal of St Ignatius Loyola, February 1544–45*, ed. and translated by W. J. Young (Woodstock, Maryland: Woodstock College Press, 1958), pp. 24, 26, 27.

⊠ Bibliography

(This Bibliography is confined to items cited in this book and amongst these to the principal references only.)

G. Ashby, *Sacrifice: Its Nature and Purpose* (London: SCM, 1988).

J. P. Audet, 'Esquisse historique du genre littéraire de la "bénédiction" juive et de l'"eucharistie" chrétienne', RB 65 (1958), pp. 371–99.

W. Barclay, *The Lord's Supper* (London: SCM, 1967).

J. Betz, *Die Eucharistie in der Zeit der griechischen Väter*: vol. I/1: *Die Aktualpräsenz der Person und des Heilwerkes Jesu im Abendmahl nach der vorephesinischen griechischen Patristik* (Freiburg–Basel–Vienna: Herder, 1955); vol. II/1: *Die Realpräsenz des Leibes und Blutes Jesu im Abendmahl nach dem neuen Testament* (Freiburg–Basel–Vienna: Herder, 1961).

J.-P. Bouhot, *Ratramn de Corbie: histoire littéraire et controverses doctrinales* (Paris: Etudes Augustiniennes, 1976).

M. F. C. Bourdillon and M. Fortes (eds), *Sacrifice* (London: Academic Press, 1980).

L. Bouyer, *Rite and Man: The Sense of the Sacral and Christian Liturgy* (London: Burns & Oates, 1963).

L. Bouyer, *Eucharist: Theology and Spirituality of the Eucharistic Prayer* (Notre Dame–London: University of Notre Dame Press, 1968).

R. Brown, *The Gospel According to John, I–XII* (New York: Doubleday/London: Geoffrey Chapman, 1966).

H. Cazelles, 'L'Anaphore et l'Ancien Testament', *Eucharisties d'Orient et d'Occident* (Lex Orandi no. 46; Semaine Liturgique de l'Institut Saint-Serge 1; Paris: Cerf, 1970), pp. 11–21.

L. M. Chauvet, *Du symbolique au symbole: essai sur les sacrements* (Paris: Cerf, 1979).

L. M. Chauvet, *Symbole et sacrement: une relecture sacramentelle de l'existence chrétienne* (Paris: Cerf, 1988).

Churches Respond to BEM: Official Responses to the 'Baptism Eucharist and Ministry' Text, edited in several volumes by M. Thurian (Geneva:

World Council of Churches, 1986–).

F. Clark, *Eucharistic Sacrifice and the Reformation* (London: Darton, Longman & Todd, 1960).

Concilium Tridentinum: diariorum, actorum, epistolarum, tractatuum nova collectio, ed. Societas Görresiana (Freiburg-im-Breisgau: Herder, 1901–).

O. Cullmann, *Early Christian Worship* (Studies in Biblical Theology, First Series no. 10; London: SCM, 1953).

N. A. Dahl, 'Anamnesis: memory and commemoration in early Christianity' in *Jesus in the Memory of the Early Church: Essays by Nils Alstrup Dahl* (Minneapolis: Augsburg Publishing House, 1976), pp. 11–29.

R. Daly, 'Sacrifice in Origen', *Studia Patristica* XI (Texte und Unter- suchungen 108; Berlin: Akademieverlag, 1972), pp. 125–9.

R. Daly, 'The soteriological significance of the sacrifice of Isaac', CBQ 39 (1977), pp. 45–75.

R. Daly, *Christian Sacrifice: The Judaeo-Christian Background Before Origen* (Washington: Catholic University of America Press, 1978).

R. Daly, *The Origins of the Christian Doctrine of Sacrifice* (London: Darton, Longman & Todd, 1978).

R. Daly, 'Sacrifice in Origen and Augustine: comparisons and contrasts', *Studia Patristica* XIX (Leuven: Peeters Press, 1989), pp. 148–53.

J. Dillenberger (ed.), *Martin Luther: Selections from His Writings* (New York: Doubleday, 1961).

G. Dix, *The Shape of the Liturgy* (Westminster: Dacre Press, 1945).

J. Doré (ed.), *Sacrements de Jésus-Christ* (Collection 'Jésus et Jésus-Christ' no. 18; Paris: Desclée, 1983).

M. Eliade, *The Sacred and the Profane* (New York: Harper & Row, 1961).

G. Fittkau, *Der Begriff des Mysteriums bei Johannes Chrysostomus. Eine Auseinandersetzung mit dem Begriff des 'Kultmysteriums' in der Lehre Odo Casels* (Theophaneia 9; Bonn: Hanstein, 1953).

S. Gero, 'The Eucharistic doctrine of the Byzantine Iconoclasts and its sources', *Byzantinische Zeitschrift* 68 (1975), pp. 4–22.

R. Girard, *Violence and the Sacred* (London–Baltimore: Johns Hopkins University Press, 1977).

C. Giraudo, *La struttura letteraria della preghiera eucaristica: Saggio sulla genesi letteraria di una forma: Toda veterotestamentaria, Beraka giudaica, Anafora cristiana* (Analecta Biblica no. 92; Rome: Biblical Institute Press, 1981).

C. Giraudo, *Eucaristia per la chiesa: prospettive teologiche sull'eucaristia a partire dalla 'lex orandi'* (Brescia: Morcelliana/Rome: Gregorian University Press, 1989).

L. Godefroy, 'Eucharistie d'après le concile de Trente', DTC, vol. V, cols. 1326–1356.

P. Gy, 'Eucharistie et "Ecclesia" dans le premier vocabulaire de la liturgie chrétienne', *La Maison-Dieu* 130 (1977), pp. 19–34.

P. Gy, 'L'Eucharistie dans la tradition de la prière et de la doctrine', *La Maison-Dieu* 137 (1979), pp. 81–102.

P. Gy, 'L'Office du Corpus Christi et S. Thomas d'Aquin: état d'une recherche', RSPT 64 (1980), pp. 491–507.

P. Gy, 'L'Office du Corpus Christi et la théologie des accidents eucharistiques', RSPT 66 (1982), pp. 81–6.

P. Gy, 'La relation au Christ dans l'Eucharistie selon S. Bonaventure et S. Thomas d'Aquin' in J. Doré (ed.), *Sacrements de Jésus-Christ* (Paris: Desclée, 1983), pp. 69–106.

A. Hamman (ed.), *The Mass: Ancient Liturgies and Patristic Texts* (Staten Island: Alba House, 1967).

A. Hänggi and I. Pahl (eds): see *Prex eucharistica*.

W. W. Harvey (ed.), *Sancti Irenaei libros quinque adversus haereses* (2 vols; Cambridge: Cambridge University Press, 1857).

J. Heinemann, *Prayer in the Talmud* (Berlin: Gruyter, 1977).

J. M. Huels, 'Trent and the chalice: forerunner of Vatican II?', *Worship* 56 (1982), pp. 386–400.

P. Hughes, *The Church in Crisis: A History of the Twenty Great Councils* (London: Burns & Oates, 1961).

R. C. D. Jasper and G. J. Cuming, *Prayers of the Eucharist, Early and Reformed* (London: Collins, 1975).

J. Jeremias, *The Eucharistic Words of Jesus* (London: SCM, 1966).

R. Johanny, *L'Eucharistie centre de l'histoire du salut chez saint Ambroise de Milan* (Paris: Beauchesne, 1968).

H. Jorissen, *Die Entfaltung der Transsubstantiationslehre bis zum Beginn der Hochscholastik* (Münster: Aschendorff, 1965).

J. Jungmann, *The Early Liturgy: To the Time of Gregory the Great* (London: Darton, Longman & Todd, 1960).

J. Jungmann, *Missarum sollemnia: eine genetische Erklärung der römischen Messe* (2 vols; Vienna–Freiburg–Basel: Herder, 1962).

E. Kilmartin, *The Eucharist in the Primitive Church* (Englewood Cliffs, NJ: Prentice-Hall, 1965).

F. de Lanversin, 'Le concept de présence et quelques-unes de ses applications théologiques', RSR 23 (1933), pp. 58–80, 176–96.

M. de la Taille, *The Mystery of Faith*, book I: *The Sacrifice of Our Lord* (London: Sheed & Ward, 1941).

K. Lehmann and W. Pannenberg (eds), *The Condemnations of the Reformation Era: Do They Still Divide?* (Minneapolis: Fortress, 1990).

X. Léon-Dufour, 'Jesus' understanding of his death', *Theology Digest* 24 (1976), pp. 293–300.

X. Léon-Dufour, *Sharing the Eucharistic Bread* (New York: Paulist, 1987).

M. Lepin, *L'idée du sacrifice de la Messe d'après les théologiens depuis l'origine jusqu'à nos jours* (Paris: Beauchesne, 1926).

L. Lies, *Wort und Eucharistie bei Origenes: Zur Spiritualisierungstendenz des Eucharistieverständnisses bei Origenes* (Innsbrucker theologische Studien, vol. I; Innsbruck: Tyrolia, 1978).

L. Ligier, *Magnae orationis eucharisticae seu anaphorae origo et significatio (ad usum privatum auditorum)* (Rome: Gregorian University, 1964).

L. Ligier, 'De la cène de Jésus à l'anaphore de l'église', *La Maison-Dieu* no. 87 (1966), pp. 7–49.

B. Lonergan, *De Deo trino* (2 vols; Rome: Gregorian University Press, 1964).

B. Lonergan, *Insight: A Study of Human Understanding* (London: Longmans, 1967).

B. Lonergan, *Verbum: Word and Idea in Aquinas* (London: Darton, Longman & Todd, 1968).

B. Lonergan, *Grace and Freedom* (London: Darton, Longman & Todd, 1971).

B. Lonergan, *Method in Theology* (London: Darton, Longman & Todd, 1972).

B. Lonergan, 'On God and secondary causes' in *Collection (Collected Works of Bernard Lonergan*, vol. 4; Toronto: Toronto University Press, 1988), pp. 53–65.

H. de Lubac, *Corpus mysticum: l'eucharistie et l'église au moyen-âge* (Collection 'Théologie' no. 3; Paris: Aubier, 1944).

H. de Lubac, *The Splendour of the Church* (London: Sheed & Ward, 1956).

Luther's Works, ed. J. Pelikan and H. T. Lehmann (56 vols; St Louis: Concordia/Philadelphia: Fortress, 1958–).

H. McAdoo (ed.), *Modern Eucharistic Agreement* (London: SPCK, 1973).

D. McCarthy, *Treaty and Covenant* (Rome: Biblical Institute Press, 1963).

J. F. McCue, 'The doctrine of transubstantiation from Berengar through the Council of Trent' in P. Empie and T. A. Murphy (eds), *Lutherans and Catholics in Dialogue* (Minneapolis: Augsburg, n.d.), pp. 89–124.

J. McKenna, *Eucharist and Holy Spirit* (London: SPCK, 1975).

B. McNamara, 'Christus Patiens in Mass and sacraments: higher perspectives', ITQ 42 (1975), pp. 17–35.

P. McPartlan, 'Eucharistic ecclesiology', *One in Christ* 22 (1986), pp. 314–31.

P. McPartlan, 'Eucharist and Church: the contribution of Henri de Lubac', *The Month* 259 (1988), pp. 847–59.

P. McPartlan, 'Tu seras transformé en moi', *Communio* (edition in French) 17, no. 103 (1992/5), pp. 38–52.

P. McPartlan, *The Eucharist Makes the Church: Henri de Lubac and John Zizioulas in Dialogue* (Edinburgh: T. & T. Clark, 1993).

G. Macy, *The Theologies of the Eucharist in the Early Scholastic Period* (Oxford: Clarendon, 1984).

A. Martimort (ed.), *L'Église en prière: Introduction à la liturgie* (3rd edn; Paris: Desclée, 1965).

A. Martimort and others, *The Church at Prayer* (revised edn, 4 vols; London: Geoffrey Chapman, 1986–87).

E. Mazza, *The Eucharistic Prayers of the Roman Rite* (New York: Pueblo, 1986).

E. Mazza, *Mystagogy: A Theology of Liturgy in the Patristic Age* (New York: Pueblo, 1989).

N. Mitchell, *Cult and Controversy: The Worship of the Eucharist Outside Mass* (Studies in the Reformed Rites of the Catholic Church, vol. IV: New York: Pueblo, 1982).

L. C. Mohlberg with L. Eizenhofer and P. Siffrin (eds), *Liber sacramentorum Romanae Ecclesiae ordinis anni circuli: sacramentarium gelasianum* (*Rerum ecclesiasticorum documenta*, series major: *Fontes* IV; Rome: Herder, 1960).

P. Neuenzeit, *Das Herrenmahl: Studien zur paulinischen Eucharistie-auffassung* (Studien zum alten und neuen Testament, vol 1; Munich: Kösel, 1960).

B. Neunheuser, *Eucharistie in Mittelalter und Neuzeit* (*Handbuch der Dogmengeschichte*, vol. IV: *Sakramentenlehre*, fascicle 4b; Freiburg–Basel–Vienna: Herder, 1963).

A. Nichols, *The Holy Eucharist* (The Oscott Series, no. 6; Dublin: Veritas, 1991).

J. T. O'Connor, *The Hidden Manna: A Theology of the Eucharist* (San Francisco: Ignatius Press, 1988).

P. F. Palmer, *Sacraments and Worship: Liturgy and Doctrinal Development of Baptism, Confirmation and the Eucharist* (*Sources of Christian Theology*, vol. I; London: Longmans, 1957).

J. Pelikan, *The Christian Tradition: A History of the Development of Doctrine* (5 vols; Chicago–London: University of Chicago Press, 1971–).

J. Pelikan and H. T. Lehmann (eds): see *Luther's Works*.

D. Power, *The Sacrifice We Offer: The Tridentine Dogma and Its Reinterpretation* (Edinburgh: T. & T. Clark, 1987).

D. Power, 'Eucharist' in F. S. Fiorenza and J. P. Galvin (eds), *Systematic Theology, Roman Catholic Perspectives* (Dublin: Gill & Macmillan, 1992), pp. 585–612.

D. Power, *The Eucharistic Mystery: Revitalizing the Tradition* (Dublin: Gill & Macmillan, 1992).

Prex eucharistica: Textus e variis liturgiis antiquioribus selecti, ed. A. Hänggi and I. Pahl (Spicilegium Friburgense, vol. 12; Fribourg: Editions Universitaires, 1968).

K. Rahner and A. Häussling, *The Celebration of the Eucharist* (London: Burns & Oates, 1968).

J. Reumann, *The Supper of the Lord: The New Testament, Ecumenical Dialogues and Faith and Order on Eucharist* (Philadelphia: Fortress, 1984).

E. Schillebeeckx, *Christ the Sacrament of the Encounter with God* (London: Sheed & Ward, 1963).

E. Schillebeeckx, *The Eucharist* (London: Sheed & Ward, 1968).

M. Schmaus, *Dogma 5: The Church as Sacrament* (London: Sheed & Ward, 1975).

H. Schürmann, *Der Einsetzungsbericht Lk 22:19–20*, part II: *Einer Quellenkritischen Untersuchung des lukanischen Abendmahlsberichtes Lk 22:7–38* (Neutestamentliche Abhandlungen, vol. XX, part 4; Münster: Aschendorff, 1955).

H. Schürmann, 'Neutestamentliche Marginalien zur Frage der "Entsakralisierung" ', *Der Seelsorger* 38 (1968), pp. 38–48.

K. Stevenson (ed.), *Liturgy Reshaped* (London: SPCK, 1982).

K. Stevenson , ' "The unbloody sacrifice": the origins and development of a description of the Eucharist' in G. Austin (ed.), *Fountain of Life* (Washington: The Pastoral Press, 1991), pp. 103–30.

D. Stone, *A History of the Doctrine of the Holy Eucharist*, vol. I (London: Longmans Green & Co., 1908).

H. L. Strack and P. Billerbeck, *Kommentar zum neuen Testament aus Talmud und Midrasch* (Munich: Beck, 1922–28).

R. Taft, 'The frequency of the Eucharist throughout history', *Concilium* 152 (1982/2), pp. 13–24.

P. Teilhard de Chardin, *Hymn of the Universe* (London: Collins Fontana, 1973).

M. Thurian, *L'Eucharistie: mémorial du Seigneur, sacrifice d'action de grâce et d'intercession* (Paris–Neuchâtel: Delachaux et Niestlé, 1959).

M. Thurian (ed.): see *Churches Respond to BEM*.

T. J. van Bavel, 'Das Sakrament der Eucharistie bei Augustinus', *Cor Unum* 39 (1981), pp. 121–135.

R. de Vaux, *Ancient Israel, Its Life and Institutions* (London: Darton, Longman & Todd, 1961).

R. de Vaux, *Studies in Old Testament Sacrifice* (Cardiff: University of Wales Press, 1964).

A. Vonier, *A Key to the Doctrine of the Eucharist* (London: Burns & Oates, 1925).

G. S. M. Walker (ed.), *Sancti Columbani Opera* (*Scriptores Latini Hiberniae*, vol. 2; Dublin: The Dublin Institute for Advanced Studies, 1957).

R. Williams, *Eucharistic Sacrifice – The Roots of a Metaphor* (Grove Liturgical Study no. 31; Bramcote: Grove Books, 1982).

F. M. Young, *The Use of Sacrificial Ideas in Greek Christian Writers from the New Testament to John Chrysostom* (Patristic Monograph Series no. 5; Cambridge, MA: The Philadelphia Patristic Foundation Ltd, 1979).

F. M. Young, *Can These Dry Bones Live?* (London: SCM, 1982).

F. M. Young, *From Nicaea to Chalcedon* (London: SCM, 1983).

F. M. Young, 'Sacrifice' in *A New Dictionary of Christian Theology* (London: SCM, 1983), pp. 516–18.

F. M. Young, *Sacrifice and the Death of Christ* (London: SCM, 1983).

W. J. Young (trans. and ed.), *The Spiritual Journal of St Ignatius Loyola, February, 1544–45* (Woodstock, Maryland: Woodstock College Press, 1958).

⊠ Biblical Index

salvation history   38, 43–4, 46, 66,
   103–4, 178, 195
Schillebeeckx, E.   111, 149, 173, 199,
   205, 209, 219, 221, 223, 235, 262
Schmaus, M.   51, 76, 97, 110, 262
Schmeelcher, W.   91
Schnackenburg, R.   75
Schürmann, H.   26, 32, 33, 41, 50, 51,
   262
Scotists   146–7, 159, 162, 164, 172,
   223–4
Scotus   146, 238
Selvaggi, F.   180
Serapion   98
Servant of Yahweh   21, 30–3, 50
spiritual communion   127
spirituality   108–9, 122–3, 233
   see also mysticism
Stanley, D. M.   75
Stevenson, K.   90, 149, 262
Stone, D.   112, 262
Strack, H. L.   60, 262
substance   40, 119–21, 129–33, 135,
   136, 138, 142–7, 154, 156, 162–4,
   172, 173, 180–4, 225
symbolism   99–102, 104, 105–7,
   109–10, 115, 119, 128–9, 134,
   140–1, 142, 155–6, 177–9, 180,
   202–3, 210, 227–9

tabernacle   56, 165, 176, 185, 231–5
   see also reservation
table rituals   6–10, 36, 37, 43, 47, 50,
   52, 57, 64, 228, 254
Taft, R.   254–5, 262
Talley, T. J.   14, 149
Teilhard de Chardin, P.   230, 236, 262
Temple   9, 11, 12, 35, 36–7, 41, 50, 56,
   65, 79, 166, 236, 250
Tertullian   86, 91, 92, 111, 236
thanksgiving   6–10, 45, 64, 79, 81–2,
   84–5, 90, 95, 152, 171, 213, 220,
   251, 256
Theodore of Mopsuestia   101–2, 112
Theodoret of Cyr   102, 112
Thérèse of Lisieux   251, 256
Thomists   146–7, 159, 162, 164, 172,
   177, 223–4, 226

Thurian, M.   104, 112, 181, 190, 257,
   262
Tonneau, R.   111–12
transelementation   101, 183
transfiguration   107, 113, 230–1, 236
transfinalization   181–4
transignification   55, 181–4, 227–9
transrhythmization   101, 183
transubstantiation   55, 117, 129–33,
   138, 141–50, 154–6, 159, 162–7,
   172, 181, 184, 224, 236
Trent   52, 67, 136, 151, 157–75, 176,
   207, 217, 232, 236, 246, 255
Trinity   72, 199–200, 229, 250–1, 253

Underhill, E.   256
Urban IV   138, 150
utraquism   126, 157, 158, 172

van Bavel, T.   113, 262
van Imschoot, P.   30, 33
Vatican II   vii, 160, 168, 180, 184, 189,
   203, 204, 206, 207, 219, 231, 233,
   236, 242, 255
Vaux, R. de   32, 33, 45, 52, 262
Vercelli, Council of   117
Vischer, L.   190
von Allmen, J.   51
von Balthasar, H. U.   75, 76
Vonier, A.   148, 177–9, 189–90,
   209–11, 262

Waldensians   122, 125, 135
Walsh, L.   148
Walsh, M. x
Wieland, F.   81, 90
William of Auxerre   131
William of Champeaux   136, 137
Williams, R.   221, 263
Witzel, G.   171
Wyclif   162, 173

Young, F. M.   90, 111, 222, 263
Young, W. J.   256, 263

Zwingli   154–6, 158, 172, 224